Disturbed Youth and Ethnic Family Patterns

Disturbed Youth and Ethnic Family Patterns

By Rita F. Stein

State University of New York Press · Albany · 1971

Disturbed Youth and Ethnic Family Patterns

First Edition

Published by State University of New York Press,
Thurlow Terrace, Albany, New York 12201
Copyright © 1971 by The Research Foundation
of State University of New York. All rights reserved

ISBN 0-87395-046-1 (clothbound)
ISBN 0-87395-146-8 (microfiche)
Library of Congress Catalog Card Number 69-14645
Printed in the United States of America

Dedicated to the
Memory of my husband
Jacob B. Stein
who learned for himself that
there is much to learn.
He was a man who reinforced my inspiration
to learn throughout our lively discussion
of people. As long as those who knew him
are alive, he will be alive.

Contents

Illustrations

Tables

Acknowledgments

I have come to believe that no one person is fully aware of all the events which have shaped the style of his or her own thinking. Many people—family members, friends, nurses, public health personnel, social scientists—have contributed to the development of the conceptions and interpretations in the present work. But among these people there are some who merit special tribute.

I am deeply indebted to Dr. Marvin K. Opler, professor of Social Psychiatry and Sociology, State University of New York at Buffalo, for his stimulating guidance and for his ever present readiness to help in shaping my thinking through the maze of findings in the human drama of adolescence. The measure of his caliber as a teacher is declared in his having stirred intellectual enthusiasm rather than demanding obedience to blind absorption. Under his direction it was possible for a graduate student like myself to amalgamate my experiences and knowledge in medicine, health, psychiatry, and sociology.

Special thanks are tendered to Dr. I. Silverman, Department of Psychology, State University of New York at Buffalo, for his many useful suggestions as the manuscript appeared in piecemeal fashion and for his assistance in the organization and presentation of data.

To Dr. H. E. Faver, esteemed psychiatrist and friend, I am thankful for support, encouragement, and guidance throughout the task of learning, studying, and writing.

To my good friend Miss Lydia Reitz, public health nurse and associate professor, State University of New York at Buffalo, I give thanks for her confidence in me and for awakening in me the excitement of intellectual adventure.

Miss Emily Holmquist, Dean of the School of Nursing, Indiana University, has demonstrated faith and has given support to the task of writing. It is a challenge to work with her and to observe her drive for the furtherance of human knowledge. Grateful appreciation is acknowledged to the Nursing Research Division of the United States Public Health Service for the support of this project. I am equally grateful for less tangible gifts: for the understanding and encouragement of Father Zielinski and the Monsignor Carr Institute Staff; for the generosity and cooperation of those students and patients who furnished the body of experience and material from which I drew while studying the theme of this manuscript.

I also wish to express my gratitude to Mrs. K. Ramsdell and Mrs. Gwen Buckley who typed the final draft. Any errors are of my own commission.

Foreword

I have known Professor Stein from the time she undertook graduate studies after a career as a psychiatric nurse and have followed her research in this study and several others with great interest and in detail. As a colleague I can safely say that this type of study is of the utmost importance, not only because of the high rate of disturbance among children and youth in the contemporary world, but also because this study sets up a careful model of scientific inquiry for investigating such phenomena.

The present book gives the major highlights of this study, which in its totality consists of between 600 and 700 manuscript pages. We can expect that Professor Stein will continue utilizing the background of this larger research design, directly or indirectly, for some time. Nevertheless, the present book is in itself a complete design of research and an exposition of important findings.

Many researchers on the problems of disturbed children and youth today limit their inquiries to such factors as social class without regard to ethnicity, or, less frequently, to cultural background without considering its economic underpinnings. But Professor Stein rightly considers a way of life, however problematic and charged with the kinds of emotion that some call "immature," as having economic, social, familistic, and hence cultural roots. To bring these factors into clear focus she has not only dealt with the variables of education, housing, and income themselves, but has insisted on clothing the mere skeleton with the flesh and blood of living human relationships and familial and subcultural interactions. Her method of analysis and use of healthy control subjects from similar backgrounds are entirely appropriate to the task of studying how these youngsters cope with the inevitable problems that arise in their lives, how some manage successfully, but how others with greater problems become enmeshed in destructive social and cultural processes.

Social or community psychiatry would be powerless without research such as Professor Stein's on group behavior; otherwise, psychiatrists and psychologists would be forced to rely entirely upon dis-
credited or hackneyed notions of invariable forces supposedly existing
everywhere in "human nature"—always to the same extent and with
the same results. Thus, Professor Stein, by introducing meaningful
social and cultural variables, and more importantly, by studying
them quantitatively and meticulously, has put the clinician and the
helping professions in her debt. This study is therefore part of a
complex movement in social and community psychiatry to utilize
actual social and community models of analysis that go beyond the
isolated presumptions of psychological and psychiatric factors. Indeed, the suggestion is that helping professions will simply have to
accommodate to these larger "facts of life," for ignoring or overlook-
ing them may lead to oversimplified, sterile, and asocial approaches.
The reader will undoubtedly feel the impact of Professor Stein's
humane personality in these pages.

Marvin K. Opler

Buffalo
24 June 1968

Special References

The following list of references emphasizes cultural effects of early learning experiences and provided the stimulus for this study.

Arensberg, Conrad, and Solon T. Kimball. *Family and Community in Ireland*. Cambridge: Harvard University Press, 1948.

Barrabee, Paul, and Otto Von Mering. "Ethnic Variations in Mental Stress in Families with Psychotic Children," *Social Problems*. Vol. 1, 1953–1954, pp. 48–53.

Benedict, Ruth. *Patterns of Culture*. New York: New Amsterdam Library, 1959.

Campisi, Paul F. "The Italian Family in the United States," in *Social Perspectives on Behavior*, edited by Herman Stein and Richard Cloward. Illinois: The Free Press of Glencoe, 1958, pp. 76–81.

Carothers, J. C. "A Study of Mental Derangement in Africans and an Attempt to Explain Its Peculiarities to Life," *Journal of Mental Science* 93 (1947): 548–560.

Child, Irvin L. *Italian or American? The Second Generation in Conflict*. New Haven: Yale University Press, 1943.

Erikson, E. H. "The Problem of Ego Identity," *Journal of American Psychoanalytic Association*. Vol. IV, No. 1, 1956, pp. 58–121.

Fishman, Joshua A. "Childhood Indoctrination for Minority Group Membership," *Daedalus* 90 (Spring 1961): 329–349.

Gans, Herbert J. *The Urban Villagers*. Illinois: The Free Press of Glencoe, 1962.

Glazer, Nathan, and Daniel Patrick Moynihan. *Beyond the Melting Pot*. Cambridge: M.I.T. Press, 1963.

Gordon, Milton. "Assimilation in America: Theory and Reality," *Daedalus* 90 (Spring 1961): 263–285.

Handlin, Oscar. *Boston's Immigrants*. Cambridge: Harvard University Press, 1941.

Handlin, Oscar. *The Uprooted.* Boston: Little Brown, 1951.

Hollingshead, August B. "Cultural Factors in the Selection of Marriage Matas," *American Sociological Review,* October 1950, pp. 627–642.

Hsu, Francis L. K., Blanche G. Watrous, and Edith M. Lord. "Culture Pattern and Adolescent Behavior," in *Studies in Adolescence,* edited by Robert E. Grinder. New York: The Macmillan Co., 1963, pp. 59–74.

Kluckhohn, Florence Rockwood. "Family Diagnosis: Variations in the Basic Values of Family Systems," *Social Casework,* XXXIX, February to March 1958, pp. 63–72.

Lord, Eliot, John J. Trenor, and Samuel J. Barrows. *The Italians in America.* New York: B. F. Buck and Co., 1906.

Mead, Margaret. "Adolescence in Primitive and Modern Society," in *Readings in Social Psychology,* edited by T. Newcomb and E. L. Hartley. New York: Henry Holt, 1947, pp. 6–13.

Mintz, N., and D. Schwartz. "Urban Ecology and Psychosis: Community Factors in the Incidence of Schizophrenia and Manic Depression Among Italians in Greater Boston," *International Journal of Social Psychiatry.* Vol. X, No. 2, Spring 1964, pp. 101–117.

Opler, Marvin K. "Cultural Differences in Mental Disorders: An Italian and Irish Contrast in the Schizophrenics," in *Culture and Mental Health,* edited by M. K. Opler. New York: Macmillan Co., 1959.

Piedmont, Eugene. "An Investigation of the Influence of Ethnic Grouping Differences in the Development of Schizophrenia," unpublished Ph.D. dissertation, Department of Sociology, University of New York at Buffalo, June 1962.

Roberts, Bertram, and Jerome K. Myers. "Religion, National Origin, Immigration and Mental Illness," *American Journal of Psychiatry,* Vol. 110, 1954, pp. 759–764.

Rose, Arnold. "The Prevalence of Mental Disorders in Italy," *International Journal of Social Psychiatry.* Vol. X, No. 2, Spring 1964, pp. 87–100.

Sanua, Victor D. "Differences in Personality Adjustment Among Different Generations of American Jews and Non-Jews," in *Culture and Mental Health,* edited by M. K. Opler. New York, Macmillan Co., 1959, pp. 443–466.

Schemerhorn, R. A. *These Our People.* Boston: D. A. Heathland Co., 1949.

Srole, Leo, Thomas Langner, Michael Stanley, Marvin Opler and

Thomas Rennie. *Mental Health in the Metropolis*. Vol. I, New York: McGraw-Hill Co., 1962.

Strodtbeck, Fred L. "Family Interaction, Values and Achievement." in *Talent and Society,* edited by McClelland, Alfred Baldwin, D. Van Nostrand Co., 1958, pp. 135–191.

Ware, Caroline F. "The Breakdown of Ethnic Solidarity: The Case of the Italian in Greenwich Village," in *Social Perspectives on Behavior,* edited by H. Stein and R. Cloward. Illinois: The Free Press, 1958.

Zborowski, Mark. "Cultural Components in Response to Pain," in *Patients, Physicians and Illness,* edited by E. Gartly Jaco. Illinois: The Free Press, 1958, pp. 256–269.

Introduction

Ethnicity as an Important Variable

in Adolescent Disturbance

This study examines the distinctive effects that different ethnic backgrounds have upon adolescent adjustment. Through the examination of two ethnic groups, Irish-Americans and Italian-Americans, it also shows the continuity of cultural effects upon emotionally disturbed adolescents. The study proposes that psychological stresses experienced by adolescents occur in subcultural ethnic configurations with their own variable stress systems and that these cultural contexts structure the largely inseparable currents of personal and social identity. Just as the biologist recognizes that study of the single organism is not the study of the individual life process, but rather the colony, in an analogous sense, the human personality requires study in the context of cultural group life.

If a culture is regarded as an adaptive and adjustive value system, then its component parts derive their systems of meanings, perceptions, and motivations from this base. The United States is built upon a variety of immigrant ethnic and cultural groups each of which varied from the others in its Old World setting and in its acculturation to the New World. The family, where value orientations are largely of ethnic origin, is the single most basic or influential institution for the adolescent and provides him with significant life meanings and patterns of behavior in interpersonal relationships.

The traditional psychiatric method of viewing patients as uniquely oriented individuals disregards in principle the individual's ethnic orientation. However, knowledge of the patient's ethnic characteristics, along with information about his symptomatic and adaptive mechanisms, are valuable for understanding typical cultural stresses encountered in a particular social environment. Knowledge of these special cultural stresses would permit more efficient diagnosis and therapy by public health and mental health personnel, but the relation of ethno-cultural backgrounds and stress systems to mental health remain to be explored in depth.

Social psychiatry attempts to link psychiatry and sociology and to show how culture, the family, and personality become connected variables. It is concerned with the impact of cultural systems and their values upon human psychology and the disorders occasioned by such psychological impact mechanisms. Thus social psychiatry is of great importance to public health practice and preventive medicine.

Since one's earliest concepts of reality develop in the home, the author chose the family to demonstrate the connection between social structure and individual mental disorder. In addition to particular effects found or conclusions drawn in this study, the data itself points out salient ethnic characteristics of the family matrix in the development of basic value orientations and points to ethnic values as determining the kind of behavior through which deviance is expressed.

1

Cultural Roots in Adolescent Adjustment

This study of adjustment problems in adolescence concentrates on certain neglected cultural aspects as a useful extension of knowledge. Different investigators pursue the same goal with different frames of reference. Kluckhohn and Murray (81:48) maintain that "the personality of an individual is the product of inherited disposition and environment. These experiences occur with the field of his biological, physical, and social environment, all of which are modified by the culture of his group." They summarize by stating that (81:35) "every man is in certain respects like all other men, like some other men, like no other man." The individual thus moves through an environment structured by the physical and cultural world and is subject to variations due to unique constitutional and situational determinants.

Biochemical and physiological reactions are well known concomitants of emotional disturbances (43), and thus this study investigates only one relevant causal factor when examining mental disorder from a sociocultural frame of reference. I have made an effort to control certain variables, or at least to acknowledge their existence when they could not be controlled. However, the physiological and biochemical processes of individuals take place in a social world with all of its cultural diversities and complexities. The material and emotional climates created by ethnic and economic groups influence biological states and the social and biological interrelationship needs to be weighed. The study excluded as subjects all adolescents with suspected or actual organic medical disorders in order to diminish the significance of physical illness or biological defect upon adolescent value patterns and personality traits.

Problems and Goals of Study

This study is primarily concerned with the distinctive effects that cultural ethnic groups have upon adolescent adjustment. The following questions motivated undertaking research on this problem: (a) Are there significant qualitative differences in adolescent adjustment as a function of ethnic background? (b) What are the patterns of values, adjustment, processes, and behavioral modalities that differentiate adolescents socialized within the frameworks of their own ethnic groups? (c) Are these differences predictive of adolescent disturbances? (d) In disturbance, will adolescents exaggerate normative reaction patterns, their disturbance modalities being a function of certain ethnic characteristics? (e) Will answer to these questions lead to more discriminating hypotheses concerning causative chains of adolescent disturbance, and potentially to more informed action programs in treatment and prevention?

The study postulates that ethnic culture does have a significant role in adolescent adjustment. It also proposes that adolescents socialized within one ethnic group are stylistically different in attitudinal and behavioral formations than those socialized in another ethnic group. These different ethnic modalities exaggerate disturbance, giving the same *psychiatric* diagnoses different behavioral expression.

Definitions

The study defines "ethnic group" as a group sharing similar biological and emotional traits that are the product of a common heritage and culture. The two ethnic groups compared in this study are American descendants of the southern Irish and the southern Italian groups.

Generally speaking one can examine the distinction between the normal and the abnormal from two viewpoints: normal as statistically usual; or normal as an approximation of an ideally healthy personality and abnormal as a deviation from this theoretical model. Yet, among the normal and the abnormal there are tremendous individual variations, and when the term "sick" is used interchangeably with "abnormal" to mean a deviation the definitions blur. If, therefore, we do not base our definition of mental health on a concept of the average and the usual people, and if we keep in mind that illness and health may co-exist in varying proportions in the same person, we can begin to define mental health as a process of balance and adaptation. Considering mental health as an equilibrating process allows us to see how an individual resolves personal conflict in the interest of maintaining his balance and adaptability. One can describe mental illness as the loss of equilibrating adaptability where conflict is poorly resolved because of inflexibility.

The Family

The psychoanalytic movement from the time of Freud, and the social sciences with even more emphasis, assign the family the fundamental role in child rearing. G. H. Mead (107) emphasizes the importance of the significant symbol between oneself and the generalized other in the child's early frame of reference. This study considers the family the basic institution for the development of fundamental attitudes in the child. Within the socio-cultural complex it provides the limits and freedoms, as well as an acculturation structure for personal identity. The family is the nuclear group representative of national origin, ethnic characteristics, class, and religious beliefs.

Even though the family may be generations removed from its immigrant ancestors, through intergenerational communication it can retain certain value patterns and methods of coping with the environment. If the adolescent reconciles his early experiences with later role expectations, he will, in the process of maturing, take with him patterns of values developed within his family and ethnic group. He will allow a selective interchange between himself and the world, not losing his subcultural values, but incorporating selectively from the community those values that fit into his scheme of life.

Theories of Personality and Adolescent Development

Since this study deals with disturbed adolescents, I will review the literature of psychiatry and the social sciences for theories of personality development and adolescent disturbances and compare the classical psychoanalytic approach, beginning with Freud, to the contemporary cultural approach of the social sciences.

Psychoanalytic literature is concerned with emotional and motivational aspects of personality structure, and with personality development in interaction with culture. Freud (38) focused attention on the role of the family in shaping the child's mental health, but in so doing he emphasized inborn instincts. He stressed the biological foundation of man while he overlooked much of the influential formative role of society. He dwelt heavily upon the first few years of life, but reduced the importance of later periods of social participation, including adolescence. Freud's concept of the superego acknowledged the role of parents and family, but his appraisal of the individual and his social group is ambiguous. Freud perceived the family as the instrument for disciplining the child's biological urges and repressing his instincts; thus, the parent personifies the restraints of society. While analyzing the phenomena of fixation and regression, Freud did not examine the maturation of the personality, except in such highly general concepts as "sublimation." He interpreted culture as the projection of man's conscience upon society.

Freud tended to design stereotypes of parental and childhood roles and contrasted parent and child in the same way that he contrasted the individual and culture. However, his theories revealed the enormous importance of childhood for subsequent personality development.

Later research eventually led to modifications of Freud's work and challenged such conclusions as the biological determination of all stages of development. Where Freud attributed childhood aggression to an inherent drive, others find it to be the result of frustration (18, 6). Other psychoanalysts such as Erich Fromm, Karen Horney, and Harry Stack Sullivan, and anthropologists Ruth Benedict, Ralph Linton, and Margaret Mead question Freud's identification of the sources of aggression and anxiety. They agree that anxiety occurs when something within the person threatens his relationship to significant people. However, the inner impulses that threaten social relationships are not conceived as forces largely created by cultural pressures. There is anthropological evidence that man's personality varies with his culture and that Freud's universal culture does not exist.

Anna Freud (37) emphasized the role of frustration and conflict in the emotional development of the child. Of historical importance is her concept that the child perceives the father as an authoritative and threatening figure. Her emphasis upon parental influences recognizes the importance of the environment of the child.

Rank (88) criticized both Freud's assertion that unconscious memory of past experiences determines behavior and Anna Freud's emphasis upon the pathological. Rank assigned primacy to the conscious ego and saw human nature as creative and productive. The core concept in his theory is that of "will," the force that actively forms the self and modifies the environment. This "will" can lead to a positive creative integration of the self. During adolescence, "will" becomes stronger and more independent until it turns against any authority not of its own choosing. Rank conceived the task of adolescent development as gaining emotional and economic independence from parents. He agrees with Erikson (29) in considering personality a continuous expansion and integration of the intrapsychic self and the self-with-other relationship. G. H. Mead (107) would call this concept the "I" and the "me."

Among those who have attempted to bridge the classical analytic and the social science approaches is the psychiatrist Adolf Meyer (71). He stresses the principle of the bio-social organism as a product of heredity and environment. The socialization of the child reflects the personality of the parent and the interpersonal relationships of the family. Heredity sets limits to the development of personality, but social experiences give it concrete form.

Around 1930 Edward Sapir advocated the collaboration of anthropology, sociology, and psychoanalysis and Eric Fromm (41) took issue with Freud's theory and pointed out that man's nature is a cultural product.

Although Karen Horney (57) does not offer specific formulations on adolescent adjustment, her theory in general highlights the adolescent phase. She reevaluated some of Freud's observations in the light of findings from the social sciences and her own experiences in therapy and she revived Alfred Adler's idea of the importance of neurotic goals, or the pursuit of false values, of which one of the most interesting examples is the "idealized image," or a defensive and erroneous picture of oneself and one's assets. A neurotic goal may be a potential source of anxiety and lead to conflicting goals, such as great ambitions combined with great need for succorance.

Harry Stack Sullivan (109) was an empirical psychoanalyst who believed theory should be based on what could be observed in therapy. He proposed that the individual is a product of interaction with other human beings, and that the personality emerges from the personal and social forces acting upon one from the day of birth. Approval of parents and others in one's culture brings a sense of well-being and security; disapproval brings a sense of insecurity and anxiety. Parataxic distortion occurs when a participant in a situation is reacting to a personification existing chiefly in fantasy. Sullivan described adolescence as a period when psycho-social involvement expands from the family to wider community contacts with an increase of sexual interests. Like Ruth Benedict (7), he pointed out the conflict for adolescents of the child-adult dichotomy in the United States.

Social psychology and anthropology approach the problem of personality through the concept of social roles played within cultural contexts. Margaret Mead (76) questions whether adolescence is always a period of development made unhappy by sexual conflicts. In Samoa, sexual experimentation among adolescents is considered natural. Girls assume increasingly mature female roles with a minimum of adolescent conflicts. Mead asserts that personality development is jointly influenced by heredity, culture, and individual life experiences.

Ruth Benedict (7) states that in American society the differences between child and adult are sharply emphasized by social and legal institutions. The change from one mode of relationship to another creates discontinuity in the natural growth of adolescence. Kurt Lewin (69) also accounts for adolescent difficulties in terms of the dichotomy between child and adult in the cultures of the West. Hsu, Watrous, and Lord (60) state in effect that the great emphasis in the United States on the transitional period and its acting-out process is not found in most other cultures; nor is it necessarily found in certain subcultures of American society. They suggest that further study be made of ethnic group patterned differences in adolescent socialization.

Instructive in cross-cultural comparisons is Jacob Fried's (39) study of the Indian migrants to Peru. These people showed ill health and anxiety when they were neither accepted by the dominant community nor supported by a strong ethnic community from which security could be gained. Victor Sanua (98) found that the social insecurity of the Jewish immigrants in the United States led to the forging of a strong ethnic in-group for psychological security. Beaglehole (5) and Carothers (13), among others, have shown that mental disorders vary in quantity and quality with different cultures and with the ways in which different cultures cope with stress.

Lewin (70), a pioneer of the field theory approach, conceives of the adolescent as one who is in a stage of "social locomotion" and is moving into an unstructured social and psychological field. Unfamiliar situations for which he is unprepared cause crises with consequent withdrawal and inhibition, or aggression and development of extreme points of view. Lewin uses the concept "lack of cognitive structure" to explain the uncertainty of the adolescent. He refers to the adolescent as the "marginal man" who neither belongs to the world of children nor to the adult world. This marginality produces conflicts in arriving at personal values, ideologies, and guides to behavior.

Coleman (19) found that adolescents look to their own peer groups to help them shape their interests and gain their social rewards, thereby creating an adolescent subculture with its own language and value system. Lewin (70) refers to this period as the culture of the "marginal man" and Erikson calls this period a "psychological moratorium." In contrast to Coleman, Friedenberg (40) envisions a vanishing adolescent society because of the increasing demands from society for conformity and bureaucratic organization. The adolescent is denied the experience of trying to establish his own identity and individuality.

Of interdisciplinary importance, Erikson's contribution lies in his approach to the study of human growth and behavior. He borrows the Freudian biological stages of development and reworks them into a theory of ego development within a social and cultural framework (28, 30). He defines eight bio-social stages of cultural conflict and resolution. The first stage, *trust-mistrust,* is developed in infancy, and is an important basic resolution potential for an adolescent's conflict in *identity-identity* diffusion. Erikson defines identity as being composed of three parts: conscious identity, or a sense of individual self; unconscious identity, or a striving for unity of character; and ego synthesis, or an unconscious and conscious solidarity with the group's ideals. Ego identity takes place:

> among men who share an ethnic area, an historical area, or an economic area, and are guided by community images of good and evil. (30:21).

In *Childhood and Society* he states:

> What the regressing and growing, rebelling and maturing youths are now primarily concerned with is who they are and what they are in the eyes of the wider circle of significant peo-

ple as compared with what they themselves have come to feel they are; and how to connect their dreams, idiosyncrasies, roles, and skills cultivated earlier with the occupational and sexual prototypes of the day.

Where such a dilemma is based on a strong doubt as to one's ethnic and sexual identity, delinquent and outright psychotic incidents are not uncommon. (28:266)

Erikson, in effect, summarizes the adolescent and personality theories of the day: Freud's biological orientation with Hartmann's ego psychology (51), Sherif's group identifications (101), and the cultural scientist's emphasis upon the importance of tradition and culture in molding children. Erikson notes that adolescents tell the older generation whether life as represented by the older ones has meaning, and whether they will renew the older generation's role model or rebel.

The Family, Ethnicity, and Social Class

Florence Kluckhohn (66) deals with the societal value systems that shape the values of the family. She differentiates with a single set of concepts the values that underlie families of different ethnic backgrounds and accounts for the kind of conflict that ethnic families may develop within the dominant American culture. The values of the middle-class American family are contrasted with the variant value orientations of ethnic families.

According to Sirjamaki (103), cultural configurations provide moral principles and patterns of behavior that guide and limit the behavior of families. He states that such generalizations are necessarily broad, since ethnic subcultures differ from that of (so-called) native-born Americans. Generally speaking, he characterizes youth as a period of innocence, energy, and enthusiasm, with antagonism existing between the generations.

Ackerman (1), in endeavoring to build a new framework germane to family diagnosis and treatment of emotional disorder, emphasizes that, like his parents, the adolescent today is scared and worried. If his parents are fearful, he is doubly fearful. If his parents are confused, he is plunged into confusion and panic. The adolescent's ever-present struggle with symbols of authority helps to shape his self-image. His need for parental protection continues, and his dependence upon them is unresolved. At the same time, he has a strong need to live his own life and to make his own decisions. The disturbed adolescent feels far from whole, and a constant tension keeps pace with his drive to extract from life that which he feels he lacks so that he may approximate more closely his ideal image of himself.

With emphasis upon the communication of behavioral traits between generations in the family, Fisher and Mendell (33) studied the transmission of neurotic patterns in the family over two to three generations. They report on the similarities of fantasy and behavior passed on from parents to child. The results of this and other studies indicate that personality traits and value orientations (as well as hidden fears and wishes) are maintained through intergenerational communication in an ethnic group.

Contemporary literature in the social sciences is abundant with studies of social stratification, and of the relationship between various human attributes and social class (22, 73). Significant studies are those by Hyman (61), Centers (14), and Clark (17). Hyman is concerned with the values placed on education and achievement by those in different social classes. Centers studied adolescent social class attitudes toward labor and labor collectivism. Clark investigated mental disorder correlated with income, occupation, and prestige in the community.

A few studies that may challenge the findings of studies on social class are those concentrating on ethnic group differences in specific variable investigations. Zborowski (117) found differences in the attitude to pain among Jewish, Italian, and "old American" families. Opler (85) found differences between Italian and Irish patients categorically diagnosed as schizophrenics. Roberts and Myers (90), in their study of national origin and mental illness, found associations of the Jewish group with high neuroticism, the Italian group with high affective disorders and illnesses of senescence, and the Irish group with high alcohol and drug intake. The finding of affective disorders in the Italian group has been corroborated by Rose (95), who studied mental disorders in Italy.

Evidence of an Old World value orientation brought to the New World is indicated by Strodtbeck (108) in his analysis of achievement motivation in two ethnic groups. In this analysis, certain ethnic groups seem to compose certain strata of society, depending upon the group's receptivity to change and challenge in the new society, and they have in turn brought changes in the dominant value system.

Gans (42), in describing an Italian-American group in an urban community, determined that the characteristics and traits of the group were due to its working-class orientation. Ethnic and class structures are kindred concepts. In order to determine differences in subcultural socialization, the social class factor needs to be held constant so that one may discover the ethnic characteristics.

Roberts and Myers (90), in their study of family and class dynamics of mental disorders, generally ignored the ethnic variable in their description of social class differences. They found two distinctly different ethnic groups in each of the social classes they studied, but these were not considered in the interpretation of their psychiatric and sociological data. Yet, Piedmont (87) found differences between the Polish and German groups in symptoms of schizophrenia.

Fishman (34) refers to the "core" culture of the minority group and starts with the assumption that the child has ambivalent feelings about loyalty to his ethnic group and loyalty to the larger American society. Fishman separates the child's attempted solution into acts of "separatism" (retain minority values), "integrationism" (preference for the American values), and "biculturism" (orientation to the behavior of both the minority and the American system).

Of significance also is Kleiner's and Parker's (64) study of status, goal striving, and mental disorder. In their review of several studies pertaining to these concepts, they come to the conclusion that no consistent relationship may be found between social class status and mental disorders or between social mobility and mental disorders, but rather that there is some tendency for aspirational frustration to be correlated with mental disorder. They write, however, that psychological meaningfulness varies with the nature of the population groups and with the nature of the community under study.

Mintz and Schwartz (79), studying urban-ethnic ecology and incidence of psychosis, found that the incidence of schizophrenia and manic-depression among Italian-Americans in Boston was inversely related to the population-density of Italian-Americans in the area. They did not find class to be significantly related to mental disorder, but ethnicity was significant. Etiologically, toleration for deviation among some ethnic groups as contrasted with others merits consideration.

Kluckhohn and Strodtbeck analyze the way in which orientations are related to ethnicity:

> Value orientations are complex but definitely patterned princi-
> ples, resulting from transactional interplay of the three analyti-
> cally distinguishable elements of the evaluative process—the
> cognitive, the affective, and directive elements—which give
> order and direction to an even flowing stream of human acts
> and thought. . . . (67:4)

> Variations in value orientations of whole societies, of subgroups
> within societies and of individual persons, who are, in the final
> analysis, the actual carriers of culture, are subjects of general
> interest. Our most basic assumption is that there is a systematic
> variation in the realm of cultural phenomena which is both as
> definite and as essential as the demonstrated systematic varia-
> tion in physical and biological phenomena. (67:3)

Kluckhohn and Strodtbeck (67) hypothesize that the rate and degree of assimilation of any ethnic group to the dominant American
culture will depend in large measure upon the compatibility of the
group's own rank ordering of values with that of the dominant culture.

These studies on ethnicity, though few in number, are a successful
beginning in differentiating stylistic patterns of response between
ethnic groups when social class has been held constant.

2

Ethnic Groups

Focus on Ethnic Groups and Social Class

It is the author's contention that sociological research on mental illness neglects the importance of ethnicity, and concentrates instead on social class categories. Lipset and Bendix (73) examine attitudes and behavior as they are related to social stratification, but do not treat ethnic variables in social-emotional research. Others describe ethnic groupings but do not consider them important in the interpretation of data (55, 91).

Socioeconomic categories, of course, should not be overlooked, for one's socioeconomic standing determines, in part, one's style of life and one's value orientations (61). Social class and ethnicity both contribute to the development of personality, but neither has been adequately analyzed either as separate or as combined dimensions in most research on mental health.

Early learning comes from familial cultural contacts that are passed on through the generations, thus, familial and cultural background with its systems of values is extremely important in studies of personality and emotional disturbances. Individuals may move across socioeconomic class lines but, ethnic value systems are not necessarily discarded when the individual changes his economic class. This is clearly demonstrated by Strodtbeck (108), who indicates that the Jewish-American group maintains values of education and social mobility regardless of class status.

Immigrants to the United States frequently find themsleves at the bottom of the socioeconomic ladder because they lack urban experience and occupational skills. As they become acculturated and learn skills, they move up the economic ladder. This process usually occurs on an intergenerational basis, the children being more sophisticated than their parents about life and its opportunities in the

new country. Children reared in these ethnic groups internalize the
values of parental ethnic orientation. Rosen (96) has recently demonstrated, in studies holding socioeconomic class constant, the influence of ethnicity and race in achievement orientation.

In view of the above, one can infer that ethnic groups have systems of values that give meanings, expectation, and motivations to
their members. Knowledge of the specific ethnic culture of the child
will give some indication of how he will value education and occupational striving, and will illustrate the style and manner in which
he interacts with other people. People with different ethnic backgrounds presumably see and experience identical experiences in different ways.

Traditional stereotypes of ethnic groups have become less common as these groups acculturate to American ways. Especially since
World War II, Old World folkways, mores, and customs have given
way to more American styles as second and third generation children become more assimilated or accepted into American society.
The assumption that minorities soon adopt the "American way of
life," however, is probably a vast over-simplification. People may
quickly discard foreign mannerisms and speech, but the overt adop-
tion of American traits by members of an ethnic group does not
truly measure the extent to which deeper values, patterns of reaction, and perceptual or cognitive peculiarities have altered.

Although adolescent peer groups contribute to the dilution of
ethnic customs in American life, the adolescent may still marry
within his own ethnic group and thus reinforce ethnic mores and
normative behavior. Hollingshead (53) agrees with Kennedy's (63)
conclusions on the importance of religious barriers (also a value system) to intermarriage in New Haven, Connecticut. Kennedy found
the incidence of marriage within the same religious group for three
groups to be: Jews, 97.1 percent; Catholics, 93.8 percent and Protestants, 74.4 percent. In cases of ethnic intermarriage, Kennedy (63)
found the percentages of Italian, Irish, and Polish people inter-
marrying with North Europeans, Germans, and Jews, as considered
ethnically, were only 17.5 percent in 1930 and 16.29 percent in
1940. Hollingshead and Kennedy conclude that the presence of cohesive ethnic groups, the existence of prejudice, loyalty to the
group, and religious adherence combine to put a check on intermarriage. Should intragroup marriage continue, the children would
continue to receive concentrated ethnic values. Intermarriage may
promote assimilation, depending upon whether the couple is loyal

to a single faith or group, whether they are loyal to their individual faiths, or whether each is loyal to neither faith.

The foregoing discussion of ethnicity as a cultural basis within social classes brings into the foreground the importance of familial orientation and childhood socialization in different kinds of value systems. One might say an individual perceives with an ethnocentric bias.

Profile of the Ethnic Groups Used in This Study

I examined literature on southern Ireland and southern Italy for descriptions of family structure and function as these affect the adjustments of the children. I will now describe the norms of these ethnic groups and follow with hypothetical frames of reference that include inferences of differential response patterns between adolescents in these two ethnic groups. I refer to these frames and their hypotheses throughout the study for verification or refutation. These general frames of reference include the following broad areas of investigation: family structure and function, goals and value orientation, projection of inner need and conflict into behavioral role, and emotional expression. These areas served as fundamental frames for the construction of a questionnaire. The literature concerning Irish and Italian cultures does not examine the effect of their values on adolescent adjustment, so clear operational categories of behavior within the different subcultures must be inferred from descriptions of practices and nuances of living.

In order to reach the more pervasive attitudinal and perceptual value patterns that differentiate the two groups, I used psychological tests and a questionnaire to determine the lessons a child learns from his family and culture. These tests investigate his version of socially sanctioned behavior patterns and how he incorporates them into his own life as part of his motivational system. One may call this internalization an integration of role and identification with dominant figures in his life. The tests emphasized economic stress, achievement orientations, and peer group affiliations in order to determine differential development of mental illness.

They also endeavored to reveal any ethnically styled orientations in the home that would organize the projection of the child's inner needs and conflicts into a pattern of behavioral roles and emotional expressions. These frames enable one to compare the disturbed and control groups on horizontal as well as vertical levels, and they also permit examination of the ethnic ground from which the attitudinal and perceptual forces spring.

Profile of the Irish Group

According to Handlin (48), northern Ireland was the primary source of immigrants to the United States until 1835. These people, about two thousand arriving annually, were chiefly artisans and well-to-do farmers. By 1850 immigration increased seven-fold and was derived chiefly from southern Ireland. These later groups were mostly of Irish peasants escaping both the great potato famine in their homeland and the rule of Britain. Since the great number of Irish immigrants to the United States came from the south of Ireland, and since most of the Irish subjects in the research sample descended from southern Irish families, it is the structure and function of family life in that area that I examined.

Although there is abundant description of the Irish-American contributions to politics, theatre, music, and journalism, there is little description of Irish-American family life. I have consequently developed and extended to the United States a description of family life in southern Ireland on the assumption that patterns of interpersonal relationships are handed down through generations.

Arensberg and Kimball (3) describe the Southern County Irish family in the middle of the nineteenth century as a nuclear one of parents and children in a rural farm economy. The wife not only attended to household chores but also had a share in the farm work. Within the family the father had in nominal control, but he was always subject to the expectations of his wife. Thus, even though acknowledged the ultimate authority figure, the father was subject to control by his wife, which shows a certain dependency in this sphere of family relationships.

Arensberg and Kimball (3) state that until the age of seven the male child was the constant companion of the mother from whom, "it learns its speech amid a flood of constant endearments, admonitions, and encouragements" (3:59). As guide and constant companion, the mother was solicitous and constantly exercised restraints and controls in teaching the child prudence, modesty, and good conduct. Her authority made itself felt through praise and persuasion. Only when a grave breach of conduct by the child demanded the intervention of ultimate authority was the father called upon to punish the child. The father then entered the son's awareness as a source of discipline. Even when the son began to help the father with the masculine work, a barrier of respect and authority made it difficult for any intimacy to develop between them. In family disputes, the mother acted as diplomat between father and son, she remained the source of his comfort, and she constantly solicited the son's affections.

During the nineteenth century, when the Irish came to the United States in great numbers, they settled in cities as unskilled laborers. The deep pessimism bred of the poor economic conditions they fled in Ireland was not relieved when they encountered discrimination in the United States (48). The practice of training sons in rural skills disappeared with emigration to the United States and an urban setting. By spending many hours away from home on the job, the father's dependency and frustration increased. He was not only more dependent upon the mother for the management of household affairs, but was dependent upon others for employment as well. It also appears that the mother's domination in nurture of the child increased, and that the social distance between father and son grew. Some (44) interpret the large alcoholic intake attributed to the Irish male as the expression of a passive-dependent role that developed because of living conditions in the new country.

We can visualize the intrafamilial relationships of the son as one controlled by maternal authority and only distantly respectful of the father, who participated little in child rearing. During adolescence, dependence upon maternal authority with its resultant identifications conceivably contributed to a more difficult adjustment to masculine role identification. Descriptions of the Southern County Irish family indicates that the son developed the same characteristics as the father in relationship to the mother. We can assume that, if the father is used as a masculine model within the nuclear family, the Irish-American son adopts the role of passive dependency as his father did before him. The son would then find it difficult to free himself from maternal domination and to develop a mature masculine independence.

The skeletal family description above can be understood only when reinforced by recognition of emotional and cognitive tenacity in the face of stress. A deep melancholy and pessimism, displayed in Irish music and lyrical poems, was brought to the New World from a poor agrarian economy and difficult economic existence (12, 59, 115). This attitude was not greatly relieved in America where the Irish found equally poor living conditions of a different order (48). Peasants in Ireland had Catholicism for consolation. Their religion assured that man received his true reward in an external scheme, not in this frustrating temporal world. Earthly affairs could become insignificant and deliverance by Divine Grace a promised reality. Discouraged in the United States by socioeconomic discrimination, the Irish turned even more to religion for consolation. They depended upon the Mother of Christ as the intercessor for Divine Grace; thus, it can be said that passive dependence by the father and son upon maternal authority was accentuated by dependency upon a greater maternal deity. The depth of their religious beliefs affected their educational patterns (48), for in the face of compulsory education, they developed parochial schools where education and religion could be unified.

The ability of the Irish to engage in fantasies of pleasure as compensatory measures against pessimism has often been noted. They possess a traditional folklore of benevolent fairies and leprechauns who would reveal great treasure if they were caught (12). Pleasurable imaging is a reality in the mind which can be enjoyed despite a dim reality of life, especially during periods of emotional stress.

If these life patterns do pass to succeeding generations we may infer that the male shows passive dependency towards the more dominant female authority. Thus, it can be inferred that the Irish-American boy exercises emotional restraint to gain social approval in interpersonal maneuvers. Consequently, they emphasize introjection rather than extrojection in the release of emotional tension. Moral and ethical values direct the Irish-American boy to a deflation of self-esteem, leading to wishful thinking and fantasies of ideal selfhood.

If we follow this logic through, then, compared to the Italian-American boy, the Irish-American boy experiences less ingroup feeling with either family or peers. In peer groups the average Irish-American boy is a follower rather than a leader. A few close friends are desired in preference to many friends. If there is a rejection of parental values, the adolescent seeks out peers he can follow for social approval and for self-esteem. Rebellious attitudes bring low-self-esteem. A compensatory device is fantasy in which the self is glorified and reality is less grim.

An apt description of Irish manhood is provided by James Joyce:

He was sure that Gallaher was inferior in birth and education. He was sure that he could do something better than his friend had ever done, or could ever do, if he only had the chance. What was it stood in his way? His unfortunate timidity! He wished to vindicate himself in some way, to assert his manhood. (62:128)

In "Uprooted," Frank O'Connor's character, Ned, felt that

He was popular because of his gentleness, but how many concessions that involved! He was hesitating, good natured, slow to see guile, slow to contradict. He felt he was constantly underestimating his own powers. He even felt he lacked spontaneity. . . . (84:101)

Magic, magic, magic! He saw it as in a children's picture-book with all its colors intolerably bright; something he had outgrown and could never return to, while the world he aspired to was as remote and intangible as it had seemed even in the despair of youth. (84:118)

Profile of the Italian Group

During the period of mass migration from Italy, the bulk of immigrants came from southern Italy or Sicily. Peak migrations occurred from 1907 to 1913 and comprised the largest single homogeneous group of all the nationalities that arrived in the United States since the year 1880 (99). Schemerhorn (99) indicates that by the depression years the majority of Italian-Americans had resided in the United States for an average of seventeen years, as compared to an average forty to fifty years for the English-Americans and Irish-Americans.

Since the Italian-American boys in this study descend from southern Italians, the study will examine the family culture of Southern Italy.

Schemerhorn describes the southern Italian way of life as a distinctive subculture representing economically deprived areas. In the southern Italian culture, peasants were considerably lower in social status than noblemen and clergy, and they considered those above them enemies. Furthermore, a peasant's title to his land or tenure on it was uncertain, which reduced his attachment to it. He did not trust the government and considered the police enemies. Self-reliance was honored. Reporting of misdeeds to the governmental authorities was a grave offense which led to social ostracism of the village betrayer.

The clergy, as part of the upper class, was also the target of hostility. The peasants believed the clergy contributed to their deprivation and uncertain living. Schemerhorn states that women, children, and old people emphasized religious observance. The young were to learn devotion and the old were to prepare for death.

Although obligations to the community were minimal, the peasant gave unquestioning allegiance to his large and extended family. Campisi (11) and Schemerhorn agree that the family was strongly patriarchal. The father's domination was based on fear. He was capable of swift and immediate physical punishment for misdeeds. The mother, as the nurturant center of domestic life, was subserviant and ingratiating to the husband but stern with the children. The parents valued well-mannered children who behaved courteously before others. The peasants had little use for education in village life, for the father preferred to view his children as potential economic assets in the interest of family solidarity and economic security. The son was subordinate to family power and was expected to work hard and contribute to the family income. The closest ties outside of the family were to godparents. Thus, the family, as a community within a community, was highly cohesive because of its members' loyalty and because it provided a specific way of life, with social and economic security for individuals within it.

Schemerhorn describes the Italian peasant as one who was not ashamed to show his emotions. The immediate present was more important than future gain. Frustrations in daily life could lead to aggressive behavior of an ephemeral sort. There was an immediate urgency for emotional expression, which just as suddenly cooled off. The Italian male showed a personal sensitivity to social ostracism, exploitation, and to ungraceful social behavior. Schemerhorn describes Italian music as dramatic and melodic, rather than reflective, with changes of mood and love of display. Schemerhorn writes of the Italian male: "As an individual, he identifies himself with actors rather than with passive admirers . . . and enters into their ardent emotions with tremendous urgency" (99:245). Thus the Italian participated with easy display of mutual group feeling in daily life and was not a participant observer (as is characteristic of the Irish).

Ware (113) supports Campisi (11) in his description of changes among Italian-Americans as a result of emigration to the United States. The second and third generations of children developed two methods of adjustment. One manner is to reject completely the Old World forms; the other is to create a marginal bi-cultural synthesis. The latter finds expression as an urgent need for Americanization and the shaping of family structure and function to the needs of the urban American family; yet, at the same time, the parental way is not rejected and the bond is not wholly broken.

The Italian-American family in the second generation is an urban, more modern, democratic, well-integrated family with a high degree of mobility. School patterns are more quickly assimilated, and sons prepare for occupations different from those of their fathers. Family in-group solidarity changes to a more limited affectionate and recreational solidarity. The Old World anticlericalism persists in the United States, which Campisi (11) indicates is especially evident when contributions and gifts are requested for support of the priesthood. An increase in divorce and separation also reflect the weakening hold of the Catholic Church and there is a decrease in the superstitious beliefs of peasant religion. (11, 99).

The father, still head of the family, has learned that American laws forbid harsh physical punishment of children. Boys still tend to be regarded as superior to girls, although this belief is waning. Children are encouraged to prepare themselves for future careers, and parents remain demonstrative in their behavior and affections. They are quick to respond to the child's behavior and needs. The mother takes on a larger role in business affairs outside the home, and the children also become more involved with the community.

In his study of marginal Italian-American adolescents, Child (16) finds three major reactions to the problem of marginality: the rebel reaction, the in-group reaction toward Italian culture, and the apathetic reaction of escape from the problem.

Hansen (50) discusses the "principle of third generation interest." The third generation, which has adopted American culture and American speech, still takes pride in its Italian ancestry:

> Whenever any immigrant group reaches the third generation stage in its development, a spontaneous and almost irresistable impulse arises which forces the thoughts of many people of different professions, different positions in life, and different points of view to interest themselves in that one factor they have in common—the heritage of blood. (50:120)

The sense of being Italian is very alive; Ware (113) also emphasizes a strong consciousness of kind. In an interview with a prominent Italian-American, she quotes:

> My people understand two things, kindness and force. . . . The rational temperate attitude of the American does not move them. You must reckon with the intense loyalty of the Italian . . . and remember that he expects loyalty, not reason or justice in return, and is very quick to suspect that by the latter treatment you are letting him down. (113:120)

This philosophy may account for some conflicts second generation Italians have with representatives of the law and community agencies.

The Italian-American adolescent has, therefore, strong ties of affection and obligation to his family. He displays this affection openly, and he acts out his other emotions within his family and peer groups. His father, dominant in the family, is easily angered by disapproved conduct. Frequent disapproval and punishment may lead to negative relations between father and son, resulting in male role confusion for the son. The parents' concern with their immediate situation, in contrast to the son's more American concern with long-range goals, results in lack of understanding and communication between parents and child.

The son, if unable to communicate with his dominant father and subserviant mother, seeks substitute group participation with such of his peers as have common attitudes and values. Within his peer group he is able to seek the power, status, and recognition accorded to his father within the family setting. His general tendency to participate, to respond quickly and openly, and to act aggressively, give him potential leadership in his chosen group. These personal traits enable him to challenge authority, and in doing so, he may become belligerent. Hatred and rebellion may encourage sociopathic escapades. Aggression and confusion in the male role generates Don Juanism in relating to the opppsite sex.

The Italian-American boy copes with life pragmatically. He strives for better paying and cleaner jobs, and he views education as a means to obtain these jobs. If Sherif's (101) concept of social group roles is correct, the foregoing description of the Italian-American adolescent indicates he learned his concept of social roles and attitudes from his family.

Frames of Reference and Hypotheses

One can infer from these descriptions of Irish and Italian ethnic groups differences in behavioral and cognitive orientations, which are maintained in child-rearing practices. The major premise of this study is that child-rearing practices, through communication of attitudes and manifest treatment of the child, determine both the nature of adolescent adjustments and some adolescent psychological problems. Child-rearing practices in the Italian-American family are different from those in the Irish-American family. In emotional disturbance, the adolescent maintains the patterns of values and behavioral modalities derived from his ethnically based family, but in reaction to stress he intensifies these modalities to uncomfortable limits for himself and others.

From the literature on the southern Irish and southern Italians and their American descendants, one can develop frames of reference that delineate the emotional and behavioral modalities of adolescents in the two groups. One can then develop hypotheses for differentiating modal reaction patterns in Irish-American and Italian-American adolescent boys.

Frame I: Relationships to Family and Authority

Dependent Action: (Irish-American)

—overtly compliant
—seeks direction for decisions and roles
—defers to authority
—follows parental expectations in behavior
—conforms to direction

Independent Action: (Italian-American)

—seeks recognition for respect and status
—argues with parents
—does not always regard parental expectations
—seeks independence in social life and vocation

Hypothetical Modalities

The Irish-American adolescent, whose mother dominates in household management, overtly complies with the dictates of his mother in household relationships and seeks parental approval. In Erikson's terms there is a basic trust in the mother-child relationship and the child tries to please his mother as much as possible.

The Italian-American adolescent is reared in a home with an extended kinship pattern where the mother, while warm and ingratiating, assumes a submissive role in child rearing and the father is dominant and quick to disapprove and punish. In Erikson's terms, the child develops a "distrust" for the father, not being able to anticipate when he will show approval or disapproval. The adolescent often quarrels with him, openly expressing his feelings as is the family pattern. He may seek recognition and self-esteem outside the home and with other substitute models.

Frame II: Sexual Identifications

Role Model Identity:

—effort made to emulate the father or substitute
—budding heterosexual strivings

Confused Identity: (Italian-American)

—effort at masculine roles with feelings of inadequacy
—dislikes father and unable to identify with him
—no adequate substitute masculine role model
—confusion in assumption of traits of both parents
—aborted efforts at heterosexual strivings—Don Juanism

Lack of Masculine Identification: (Irish-American)

—unable to identify with masculine role
—identifies with mother or other female figure
—passive heterosexual strivings
—feminine in characteristics

Hypothetical Modalities

The Irish-American adolescent, dependent and close to the mother, develops problems assuming an adult masculine role. If the boy has an American image of the social and economic masculine role with its attendant independence and male adequacy, the dependent position of the father makes identification with him difficult and emulation abortive. He may perceive the father as unsupportive in time of need. The nuclear family structure, in contrast to the extended family of the Italian-American boy, does not provide the boy with a range of father substitutes. If he does identify with the father, he assumes a passive-dependent male role consistent with his childhood dependence on his mother. He comes to exhibit passivity in relation to all females. He may adopt desirable traits from both parents, with an inability to determine what his masculine role should be. When he turns to his peers for help he assumes a passive-dependent position within the group, but makes an effort to go along with masculine activities.

The Italian-American adolescent feels kindly toward his submissive mother. He may resent and distrust his more dominant father whom he cannot better in an argument, so in striving for a masculine image, he seeks a father substitute within his extended family. His efforts at dominance and independence within his peer group lead him to braggadocio. Identification with his mother and distance from his father intensify his heterosexual strivings which results in restless Don Juanism to express his identity confusion.

Frame III: Relationship to Peers

In-group Directed: (Italian-American)

—heavy reliance upon peer group sanctions
—regulates own wishes to accord with peer group norms
—seeks deference from associates
—strives for status and power
—has several friends
—sees self from other viewpoint
—often a leader of group, enhancing group activity

Less In-group Directed: (Irish-American)

—wishes and desires not always part of peer group norms
—may follow parental expectations
—prefers few friends to several friends
—seeks group for social intercourse, not leadership
—may be fringe member of many groups
—belongs to large community groups
—does not originate sociopathic group behavior

Hypothetical Modalities

The Irish-American adolescent tends to participate as a member of a group rather than as a leader. He seeks peers for social intercourse and for empathy. His restrained emotional expression and self-conscious thinking allow him a few close friends, while his relationships in larger community organizations are more superficial. He rejects parental values only to enact a similar dependent role in the peer group he has joined for thrills and gratification. Although rebelling from home he follows the rebellious activities of his group, rather than initiate them himself. He is a joiner rather than a leader in delinquent acts. This dependence reinforces his doubts concerning the reliability of his own decisions.

Although his peer group provides him with the potential for masculine identification, the assumption of masculine values poses egocentric uncertainty for the Irish-American boy. The boy, in attempting to gain independence from his mother, becomes dependent and compliant as his father is in social relationships.

Beginning at an early age, the Italian-American adolescent learns in-group give-and-take methods of interpersonal relations with his extended family. He learns to think and act openly in defense of his rights. He learns to value the generalized other as an important frame of reference from which to view himself. Home stresses in early childhood teach him to seek status and recognition among his peers and extended family. Gratified with this recognition and conditioned in this method of social intercourse, he belongs to informal groups and clubs. His autonomy and self-image are derived from overt manipulation of his social environment.

Frame IV: Hostility and Anxiety

Anxiety: (Irish-American)

—inner diffuse tension and uneasiness
—guilt over transgressions
—loss of self-esteem
—feelings of inadequacy, helplessness
—self-conscious feelings
—feelings of isolation and being misunderstood

Hostility: (Italian-American)

—hatred, anger
—distrust, suspicion
—overt challenge of authority
—desire to injure
—desire to conquer or to get even
—rebellion, belligerency, ridicule

Hypothetical Modalities

The Irish-American boy's code of ethics (which is derived from the maternal code of ethics) induces feelings of anxiety and introjected guilt for perceived transgressions. His dependence, religious orientation, and constraint in emotional expression combine to make him anxious when he fails to comply with parental expectations or the moral code. His sensitivity to disapproval, his difficulty in overt manipulative relationships with peers, and his lack of confidence in self-assertion create uneasiness when he attempts to make his own decisions. His moral-ethical code is binding, and transgressions lower his self-esteem. Lack of parental harmony, disillusionment in his ego ideal, and lack of solid masculine identification create introjected diffuse anxiety and uneasiness which may be made manifest in hypochondriacal complaints. The desire for change is converted into daydreams of what could be a better life at another time and in another world.

The Italian-American adolescent's code of ethics is pragmatically derived from the give and take of overt, daily social intercourse. His affective conditioning enables him to express his hostility openly and to challenge authority. He transforms his anxiety and sense of inadequacy by the projection of blame onto other people. He is able to mold his anxieties to the needs of his peer groups and their action programs. Intensive group participation enables him to cooperate actively with the group in delinquent acts. His dominance and aggression may drive him to leadership in delinquency. Where overwhelming hostility and aggression are not gratified by defiance and when despair threatens ego-integration, he saves face through conversion symptoms when his behavior and attitudes cannot be otherwise excused or rationalized.

Frame V: Emotional Expression

Lack of Constraint: (Italian-American)

—angry, defiant, sarcastic
—rebellious, belligerent
—happy, euphoric

In Constraint: (Irish-American)

—appears undisturbed and unable to appreciate one's circumstances

—denial of disturbance
—unwilling and unable to express oneself, defensive
—withdrawn

Hypothetical Modalities

The Irish-American adolescent has learned emotional constraint and he complies in order to gain the social approval that reduces his tensions. He resorts to autistic thinking and fantasy in the ventilation of his feelings. This boy may be unable to verbalize his feelings adequately, unwilling to express himself, or he may be self-conscious and defensive to save face. His emotional constraint often makes interpretation of his behavior by others difficult. His attention-getting behavior and desire for succor constrast vividly to the overt, distrustful projection of anger by the Italian-American boy.

The Italian-American boy is equally quick in the acting out of affection or of distrust and anger. He anticipates action and reaction and can react defiantly and belligerently to authority or his peers in both speech and action.

Frame VI: Role and Behavior

Compliant: (Irish-American)

—seeks overt signs of approval
—obeys authority, respects authority
—wants to be told what to do
—questions little, afraid to disagree
—passive with opposite sex
—allows leader to give orders

Aggressive: (Italian-American)

—questions forcefully
—seeks status, leadership, power, recognition
—behavior defies social norms of conduct
—overt effort to harm someone or get even
—overt heterosexual advances

Hypothetical Modalities

The Irish-American adolescent, to preserve his self-esteem and to reduce guilt for transgressions, respects and complies with authority. He may, in his efforts at identification, comply with older boys who teach him masculine acting-out patterns. His behavior seeks approval from others through subordinating himself. Success in this maneuver minimizes anxiety and guilt and increases self-esteem. In sociopathic escapades he seeks approval of masculine-appearing and seemingly masculine-behaving peers.

The Italian-American boy acts out spontaneously. His sociopathic escapades and behavior that defy the norms of social conduct show little prior reflection especially in contrast to the Irish-American boy. His aggressive behavior also leads to status-seeking of a socially acceptable sort for he is outgoing in seeking any power and status that enhance him in the eyes of others and therefore also in himself.

Frame VII: Patterns of Values

Egocentric and Idealistic: (Irish-American)

—religious morals—emphasize golden rule and honoring parents
—honesty, sincerity
—brotherhood, friendliness
—responsibility
—reliance upon one's desires and desires of authoritative figures
—desire to achieve the end one wishes, whether reality permits it or not

Sociocentric and Pragmatic: (Italian-American)

—gets along with people, makes friends
—works with group orientation
—knows the right people
—respects people's rights
—manipulates people
—fights for rights
—be seen in the right places
—deals with reality as one finds it, rather than as one wishes to find it
—enjoys outgoing occupations
—seeks material rewards

Hypothetical Modalities

The Irish-American boy lives by the moral code of his parents, the law, and religion. Loyalty, friendliness, and sincerity are his ideals of work and play. He believes that a man should be kind and good to other men, that the individual is responsible for his own actions before the law, and he is concerned with good and evil. When his achievement orientation is frustrated, he suppresses aggression and resorts to compensatory fantasy where he creates an ideal self-image. Isolation and identity diffusion serve to intensify his subordination to authority.

The Italian-American has a religious and moral code but dilutes it with his more pragmatic attitude and behavior. His orientation emphasizes in-group friendships and contacts with the right people. In the face of anxiety and frustration, he shows active aggression in overt manipulation of the environment for the enhancement of self-esteem.

3

Methodological Procedures

Briefly, the principal methodological operations used in this study are: (a) the enumeration of individuals receiving psychiatric care; (b) sample selection of community control adolescents; (c) description of the index of social position; (d) description of the method of study and the administration of the research instruments. Each of these operations will be described in succeeding sections of this chapter.

Selection of Samples

Control Criteria

Basically the research design is a four-cell table, split one way into two ethnic groups and the other way into disturbed and control groups. In order to separate out certain factors that might distort the results, certain controls were placed upon selection of the sample.

The sample groups were limited to white males to control for racial factors. Boys chosen for the samples were Roman Catholics since Catholicism was the modal faith of the Irish-American and Italian-American adolescents. Controls for religion were made in order to eliminate any effect from mixed religions in small sample studies. Adolescents from thirteen to nineteen years of age with at least one sibling were chosen, for an only child may exhibit behavior patterns masking the purely ethnic factors. No adolescent who had, or was suspected of having, organic disease was chosen for study in order to control for emotional reactions to physical and biochemical disturbances. Only those adolescents were accepted who exhibited intelligence ratings within the "normal" range of 90–110 intelligence quotient or above. This procedure was to insure that the boys had sufficient reading ability and comprehension to understand the test instruments and to form conceptual images of themselves. Known mentally defective children and those with central nervous system diseases or defects were excluded from the samples.

All of the adolescents were at least third generation Americans with the exception of one boy in a control group who was of the first generation, and one disturbed boy who was second generation. Only those adolescents of Irish or Italian descent on the side of both parents were accepted for study.

The most frequent adolescent diagnosis in the files of the mental health clinic was chosen as a control in disturbance. This diagnosis, termed the "Adjustment Reaction of Adolescents," was considered desirable because of the variety of reactions that appear under this title, and that are applicable to a test of the frames of reference hypothesized about the two groups. This diagnosis is defined in the American Psychiatric Association's *Diagnostic and Statistical Manual* (2:42) as follows:

> Under this diagnosis are to be included those transient reactions of the adolescent which are the expression of his emancipatory strivings and vacillations with reference to impulses and emotional tendencies. The superficial pattern of the behavior may resemble any of the personality or psychoneurotic disorders. Differentiation between transient adolescent reactions and deepseated personality trait disorders or psychoneurotic reactions must be made.

Within each ethnic group, social classes were examined for suggestive differences in phenomena under examination. Although this was not a study in social class differentiation, it appeared that ethnic groups cut across class lines and that social classes contain diverse ethnic groups. In studying the ethnic factor, it is therefore important to determine if a behavioral trait significant to an ethnic group is in evidence regardless of their social class. The study defines social class operationally according to an index devised by A. B. Hollingshead (56). His index of social position is based on the two factors of occupation and education, each of which is measured by a seven point scale. The scores are grouped into five social classes or strata in the community. The study assigned each boy in the total sample a position in the Hollingshead social scale.

The Disturbed Adolescents

The study defines a disturbed adolescent as one who is being treated by a psychiatrist or is under the care of a psychiatric clinic or mental hospital. This definition may well omit a significant percentage of mentally ill persons, for we did not count those in therapeutic relationships with physicians other than psychiatrists and allied professional workers. This group would have been difficult to determine and undesirable to include in this study, for medical disorders are certainly a major factor in their mental disturbance.

The author contacted authorized personnel representing all of the outpatient mental health clinics of the Buffalo, New York, metropolitan area. I made this initial investigation to determine the purpose of the clinic, types of referrals, age range of patients, diagnoses, range of socioeconomic classes represented, and the ethnic and religious composition of the patients.

Of the four mental health facilities in the area, three of the clinics were unsuitable because of such factors as patients' medical disorders, limited age range, severity of illness and withdrawal, and insufficient number of patients with the desired ethnic backgrounds. I subsequently contacted a representative of the Monsignor Carr Institute, an outpatient mental health clinic accepting those in need of treatment without age, race, or religious limits. A review of the Institute's statistical sheet for 1963 revealed a census of 153 active adolescent outpatients ranging in age from fourteen to twenty-one.

Description of Monsignor Carr Institute

The Monsignor Carr Institute is licensed by New York State and jointly supported by the Erie County Community Welfare Board. It is a multiple service clinic treating children, adolescents, and adults. The clinic provides free treatment at its discretion.

Since the Monsignor Carr Institute had the greatest number of adolescent patients upon which sampling controls could be exerted, a pilot sampling of adolescent outpatients, ranging from thirteen to nineteen years of age, was selected in November 1963. The study considered the following variables for estimation purposes: ethnic background, religion, diagnosis, father's occupation and education, source of referrals for treatment, and school placement of the adolescent under treatment.

The pilot sampling had a double purpose: to estimate roughly the ethnic composition of adolescents at the Institute in order to anticipate sampling opportunities and problems; and to obtain some idea of adolescent representation in the clinic as compared with the community population at large. I compared these findings to the census representation of the Buffalo standard metropolitan area, for it was especially important to know whether the ethnic and socioeconomic backgrounds of the Institute patients were representative of those found in the standard metropolitan area of Buffalo. A pilot study of a few weeks' duration is not an exact description of the Institute's patients, for attendance, new admissions, readmissions, and closures fluctuate throughout the year, which in turn cause fluctuation in ethnic group proportions and socioeconomic class representation. Some underlying continuity, however, does exist, and a background picture with regard to the above variables can be drawn for comparative evaluation purposes.

The tables with census comparisons are in Appendix I. Comparison of the ethnic composition of the Institute's adolescent population with that of the general population of the Buffalo metropolitan area is not a valid one, even though there is a significant difference between them $(p > .001)$. This is because the study's fourth and fifth generation Irish-American boys were compared to foreign-born and native white of foreign-born populations in the census. This is the only way in which the census (111:433) statistically defines its ethnic populations.

Italian immigration declined more gradually in recent years than did the Irish, and the case was similar for the Polish-American population. These populations then more closely resemble second generation Americans.

In its annual report of 1963, the Institute claimed that 19 percent of the total clinic population consisted of adolescents between thirteen and twenty years of age. This proportion is not significantly different from the proportion of adolescents reported in the United States Census of Population and Housing, 1960 (112).

The distribution of occupations of the disturbed adolescents' fathers was roughly equivalent to that reported in the census for white male heads of households in New York State (Table 2, Appendix I). According to Hollingshead's two factor index (56) of social position, 12 percent of the sample is in class II (professional and executive) and 10 percent is in class V (unskilled laborers). Classes III and IV (clerical and skilled workers to semiskilled workers) predominate, the mean index social position being 39.3 (the lower level of class III).

More fathers of adolescents in the Institute graduated from high school as compared with the general population of the Buffalo Metropolitan area (Table 3, Appendix I). More Institute fathers were service workers and more were college graduates.

Referrals to the Institute came from such sources as the parent of the boy, family court, schools, social agencies, physicians, and clergy. All of the adolescents had attended parochial elementary schools, and half of them were attending parochial high schools.

If the adolescent population of this clinic is roughly representative of the adolescent outpatient mental health clinic population of Buffalo, one cannot say this is a random sample. Neither the groups studied nor the clinic were selected randomly. They were selected on the basis of the greatest number of adolescents attending a clinic that was treating the greatest number of patients who fulfilled the requirements for this study. The number of adolescents receiving psychiatric treatment in the community is not known, for the various sources of private treatment and counseling are not recorded. Establishing the true number of maladjusted adolescents in the community is problematical for other reasons. In cases of juvenile delinquents a judge may favor punishment, over the physician's recommendation of psychiatric treatment. Professional disagreements can lead to different modes of treatment. These considerations, however, only narrow the findings to the outpatient clinic population without altering the purpose of the study. It was still possible to explore significant differences in ethnic behavior. Comparisons of these disturbed adolescents with their peers in the community who are not being treated will increase the validity and reliability of the findings. The study also includes tests of statistical significance to determine whether significant differences at given levels of probability exist between variables for the groups studied.

Ethnic Control Groups

The study utilizes ethnic control groups in the community to clarify significant areas of ethnicity in adolescent socialization and disturbance modalities and to open further areas for consideration. This allows for more reliable prediction of ethnicity as a possible predictor of modal adjustments and emotional disturbances.

Many people with varying degrees of emotional illness exist in the population at large untreated. It is possible that boys whose emotional disturbances are unrecognized or unacknowledged may be found in the control groups, therefore the study calls these groups ethnic groups rather than normal groups.

Of the total number of boys attending the Institute and meeting the study criteria, thirty-seven were attending parochial grade or high schools, and eight were attending five different high schools scattered throughout the standard metropolitan area.

Since the majority of the disturbed boys in parochial high schools attended two particular diocesan high schools (four attending a private parochial high school), the author selected these schools for research purposes. Bishop Timon and Bishop Fallon High Schools were the diocesan high schools most frequently attended, while Canisius High School was the only private parochial high school of choice.

The author went to the guidance counselor of each school to make arrangements for selecting suitable students for participation as control subjects. All boys of the appropriate ethnicity and age whose last period in school was a study period were chosen as control subjects. The study period enabled them to stay after school for testing. The age range remained from thirteen to nineteen but exact matching of disturbed boys with control boys by age was found to be impossible.

Bishop Timon High School is in a traditionally Irish section of the city, although boys from the large diocese that encompasses areas outside this ethnic section attend the school as well. Twenty were chosen, thirteen were of Irish descent and seven were of Italian descent.

Bishop Fallon High School is a diocesan school serving many Italian boys whose homes lie within or near the vicinity of the diocese. Under the same conditions of selection, twenty-eight boys of Italian extraction and seven of Irish extraction were selected.

In Canisius High School (a private parochial high school serving all sections of the city) twenty Irish boys were obtained who met the controlling requirements.

In the judgment of the counselor, all of the boys had normal to superior intelligence. There were no histories of emotional disturbances or attendance at a mental health clinic. All of the boys filled out census schedules to determine ethnicity, age, religion, and generation level. In some instances the author had to make second and third visits to finish testing the boys because some had after-school employment.

The Measuring Instruments

The use of several testing instruments in a standardized, orderly sequence can verify the validity and consistency of responses, and amplification of the life experiences which these tests elicit can increase understanding of the social components of personality formation. Operational tests and measures are effective only to the extent that the adolescent perceives a situation to be true and real to him. In testing hypothetical frames of reference, polydimensional testing approaches are valid and reliable to the extent that they measure what we are attempting to find. In this study they measure both how the two ethnic groups differ and how the disturbed groups differ from the control groups. The polydimensional approach is itself a test of validity and consistency, since each test measures different aspects of the intellectual and emotional spheres of living. The different testing procedures should complement each other in describing the variations of ethnic personality.

Administration of Instruments

All of the instruments were given in the following order: a census schedule, the Edwards Personal Preference Schedule, the Life-Space Drawing, The Tennessee Department of Mental Health Self Concept Scale, and a questionnaire devised and supervised by the author. The time taken for the administration of this group of instruments varied with the individual adolescent. Some of the adolescents answered the questions rapidly; others required two to three visits. There were no differences in this respect between the community control groups and the groups of disturbed adolescents.

On the whole, both the control and disturbed boys exhibited cooperation and interest. In orienting the adolescents to the study, I did not stress the investigation of ethnicity but rather that the study was general research in the interest of understanding contemporary youth.

A form entitled "Presenting Problem," with its accompanying

"Face Sheet," was used to abstract descriptions of disturbance and central conflicts from the confidential folders of the adolescents attending the Institute. These data were compared with the results of the disturbed boys' responses to the testing instruments.

All boys were given identification numbers to eliminate personal identification. This not only eliminated subjective bias on the part of the examiner, but also allowed examinees to answer more freely. Anonymity also freed the boys from restricting authority and reduced their possible attempts to provide answers they might think were expected of them. The boys seemed to appreciate not having to answer for negative reasons. My experience in testing senior nursing students indicates this freedom from identity prompted more honest replies because fear of reprisal was eliminated.

A systematic control factor built into the design was the comparison of the ethnic groupings with each other and with the representative normative groupings as described in Edwards (23) and Fitts (35).

The Census Schedule

The purpose of this schedule was to evaluate the adolescent for eligibility and to gain current essential data for the description of the subject as to age, birthplace, generation level, ethnic descent, grade level, and school attended.

The Edwards Personal Preference Schedule (EPPS)

This instrument tested for predominant modes of behavior patterns that appeared appropriate to the frames of reference and consequently served as an objective measure of ethnic differences. This schedule measures fifteen relatively independent personality variables (definitions of these variables are in Appendix II). These variables were conceived and named by H. A. Murray and others (80).

In this scale, Edwards purports to minimize the answering of personal questions according to what the subjects think is socially acceptable or desirable even if such answers contradict their true feelings. Edwards and his associates attempt to scale values on a psychological continuum, out of which two statements are taken that are *equal* in social desirability, thereby increasing the ease of the free honest choice.

The EPPS also measures consistency by comparing a number of

identical choices made in two sets of the same fifteen items. Different groups have validated this test over a period of time (23), and there are normative scores for comparative purposes. The EPPS personality variables can be integrated into this study's frames of reference and serve as an objective measure of ethnic and personal trait differences. The study predicted that the Italian-American boys would choose statements that would show dominance, exhibitionism, aggression, and overt heterosexuality, and that they would choose fewer statements of endurance and be less consistent on the test as a whole than the Irish-American boys. The study also predicted the Italian-American boys would have wider circles of friends with more varied and outgoing social activities than the Irish-American boys.

The Irish-American boy, in contrast, was predicted to choose deference-for-authority statements and those indicating compliance with authority figures. He would presumably have greater preference for ordered organization and consistency of life experiences. These predictions postulate the average Italian-American boy as sociocentric with gregarious tendencies, while the average Irish-American boy would be egocentric in his tendency to accept nurturance and seek social approval for the maintenance of his self-esteem.

The study did not intend these variables to stand alone as explanations of the frames of reference, but rather as tests of compatibility, to be validated and explained by the subjects' choice and by amplification of perceptual experiences in succeeding research instruments.

The Life-Space Drawing

Each subject was told to draw a circle designating himself, and then to indicate those persons important in his life by drawing smaller circles around himself. Those to whom he felt closest in life-space were placed closest to his own circle, while those to whom he felt less close were placed proportionately further from his own circle. This produced a pictorial range of orientation and direction to his world of relations. The concept of the adolescent's social world and his place within it became a life-space schema for either the construction of his relationships or their extension to horizons outside his family. This was an experimental procedure in the midst of the already established methodology and was purely exploratory in nature.

The study postulated that the Italian-American boy would show a wider sphere of family relationships and would include more people outside his immediate family. The study predicted the Irish-American boy would draw a smaller world of perceptual social relations, with restricted choices in social intimacy. The Irish-American boy would also gravitate toward extrafamilial relationships instead of extended family. Because the Irish-American boy came from a nuclear family the study assumed he would emphasize the mother in contrast to the lesser importance assigned her by the Italian-American boy. In view of maternal domination and his nuclear family, the Irish-American boy could be expected to have greater difficulty in masculine identification while the Italian-American boy would have greater choice of substitute paternal figures in his extended family.

The study expected the Irish-American boy to draw smaller "me" circles in his life-space field. This would accord with the self-image and the hypothesized EPPS choices showing dependency, compliance with the dictates of authority, and the relative feelings of inadequacy. The Italian-American boy could be expected to see himself as a more significant figure around whom other people revolve. The study anticipated that the Life-Space Drawings would indicate contrasting worlds of expansiveness and active aggression as opposed to restriction and passive aggression.

The Life-Space Drawing is an exploratory procedure that may vividly portray how the boys in the two ethnic groups are oriented to their environment. The study employed this drawing to corroborate the adolescents' realities and ethnic realities revealed by the other research instruments. Such drawings can bring to the social workers of neighborhood houses and to psychotherapists in general a wealth of material for adolescent and ethnic action programs, and for social science this research instrument may indicate that subcultural orientations, as well as sex role orientations, are decisive in the study of society.

The Tennessee Department of Mental Health Self-Concept Scale (TDMH)

The study demanded a necessary cognitive corollary to be compared with the Edwards Personal Preference Schedule the self-concept, as an index of self-evaluation and self-satisfaction. The TDMH indicates a positive feeling to oneself in relation to others in the social world. The self-concept has usually been identified with Roger's personality theory. He states:

> The self concept or self structure may be thought of as an organized configuration of perceptions of the self which are admissible to awareness. It is composed of such elements as the perceptions of one's characteristics and abilities; the percepts and concepts of the self in relation to others and to the environment; the value qualities which are perceived as associated with experiences and objects; and goals and ideals which are perceived as having positive or negative valence. (93:136)

Wylie (116) states that knowledge of a subject's perception of his self and his environment provides a means of understanding and predicting his behavior. Here environmental events influence self-satisfaction which also depends on perceived successes and failures. Self-satisfaction is the consequence of learning, motivation, and perception.

The author inferred that the conscious self-percept is a self-recognizable function, and that these can be measured and their differential patterns compared in adolescent ethnic groups. Testing the self-concept may show differentiation in ethnic group patterns of positive self-evaluation as opposed to negative self-evaluation, and in the differentiation in ethnic group patterns of positive self-evaluation as opposed to negative self-evaluation, and in the ability for introspection as opposed to defensiveness and stereotyping the self. The self-concept differentiates between areas of attitudes to one's physical, psychological, and social self. Quantitative and qualitative comparisons show self-conceptions with regard to the self-and-other relations, and point out conflicts within the self in such areas. If the subject has a negative self-conception he will conceive of the world around him in the same way, but if the subject conceives of himself positively, he may still show dissatisfaction in relation to his ego ideal and to his perceptions of the way others see him.

The study anticipated that the ethnic groups would show different patterns of self-conception because one's self-concept develops in the family. The author's hypothesis was that the Italian-American group would show more positive feelings towards the self and others because of less restrained nurturance and more relaxed interpersonal relations. On the other hand, the Irish-American group would show greater introspection, with the self-concept dependent upon social approval from important others. The Irish-American members were expected to score higher on deference to authority and on intraception, and their moral ideals presumably would lead them into conflict regarding satisfaction with their personal, physical, and social selves on the TDMH scale. It was also anticipated that the Italian-American boys would be capable of overtly displaying negative self-evaluation and self-satisfaction with this evaluation. The Irish-American boy, in contrast, would show covert negative self-evaluation and dissatisfaction with the self which he translates into an idealistic conception of what the self should be. We thus have contrasting self-concepts: tendencies toward idealism for the Irish-American boy and tendencies toward pragmatism for the Italian-American boy.

The Edwards Personal Preference test makes the self-concept obvious and the adolescent explains it further as he illustrates his life experiences in the questionnaire. The development of the self-image begins in the home and this early image reinforces the perceptions of later experiences and goals. Illustrations of differences in self-concept between ethnic groups clarify the findings of the other research instruments and help determine the influence the family has in personality development.

Engel (25) tested one aspect of the stability of the self-concept in adolescents. In a test-retest done with one group in grades eight to ten and another grades ten and eleven, she established the reliability of self-concept early in child development. William Fitts (author of the TDMH Self-Concept Test), in a personal communication to the author, states: "Data thus far indicate no particular differences on this scale between adolescents and adults or between Negroes and whites." The author assumed, therefore, that the TDMH scale would be applicable to the adolescent group under study.

The test is broken up into a five-by-three category analysis. The five categories represent the major frames of reference that individuals employ in self-perceptions. These are: physical characteristics, moral and ethical characteristics, psychological traits, primary group membership (self in relation to family and friends), and secondary group membership (social self in relation to other people).

The five horizontal categories are answered by three measures of internal consistency: the abstract self, self-satisfaction, and functional behavior. The answers, on a true-false, five-point continuum, are made to positive and negative statements about the self. The description of the abstract self allows the individual to stand back and look at himself. The self-satisfaction section seeks to determine how the person reacts to what he is. It is an index of self-acceptance and, according to Fitts (35), represents in a measure, the super-ego. The measure of functional behavior examines what the individual actually does. These categories of internal measurements are pursued in each of the five external categories on a horizontal basis.

The consistency scores, distribution scores, and the positive-negative continuum provide measures for the analysis of personality adjustment and for the clarity and certainty of the self-concept. The author anticipated that the test would reveal whether one ethnic group is more positive than the other in its orientations to primary and secondary group relations, and whether one group places greater emphasis upon moral-ethical standards. This test reveals differences in perceptual dimensions when the description of the abstract self is compared to measures of self-satisfaction and to the functional behavior. If the proposals in the frames of reference are correct, the self-concepts of the Irish-American and the Italian-American groups should show amplifications of the EPPS choice of variables and the questionnaire.

Fitts (86) reports that the TDMH was given to both normative and psychiatrically ill groups and comments on its value:

> There are many different features of the self concept which a person reports on this scale which can be quantified and reliably measured. These different features of the self concept are relatively independent of each other and all show certain types of validity. This report adds to the cumulative evidence that the self concept is an important psychological construct in the understanding of people and their behavior. (86:24)

The subject may misrepresent himself in answering the TDMH as Crowne and Stephens (20) outline. Subjects differ in insight, in their depth of knowledge of themselves, and in their ability to remember and judge their own acts. Some can see themselves as others see them (the looking-glass self), while others are protected from this perception by repressions and projections. Subjects also may desire to ingratiate themselves with the tester or interviewer. The test attempts to account for these factors through consistency scores and the built-in honesty scale.

In the case of disturbed adolescents, we may conjecture that successful counselling or psychiatric treatment can produce a greater congruence between the self-concept and ideal self, together with a more realistic and objective estimation of the self. Wylie (116:161) discusses this problem from the clinical viewpoint. The disturbed adolescents in this study have not yet had the time through therapy to achieve self-congruence on a long-range basis, but nevertheless the study postulates that the ethnic groups might show variant patterns of self-conceptualization. Since patterns of personality are enduring characteristics, any values gained to date in therapy are incorporated into a basic perceptual and motivational system of past orientations. Since the study used control groups for comparative purposes, the self-concept can be objectively studied for phenomena peculiar to an ethnic group.

The Questionnaire

The individual adolescent's interpretation of a frame of reference is the important definition of his singular social situation. This is essentially the practical working situation in individual psychotherapy, and it is the perceptual condition that motivates feelings and behavior, rather than the situation as it actually is, or should be, or can be.

Considering the necessity to balance group statistics with individual experience, the study questionnaire included a conceptual scheme systematically ordered according to the three broad areas of investigation: family structure and function, attitudinal orientations, and projections of inner needs and conflicts into roles. The schedule of inquiry outlines intrafamilial relations, attitudes toward school and peers, vocational aspirations, attitudes toward females, and differences in self-awareness, and these areas of inquiry were compared one by one to the frames of reference. This conceptual scheme produced an outline of the characteristics that differentiated the Italian-American boy from the Irish-American boy and thus made possible a comparison of cases.

The questionnaire was administered under supervision in standardized order, following the administration of the TDMH Scale. The subjects answered the questions and were encouraged to ask questions as often as desired. Since all of the subjects were given numbers to identify themselves on all of the tests, they were encouraged to make written comments as freely as they wished. The average time taken to complete the questionnaire was about forty minutes. The author reviewed the completed questionnaires and returned them for clarification whenever further explanations seemed desirable.

Problems of Sampling and Data Collection

The Disturbed Adolescents

In the summer of 1964 the author attempted to select suitable Irish-American and Italian-American subjects at the Monsignor Carr Institute which at this time had a total adolescent enrollment of forty-nine. Thirty-eight of the boys were undergoing active psychotherapy. Nineteen were of Irish descent and thirteen of Italian. Six had one Irish and one Italian parent, but they had been raised by one parent and had no contact with the other. There were grandparents in two of these cases. The author considered these boys to have the ethnic background of the parent responsible for their care. One boy refused to cooperate in the study.

Of the cooperating adolescents, seventeen lived in the Immaculate Heart of Mary Home for neglected children and those with behavior problems. Of these, eleven were of Irish and six of Italian descent. This home takes the child from poor social surroundings into a more constructive group therapy atmosphere. An adjunct to this home is Baker Hall, a residence for boys beyond the eighth grade in school. The residences carry out group therapy and the Institute conducts clinical therapy. Only those boys who spent most of their life—up to at least ages ten or eleven—with both parents of the same ethnic origin were accepted for study. Five boys from Baker Hall met the requirements for participation in the study.

Inasmuch as only nineteen Irish-American boys and thirteen Italian-American boys were eligible subjects because they were regularly attending therapy sessions at the Institute, the author attempted to increase the size of the sample by approaching the parents of boys whose cases had been closed because the boys had not kept their appointments for therapy. The reason for closure indicated that some disturbance still existed, and an examination of the folders indicated the boys required further therapy. Reasons for non-attendance were various: parents' desire to handle the situation, boy's resistance to therapy and lack of insight into the need for it, moving out of town, acute disturbance and transfer to a hospital for treatment, suggested institutional placement for more constructive environmental surroundings, and lack of cooperation.

After those cases most recently closed were examined for appropriate controlling factors, the author approached the parents through a letter explaining the purpose of the study. The parents were given two days to receive the letter, and then were telephoned in order to provide further explanations and to set up appointments so that the study could be discussed, if desired. The greatest obstacle in this procedure was that families had moved, or the boy could not be located. Two boys were too disturbed to be approached. Four percent of the forty-seven parents refused to cooperate. Following the disqualification of four boys due to mixed ethnic parentage, seventeen boys were found suitable for study.

The Community Control Group

The study originally planned to match the disturbed adolescent boys attending the Institute and the boys in the control groups by age, ethnicity, and school attended. Exact matching by these variables, however, proved impossible.

Since the public schools had recently adopted a rule forbidding the use of psychological questionnaires and research instruments, the author considered three parochial high schools, those most frequently attended by the boys under treatment at the Institute, as sources for data collection.

The author felt the parochial school was a valid data source, for one learns ethnic traits in the home and these develop through interpersonal relationships within the family and the more immediate social environment; such ethnic trait patterns will be carried into both the parochial and public school classroom.

The possibility that a sample drawn only from parochial schools might exaggerate the significance of religion in their lives seemed insignificant, since Gans (42) states that Italian parents favor parochial schools because they are thought to produce more cultured and well-mannered students. Attending parochial school need not necessarily indicate greater religiosity. Another justification for using parochial schools is that all of the disturbed boys attended parochial grade schools, and the majority were attending parochial grade or high schools at the time of this study.

Plan of Analysis

The author was concerned with analyzing inductively the subjects' responses on each of the five instruments. I emphasized throughout the study the testing of hypotheses on relationships between ethnicity and modal group responses. I must stress at this point that the social and psychiatric characteristics found among the majority of disturbed boys in each ethnic group did not apply to all of them. There were some individuals in the group who did not display the behavior of the majority. Likewise, all members of the control group did not exhibit the pattern of the majority. In short, there was considerable individual deviation.

We scored the Edwards Personal Preference Schedule and the Tennessee Department of Mental Health Scale individually and obtained group averages and standard deviations. These averages pertained to all of the fifteen personality traits in the EPPS and to the eight areas of measurement in the TDMH Scale. In these two tests we have a series of scores or numerical values representing each case within the ethnic group. Analysis of variance was used to test whether the variability between the ethnic groups was significantly greater than the variability within the ethnic groups at a given level of probability. By performing a two-way analysis of variance, we can make determinations as to whether the variability between the disturbed-control categories is significantly greater than the variability within the disturbed-control categories. Thus, we can make a determination as to whether ethnic differences and disturbed-control differences interact or are interpreted more meaningfully on an ethnic basis.

Certain problems arose in the social class analysis, which entailed grouping the boys into upper and lower classes, or, according to the United States Census, as white-collar and blue-collar classes. Due to the small numbers of boys in each social class, and the disproportionate numbers in social class groupings between the Irish-Italian and control-disturbed groups, we analyzed these data by *t* tests rather than in the analyses of variance. This applies to all tabular analyses.

Class positions for all the adolescents under study came from Hollingshead Index (56). In studying differences between social class means in each ethnic group, we combined social classes I, II, and III for a common upper-class mean score (professional, executive and administrative positions). This was done for several reasons. Most of the boys in the disturbed and control groups were placed in social classes III (clerical and skilled worker) and IV (semiskilled workers), which were the predominant classes of both ethnic groups. It is relevant to make a division between these two socioeconomic classes, since class III represents the majority of heads of households in the upper administrative and business pursuits with high school to college education. Class IV represents skilled workers, the majority of whom had some high school education or were high school graduates. Classes I and II in each group were represented by only two to four subjects of professional status (with the exception of the Irish-American control group, which included eight subjects). The mean score values attained for the sons of professional people were not significantly different from those obtained for the class III heads of households. This may have been due to the small size of this group which produced greater variability of scores that in turn increased the within-group variation. The study refers to this combined class score as the upper class, or white-collar class. This combination also is in line with Hollingshead's two-factor index (56) where he makes marked descriptive divisions between the middle class, working class, and class V.

In Hollingshead's categories (55), class V is a distinct subculture at the bottom of the working class and represents a way of life found in the worst slum areas of the city. None of the subjects in this study were part of this distinctive slum subculture. We found, for the most part, that *t* tests of significant differences yielded greater variance between upper-class mean scores and class IV mean scores than between upper-class and class V mean score values. Since *t* tests did not yield significant differences to warrant maintenance of class V as an entity, we incorporated this class into class IV as a part of the blue-collar class structure.

We analyzed the Life-Space Drawing in terms of attribute choice by expressing what percentage of boys in a given group exhibited a characteristic choice. These choices were weighted, with the heaviest weight given to the most distant choice. We used the chi-square test to determine whether significant differences existed between frequency distributions. We used actual numbers in the computations and employed Yates correction if we expected less than ten cases in any one call. We made graphs and pictorial representations from the weighted percentages calculated for this purpose.

In the questionnaire the first step was to select an area of inquiry, such as intrafamilial relationships, which was followed by a more specific subject within the area such as parental attitude toward choice of vocational career. We used the chi-square test to determine whether an attribute appeared more frequently in one grouping than in another and whether there were significant differences between the ethnic groups in specific attributes. In this respect we investigated social class differences as well. In statistical analysis, we defined high significance at the .05 percent level. However, since there are innumerable individual behavioral deviations from the average in any specific grouping of human beings, we considered probability levels of .10 highly suggestive results for consideration and exploration. This means that under the null hypotheses of no difference, an observed distribution differs from expectation by sampling error alone no more than five to ten out of one hundred times. We can reject the null hypothesis when the observed distribution differs from this expectation.

Statistical evaluations in this study were utilized as objective tools. Sociological and psychiatric interpretations were made from the resulting mathematical distinctions.

This research design enables the author to learn what experiences are shared by and what experiences are specific to two types of adolescents in each of two ethnic groups. It also enables the investigator to indicate aspects of ethnic background significant in the understanding of adolescent adjustment problems.

4

The Census Schedule

This chapter describes the demographic characteristics and kinship structures of the study subjects. This background information is a preparation for analysis of the subsequent tests of control-disturbed phenomena of ethnicity in adolescence.

Demographic Characteristics

Age

The one hundred and twenty-three subjects in this study range in age from thirteen to nineteen years. Although the mean ages are nearly equal among the four groups, the standard deviation indicates that there is greater variability and spread in age range in each of the two disturbed groups. Chi-square analysis in Table 1 corroborates this and indicates that there are more younger adolescents in the disturbed groups than there are in the control groups. In contrast, over half the control boys are sixteen to nineteen years of age, the Irish control group having more boys in higher teen categories.

Certain factors among the control subjects placed priority on selection of sophomores, juniors, and seniors who had a home room study period at the end of the day and no outside employment or undemanding employment.

The mean age for disturbed boys living at the Immaculate Heart of Mary Home was fourteen. The five Baker Hall boys had a mean age of sixteen. All of these disturbed boys were in their constructive group living placements for an average time of one year and one month. The youngest boy was twelve on placement. All of the boys

Table 1

Age Distribution of Subjects at Last Birthday at Time of Study

Group	Age in years and months			Mean	S.D.	Total	N
	13-15.11 %	16-16.11 %	17-19.11 %				
Irish-American Control	17.50	45.00	37.50	16.20	1.01	100	40
Italian-American Control	47.05	26.47	26.48	15.10	0.27	100	34
Irish-American Disturbed	72.00	8.00	20.00	15.20	2.01	100	25
Italian-American Disturbed	62.51	20.83	16.66	14.96	1.72	100	24

Second and third columns combined for chi-square analysis.
$X^2 = 22.36$, 3 d.f.; $p < .001$

were able to verbalize and to remember vividly their earlier intra-familial relationships, in most cases with deep emotional overtones.

Education

Table 2 shows the types of schools the study subjects attended. All the control subjects attended parochial high school, and 52 percent of them had attended parochial grammar schools, so that they had common orientations in education with the disturbed boys. There were more disturbed boys in parochial grammar schools, and all the disturbed boys had a higher rate of transfer between parochial schools and public schools than did the control boys.

The mean school grade achieved by the Irish-American and Italian-American disturbed boys at the time of this study was grade eight. The low grade level these boys had attained was due to difficult home environments and poor social adjustments which often required change in residence and in schools with consequent poor achievement. Clinic psychologists scored the intelligence quotients of all the disturbed boys average to high; one boy attended a special school for the gifted.

One-third of the disturbed boys attended public school because

Table 2
Type of School Attended by Subjects at Time of Study

School	Parochial Grammar	Parochial High School	Public Grammar	Public High School	Special School for Gifted	Above High School	Total
Irish-American Control	0	40	0	0	0	0	40
Italian-American Control	0	34	0	0	0	0	34
Irish-American Disturbed	14	4	0	5	1	1	25
Italian-American Disturbed	7	8	4	4	0	1	24

they were not accepted at parochial schools, or because public schools were deemed therapeutically desirable.

While 32 percent of the Irish-American disturbed boys were in grades nine to eleven, 64 percent of the Italian-American boys were doing this level of work. This higher percentage may be related to the fact that more of the Italian-Americans lived at home and had moved about less, and suffered less as a consequence. On the other hand, as the Italian-American boys may have encountered equally difficult adjustment problems at home, they may have developed other ways of coping with demands for achievement while undergoing emotional difficulties. This possibility will be considered in examining the test results.

Adolescent Employment

Fourteen percent of the Italian-American control group boys and 25 percent of the Irish-American control group boys had part-time jobs after school as news carriers, car washers, waiters, stockboys, salesmen, and caddies. The seventeen adolescents housed away from home were assigned tasks in cooperative group work, depending upon age, desires, and abilities. In the disturbed groups, 12 percent of Irish-American boys and 21 percent of Italian-American boys worked part time in the following jobs: baker, shoeshine boy, bartender, clothes presser, and lens grinder.

Home Status and Kinship Structure

Residence

There was a difference between the proportion of Italian-American and the proportion of Irish-American disturbed boys who were placed in outside residence. Inversely, there was a difference between the two disturbed groups in the proportion of those remaining at home with one or both parents.

It is appropriate at this time to examine the reasons for transfer to group residence outside the home as a possible clue to familial structure and strength. The study follows with an explanation of kinship structure itself.

Table 3
Distribution of Groups by Residence

	At Home with:		Home Status One Parent:			
	Both Parents	Step-parent	Parent Deceased	Divorced Separated	Institutional Residence	Total
Irish-American Control	39	0	1	0	0	40
Irish-American Disturbed	8	1	1	1	14	25
Italian-American Control	33	0	1	0	0	34
Italian-American Disturbed	12	1	1	2	8	24

The boys in the Italian-American disturbed group were most frequently referred to the Institute by their mother or father or both. The parents either applied to the Catholic Charities Social Agency for help in guiding their sons or were referred to the Monsignor

Carr Institute by their son's principal or school guidance counsellor. The reasons for referral were poor school adjustment and behavior problems, incriminating defiance of authority and refusal to accept responsibility.

Parental physical or mental illness necessitated placing four of the boys outside their homes. In only one case was actual neglect cited on the part of the remaining parent after parental separation. Four working mothers enlisted grandparents' help after separation from their husbands but found themselves unable to cope with the defiant behavior of their sons and sought help from community agencies. In most of the cases, the ill or separated parents were aided by relatives in caring for the boy and sought agency help when the boy became disturbed.

In the Irish-American disturbed group, the boys were referred for emotional disturbance by separated mothers, private physicians, and family court. The family court made recommendations after court arraignment for stealing, setting off fire alarms, and disorderly conduct with others in gangs. Eighty percent were placed outside the home on the appeal of a working mother who was separated from her husband. In this group the boy's parents were more often divorced or legally separated and this had occurred when the boys were between nine and ten years old. The mothers worked, leaving the boys to fend for themselves most of the day. At the onset of adolescence, the drive for masculine independence from maternal domination and lack of paternal identification brought on emotional reactions requiring professional help. The psychiatric evaluation was that the boys required group therapy in supervised professional settings. In none of the instances were other relatives willing or able to help the parent in his or her dilemma, nor did the parent want to solicit family aid. In only one case was parental sickness and mental illness a possible counterpart of the boy's emotional disturbance, and in this case the social welfare department established neglect as reason for institutionalizing the boy. This is in contrast to the emergency measures taken to institutionalize the Italian-American boys because of sickness and incapacity of both parents, leaving only three cases of separation and consequent disturbance among the Italian-American boys.

Whether enlistment of relatives to keep the family intact prevents mental illness remains to be proven. Although family aid may be given with the best of intentions, the boys remaining at home in the care of relatives, as is the case with the Italian-American disturbed

FIGURE 1

Mean Number of Kin and Percentage of Italian-American Contact with Relatives

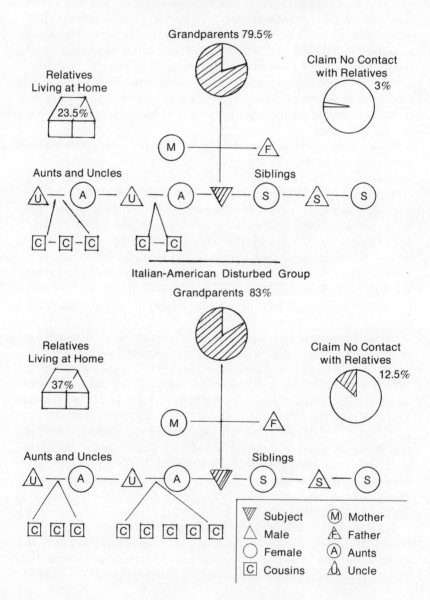

Italian-American Control Group

Grandparents 79.5%

Relatives Living at Home 23.5%

Claim No Contact with Relatives 3%

Aunts and Uncles

Siblings

Italian-American Disturbed Group

Grandparents 83%

Relatives Living at Home 37%

Claim No Contact with Relatives 12.5%

Aunts and Uncles

Siblings

▽ Subject   Ⓜ Mother
△ Male   Ⓕ Father
◯ Female   Ⓐ Aunts
☐ Cousins   △ Uncle

FIGURE 2

Mean Number of Kin and Percentage
of Irish-American Contact with Relatives

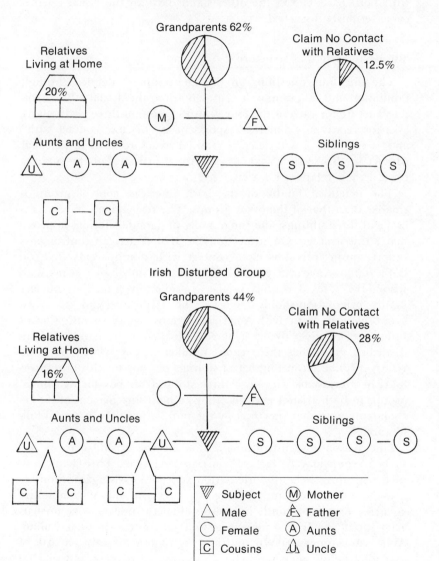

Irish-American Control Group

Grandparents 62%

Relatives
Living at Home

20%

Claim No Contact
with Relatives

12.5%

M — F

Aunts and Uncles

U — A — A — ▽ — S — S — S

Siblings

C — C

Irish Disturbed Group

Grandparents 44%

Relatives
Living at Home

16%

Claim No Contact
with Relatives

28%

F

Aunts and Uncles

U — A — A — U — ▽ — S — S — S — S

Siblings

C — C   C — C

▽ Subject	M Mother
△ Male	F Father
○ Female	A Aunts
C Cousins	U Uncle

boys, can still show disturbances that require professional help. These problems usually involve interpersonal relationships, especially those with authority figures. While the boys in institutions enjoy a more peaceful group setting, they still dream of a home life with both parents. On the other hand, boys in the home can become seriously disturbed.

Sibling and Familial Structure

The first four questions on the questionnaire defined through tabulation and diagrammatic representation, the modal ethnic family structure for each of the four groups. Question three particularly asks for relatives whom the respondent is "in close contact with" and "sees often." I will describe familial structure through personal contact in this section, leaving perceptual attitudes of the subjects toward their relatives for a later section.

The extended family of the Irish-American control group is smaller than that of the other groups. The respondents have an average of three siblings, and the number of parental siblings approximates this average. On inspection the Irish-American control boys report significantly less close contact with grandparents than do both Italian-American groups. The mean number of cousins with whom they are in contact is also considerably less. This nuclear family orientation holds true for the Irish-American disturbed group as well. Both Irish-American groups report an insignificant number of relatives living at home with them. The Irish-American disturbed group has the greatest number of boys who report "no relatives." The mean number of siblings per boy for this group was four, in contrast to a mean of three siblings per boy for its control group. In both Irish-American groups almost fifty percent of the respondents state that they occupy the middle position in the sibling hierarchy.

One reason for institutionalization in the Irish-American disturbed group may be lack of concerned relatives. This factor, coupled with nuclear family orientation and family disorganization because of separation and divorce, requires the aid of community agencies. Extended family in-group solidarity appears to be uncharacteristic of the Irish-American groups, in contrast to their Italian-American counterparts. In addition, high moral-ethical standards of extended family members who disapprove of divorce and marital strife may lead to their abandoning the children of a disorganized family.

In contrast to both Irish-American groups, the Italian-American groups have more extensive families and greater numbers of relatives living at home with them. There are more cousins and parental siblings, however the average number of siblings per respondent in both Italian-American groups was two. In the Italian-American disturbed group, fifty percent of the respondents are the oldest sibling. The difference in sibling position between the two ethnic groups may have an ethnic connotation with regard to length of marriage and emotional crises at adolescence.

The confidential records indicate that the psychiatric institute counselled six Italian-American mothers regarding their children and the mothers themselves were seeing psychotherapists for their own psychiatric disorders. In contrast, only two Irish-American mothers received counsel for their own psychiatric disorders during the times their sons were in therapy.

The above factors may derive from the emphasis upon affective overtones in the Italian-American household as opposed to emphasis upon constraint in emotional expression in the Irish-American household. Thus, sharper and quicker marital cleavages occur in the Italian-American household and these affect the older sons. Close and extended kinship patterns persist, however, in spite of emotional outbursts.

If Campisi (11) is correct in describing the post-immigrant Italian family in the United States as one that has grown smaller and more nuclear in its urbanization, this study shows the Italian family still has more extended relationship ties than the Irish groups. An atmosphere of greater in-group solidarity is still evident, not only through close contact with relatives, but also through the greater number of grandparents and other parental kin living at home with the nuclear family.

Generation Level

There is a definite difference in generation level between the Irish and Italian groups. The greatest number of Irish immigrant relatives were great-grandparents and "at least great-grandparents." Whereas the Irish-American control group mention a great-grandparent most frequently as first immigrant, the disturbed group pre-

Table 4
Distribution of Groups by Percent in Each Generation Level,
Indicated by First Relative to Enter the United States

Group	Generation Level					
	1	2	3	4	5	
				Great	At Least	
			Grand-	Grand-	Great	
	Self	Parent	parent	parent	Grandparent	Total
	%	%	%	%	%	%
Irish-American						
Control	0.00	2.50	15.00	47.50	35.00	100
Disturbed	0.00	4.00	16.00	28.00	52.00	100
Italian-American						
Control	1.40	1.40	75.00	17.70	4.50	100
Disturbed	0.00	0.00	87.50	8.30	4.20	100

First and second generations combined with third for analysis—due to cells less than 10 and rationale of split between "newly established" and "long established" Americans.
$x^2 = 110.98$, 6 d.f.; $p < .001$

dominates in the "at least great-grandparent" category—making over 50 percent of this group fifth generation level. The boys gave this answer when they knew that the first immigrant clearly came to America well over one hundred years ago. If one calculates twenty-five years for a generation, this category signified one hundred and twenty-five years of family residence in the United States. Curiously, at this generation level, the great-grandfather on the mother's side predominated as first immigrant. As the levels recede to the fourth generation, the great grandfather immigrated. At the third level the grandparents were immigrants to this country. Most of the Irish immigrants were single while the Italian immigrants were married couples. The great majority of Irish-American respondents claimed Eire or Dublin as the source of immigration (89%).

The Italian groups are mostly third generation, their grandparents on both sides having arrived in the United States as first generation immigrants. Only one boy arrived here as a first immigrant. Another boy is of second generation Italian-American descent. The boys' responses, interestingly, indicate that a preponderance of both grandparents on either side arrived in the United States together and already married. Forty-seven percent of the boys stated that their grandparents came from Sicily, while 41.37 percent stated that their first relative came from Southern Italy. Only 6 percent of the boys gave northern Italy as the source of origin. Three boys claimed that their immigrant relatives were mixed marriages of northern Italians and Sicilians.

Neighborhood

In answer to the question on ethnic predominance in their neighborhood, 62 percent of the Irish-American control boys and 68 percent of the disturbed boys stated that their neighborhoods had several different ethnic groups, with no one group predominating. Only 17.5 percent of the control boys and 12 percent of the disturbed boys claimed predominantly Irish neighborhoods. Twenty percent of the control boys and 8 percent of the disturbed boys stated that they lived in Italian or German neighborhoods, and a small percentage of the boys in both Irish-American groups lived in areas where other ethnic and racial groups predominated.

In comparison, 41.7 percent of the Italian-American control adolescents and 37.5 percent of the disturbed adolescents live in Italian areas. At the same time, 41.7 percent of the control boys and 54 percent of the disturbed boys stated that they lived in ethnically mixed areas. The remaining percentages of boys in both Italian-American groups claimed other ethnic and racial neighborhoods in various assortments. The Italian-American groups, to a much greater extent than the Irish-Americans, lived in areas that predominated ethnically. This pattern, however, may indicate generation level as a measure of acculturation and of increasing social and psychological security in America.

Index of Social Position

The occupation and education of the adolescent's father determined social class position. In the chapter on methodology, I discussed how I would calculate the index of social position. I mentioned that since the representatives per class were a very small number and since the subclass frequencies were disproportionate, I would combine the upper classes and then the lower classes for comparative analysis. I also stated that comparative analyses between the upper and the lower classes of boys in each ethnic group were roughly indicated in order to determine whether social class boundaries influence behavior found significant on ethnic levels. I used Hollingshead's index of social position (56) to separate the boys into five social classes. Subsequently, for purposes of chi-square analysis, the social classes were divided into white-collar and blue-collar classes. Reasons for these combinations will be more apparent in the descriptions which follow.

Class I

In class I, 66 percent of the fathers were lawyers, physicians, engineers, and architects, all of whom had college degrees. All of the mothers, with the exception of one business representative in the Italian-American control group, were housewives. In the Irish-American control group, most of the mothers had completed college. In the other groups, the mothers had less education than the fathers (education range from partial high school to partial college).

Table 5
Percentage Distribution of Adolescents in Social Classes
According to the Classification of Heads of Households
by Hollingshead's Index of Social Position

| | Social Classes | | | | | | |
| | I | II | III | IV | V | Total | |
Group	%	%	%	%	%	%	N
Irish-American							
Control	10	10	25	55	00	100	40
Disturbed	4	12	16	52	16	100	25
Italian-American							
Control	5	3	32	43	17	100	34
Disturbed	4	4	38	29	25	100	24

Although this class is at the top in social and economic status, they were eligible for free psychiatric care at the mental health clinic, because of financial stress, size of family, amount of illness, or a number of other reasons. Although residence is not a factor in this index, we noted that these people did not live in the most expensive neighborhoods of the city or its standard metropolitan area, as such neighborhoods are described by Hollingshead and Redlich (55).

Class II

Class II consists of teachers, a pharmacist, a school principal, a city comptroller, and an examining engineer; all but one are college graduates. Both Irish-American groups had significantly more professional working mothers in this class than did the Italian-American groups. Only 20 percent were housewives, while the larger proportion pursued secretarial work, nursing, teaching, and social work. The Irish-American control group had more professional men in class I, while both Irish-American groups had more professional working people in class II than did the Italian-American groups.

Class III

The Italian-American groups, especially the disturbed one, have a greater percentage of fathers in this class than do the Irish-American groups.

In the Irish-American groups, 80 percent of the employed fathers were in various administrative occupations: business managers, sales managers, bank examiners, estimators, and sales directors. In the control group, 10 percent of the fathers were semi-professional and 10 percent were skilled workers. Twenty-five percent of the fathers in the Irish-American disturbed group owned small businesses. In this disturbed group, 50 percent of the fathers were high school graduates, and 50 percent of them were college graduates. This educational level is somewhat above that for the control group where education is evenly divided between high school completion, partial college, and college completion. In the Irish-American disturbed group, 50 percent of the mothers had some college education and were gainfully employed in sales work. In the control group, 80 percent of the mothers were housewives, although 50 percent of them were college graduates.

In the Italian-American groups, approximately 55 percent of the fathers owned small businesses. While 27 percent of the fathers of the Italian-American control boys were in administrative and sales occupations, 44 percent of the fathers of the Italian-American disturbed boys were in sales occupations. Eighteen percent of the control group fathers were technicians, while 1 percent of the disturbed group fathers were in semi-professional work. As for education, 54.5 percent of the fathers in the control group were high school graduates, and 78 percent of the fathers in the disturbed group had high school diplomas. Eighteen percent of the control group fathers and 11 percent of the disturbed group fathers were college graduates.

The pattern of maternal employment in the control and disturbed groups is similar to that of the Irish-American groups. In the control group, only 28 percent of the mothers were gainfully employed, while 72 percent were housewives. Somewhat behind their husbands, 45 percent were high school graduates while only 9 percent were college graduates. In the disturbed group, 45 percent of the mothers were gainfully employed outside of the home in such fields as sales, teaching, and music. In this group, 11 percent were college graduates and 22 percent were high school graduates.

The fact that the Italian-American groups led in the number of small businesses and in high school graduates supports the assumption that second-generation upward mobility focuses upon the independent, self-propelled business enterprise as a symbol of opportunity, with education uppermost as a tool for forging ahead. Although upward mobility aspiration in disturbed groups may produce the greater percentage of working mothers, another consideration may be these mothers wished to get out of the home for relief of anxiety and tension. Whatever the reason, less parental supervision and less stable emotional support in time of need may be a factor in adolescent crises.

Class IV

In the Irish-American groups, over 90 percent of the control fathers were skilled manual workers, while 46 percent of the disturbed fathers were skilled workers. In the disturbed group, 30.7 percent of the fathers were semi-skilled and only 7 percent were sales workers. Fathers in skilled trades were policemen, brakemen, firemen, tool and die workers, bricklayers, and mailmen. In both Irish-American groups, approximately 50 percent of the fathers were high school graduates. The level of education was somewhat higher in the control group, since 32 percent of the fathers had partial or complete college educations. In contrast to the control group, 50 percent of the fathers in the disturbed group were only grammar school graduates. The education of the disturbed group housewives was nearly equivalent to that of their husbands. This educational pattern differed somewhat from that of the control group where 59 percent of the mothers were high school graduates and 27 percent had completed college. The pattern of education for control group mothers was somewhat above that of their husbands and could be interpreted as an active economic asset to the Irish-American class IV household.

In contrast to the Irish-American groups, the occupations of fathers in the Italian-American groups were divided between skilled labor and semi-skilled labor. Fifty percent of the fathers in the Italian-American control group were skilled workers, while 71.4 percent of the fathers in the disturbed group were semi-skilled workers. In contrast to 28.5 percent of the control group fathers who were unskilled workers, none of the fathers in this disturbed group were unskilled workers. Instead, 28 percent were equally divided between skilled workers and sales workers. Seventy-one percent of the fathers of both Italian-American groups were high school graduates. Seven percent of the control group fathers had completed some college while 28 percent of the disturbed group fathers had completed only grammar school.

Over 75 percent of the mothers in both Italian-American groups were housewives. Those who did work were engaged in semi-skilled work. Approximately half of the mothers in both Italian-American groups were high school graduates, while approximately 40 percent of the mothers were grammar school graduates. Seven percent of the mothers in the control group were college graduates.

The percentage of high school graduation indicates again the Italian-American stress on education as a means of upward mobility for those who more recently immigrated.

Class V

The index of social position places approximately 16.5 percent of the Irish-American disturbed boys and the Italian-American boys in this class. There were no Irish-American control group fathers holding this social status.

I must state again that none of the class V adolescents lived in large tenements or in the worst slum areas of the city as Hollingshead (55) attributes to this position. The fathers were classified by occupation and education, not by residence, and the general impression of the modal class V residence was, like the class IV residence, an area of well-kept two-family homes, modest but adequate for comfort.

In the Irish-American group the fathers were equally divided into semi-skilled and unskilled workers. Fifty percent were grammar school graduates and 50 percent had completed some high school. The mothers were equally divided between housewifery and gainful employment. Those who worked did part-time nursing and dental technician work. Fifty percent were grammar school graduates and the other 50 percent not only completed high school but also had some college education. This pattern of working wives and mothers raises the family from the hand-to-mouth existence described by Hollingshead and Redlich (55) to a way of life more similar to class IV status.

In the Italian-American groups, the majority of the fathers were semi-skilled workers: porters, busdrivers and watchmen. In the disturbed group, 33 percent of the fathers were skilled workers. The larger number of men working in skilled jobs in this group could be due to the acquisition of skills from the Old World immigrant father, or to the fact that a greater number of fathers had completed high school. In the control group, 33 percent of the fathers were high school graduates, and over 60 percent of the fathers were grammar school graduates. In the disturbed group, 33 percent of the fathers had some high school education, and only 17 percent had completed high school.

Approximately 66 percent of the mothers in the control group were housewives, while 34 percent pursued semi-skilled work. Fifty percent of the mothers were high school graduates. In the disturbed group, all of the mothers were housewives, pursuing no work outside the home. Again, 50 percent of them were high school graduates, while one mother had some college education.

Both Italian-American groups again lead in high school graduates among the heads of households. Both Italian-American groups not only present a larger number of fathers in semi-skilled work, but there are also more skilled workers in this class. More of the mothers in these groups are housewives who remain at home with their children.

Chi-square evaluation reveals that there is a significant difference at the .001 percent level of probability ($X^2 = 16.29$, 3d.f.) in the proportion of working mothers on an ethnic basis. The Irish-American groups have, as a whole, more working mothers than do the Italian-American groups. When the distribution of education of mothers in the four groups is expressed in percentages and chi-square evaluation is made, there is a significant difference between the mothers in each group and the amount of education completed ($X^2 = 19.39$, 6d.f., $p < .001$). Fewer of the mothers in the disturbed groups finished high school than did the control group mothers, and fewer of the disturbed group mothers completed college.

More of the mothers in the Irish-American groups completed high school and college than did Italian-American mothers. Differences between the Italian-American and the Irish-American mothers in education levels could well reflect generation level in America, since the Italian-American groups were one to two generations behind in adapting to the American scene.

I noted that Italian-American fathers had educational attainments on a par with and often ahead of Irish-American fathers. Italian-Americans conceivably value education more for the breadwinner, while they value women more highly as housewives and mothers. This is a practical point of view for immigrants who need to adjust to the American business and industrial pattern. Small businesses are common in the Italian-American middle class as compared to the administrative opportunities in industry open to the more fully Americanized Irish-American fathers. Small business is independent and free and can symbolize American opportunity for self-advancement. The present generation Italian-American boy may find opportunity in professional preparation when he discovers the financial reward and consequent economic security it offers.

5

Clinical Abstracts

This chapter is concerned with clinical descriptions of the disturbed boys and with ethnic variations in symptom patterns. The diagnostic scheme used in this study is the nosological system developed by the American Psychiatric Association (2) and utilized by the psychiatrists at the Monsignor Carr Institute. The diagnostic category into which all of the adolescents were placed was "Adjustment Reaction of Adolescents."

We investigated the clinical records with regard to the emotional descriptions, summary of behavioral characteristics, and the central conflicts that prevailed in each disturbed group. The clinical records at the Monsignor Carr Clinic and at the residential care institutions were summarized according to an assessment schedule. This schedule outlined the following areas of inquiry: personal history, psychological testing, physical illness, emotion, conduct, hostilities and anxieties, attitude to mental health clinic and authority, and central conflicts.

Analysis of the clinical records proceeded with content analysis of record abstractions. We scanned the records for behavioral and emotional descriptions which the therapists and psychologists at the Institute used and then tabulated these expressions for each group. Since there were generally several expressions for each individual, emotional and behavioral descriptions exceed the number of boys in each group.

Since other studies (89) link class status with certain kinds of disorders, this study investigated class differences as well. Tests of significance for adolescent disorders and class status failed to reveal probability levels for relationships, other than chance distribution. Those personality traits found in the Edwards Personal Preference Schedule to rise with decreasing class status (endurance, heterosexuality, exhibitionism) also characterized the clinical findings. In disturbance, the traits appear to fuse in favor of ethnic phenomena, however, in view of the small number of boys in each social class, increased intra class variations may reduce the sharpness and clarity in tests of significance.

The following compendiums are derived from clinical descriptions of psychiatric disorders. In order to determine differences, if any, between boys with differing family structures, we grouped the clinical descriptions according to parental status and patient residence: at home with both parents, at home with one parent, or not living at home. All psychiatric descriptions were thus compounded for each category of residence. These grouped abstracts refer to more than one boy. The boy described is compounded of all descriptions in that category.

The Irish-American Disturbed Group

Most of the behavioral adjectives and emotional expressions tabulated in Table 6 refer to mechanisms of detachment, isolation, and rigid control.

Table 6 presents a picture of a boy who basically withdraws into a self-made fantasy. He is compliant, passive, and self-conscious in interpersonal relationships. Somatic manifestations reveal inner tension and suppressed aggression that often serve as secondary motivations for succorance (human concern) in his dilemma. Feelings of being unwanted and abandoned, coupled with feelings of inferiority and inadequacy dramatize his psychological reaction to the social dilemma. This boy is moody and dejected, and is uneasy and anxious in the face of his own hostility.

The therapeutic personnel in the clinic described the boys in this group as attempting to control their behavior and emotions by "conscious suppression of aggression," "passive-aggressive attitudes," and "suppression of aggression by neutral, compliant forms of behavior with dependent actions." Considering this picture, the boys' reactions to social situations will cause aggressive phenomena to turn inward with depressive guilt and self-conscious isolation. Their feelings of inferiority and inadequacy will produce compensatory fantasies of a better world, but since the desire for change and emotional comfort has become an impractical daydream, they make no constructive effort to bring about this better world.

In accordance with the clinic form, we tabulated the summarizing notes of illness and central conflicts by content analysis. The report described twelve of the boys as having dominant mothers who were rigid and overprotective in their maternal behavior, so that the boys found it too difficult to strive for independence. Adjectival descriptions present these boys as having poor and difficult mascu-

Table 6

Frequency of Behavioral Descriptions and Emotional Expressions
from the Clinical Records of the Irish-American Disturbed Boys

Behavioral Descriptions	No.	Emotional Expression	No.
Shy	7	Feels rejected	4
Quiet	6	Feels depressed	2
Too compliant	8	Broods	2
Withdrawn	9	Constriction	2
Inattentive	3	Sad	3
Isolates self	8	Uneasy, anxious	1
Moody	1	Feels abandoned	3
Detached	3	Feels inadequate	3
Fantasy	9	Feels inferior	5
Introversion	1	Feels unwanted	2
Under-achievement	4	Bitter	2
Too polite	1	Lonely	3
Infantile	1	Desires independence	
Seeks attention	2	from mother	3
Hypochondriasis	2		
Sado-masochistic	1		
Stealing, lying	2		
Defiant	1		
Follows delinquent gangs	3		
Total	72	Total	35
	N＝25		N＝25

line identifications and father figures, or as having "lacked" paternal images at a crucial period in their lives. This is in contrast to the Italian-American disturbed group where there was no complete rejection but rather a more confused orientation towards the masculine role.

Boy Living With Both Parents

Summary

Summary of psychological tests indicate that the boy's intelligence quotient is superior, but in view of severe maladjustments, perceptions of life are found to fit in with fantasy life. There is extremely uninhibited imaginative play and rigid and

Table 7
Central Conflicts Abstracted and Summarized
from the Clinical Records for the
Irish-American Disturbed Boys

CENTRAL CONFLICTS	No.
Mother domination	12
Little respect for father	1
Conflict over male figure	2
Disappointed in father	1
No male figure	1
Poor father image	3
Rejected by father	4
Father is threatening	2
No ideal masculine figure	1
Clings to father image	1
Clings to maternal image	1
Difficult male identification	1
Almost feminine identification	1
Needs strong male identification	2
Total	33
	N = 25

inhibited ego patterns. Psychological tests indicate that this boy finds it difficult to profit from experience, since he couples feelings of identity with feelings of worthlessness and the rejection of other people. There is much anxiety and tension with intellectual-type defenses. Emotionally, this boy spends time seeking attention through histrionic, hypochondriacal displays (overbreathing, hand rigid). There are blocks in intellectual learning and consequent poor scholastic work in school. This boy is extremely negative to his sibling and is superficial in his conversation. He wanders off, does not return affection, and is, in general, too controlled and proper in his social relationships. He expresses control of emotional hostility through detachment from family, the appearance of self-sufficiency, extreme conformity, and efforts to please the parents. He often regresses to infantile behavior in hypochondriacal displays.

His central conflict revolves around parental conflict and discord. The mother is the more dominant of the parents in the home, and the father is away from home a great deal as a traveling salesman. As a consequence of marital difficulty, the father objects to maternal domination and is openly critical of the child. The boy feels that he is constantly being punished and threatened by his mother. He feels rejected by his mother, who is somewhat intolerant and impatient with him. The mother feels that the father estranges himself from the child, and there is poor role model identification. This, coupled with her own dominance, indicates confused parental supervision. The boy as a consequence endures feelings of rejection and feelings of being abandoned and senses lack of paternal interest. In an excessive effort to achieve parental approval, this boy plays with younger children in order to be the leader. This boy has few close friends because of his fantasy life, retreatism, hypersensitivity to disapproval, and histrionic need for attention. Beneath the excessive conforming behavior, there is an infantile and immature attention-getting behavior toward both the father and the mother. Part of this reaction is exhibited in underachievement in school. Although the parents want this boy to attend college, he is bent on leaving school as soon as possible.

The therapist feels that there is a confused and difficult identification problem coupled with an environment of maternal domination. The father's own dependence on alcohol, his criticism of maternal authority, and his own part in marital discord were made features for parental counseling. Further therapeutic goals included community-wide masculine affiliations in peer groups.

Boy Living At Home With Stepfather and Mother

Summary

This summary is that of a boy living at home with his mother and stepfather. The stepfather's alcholism and extreme rejection of the boy reveal his poor family environment. The stepfather is jealous of the mother's maternal attention to the boy and competes for her affection. The mother is not only dominant but also devoted to the boy in her overprotection. The boy turned to the grandmother for support and love in view of the confusing parental situation. The boy in this compendium was referred to the clinic because of extreme underachievement in school and lack of motivation in doing his homework. This boy seeks attention by hypochondriacal complaints of dizziness and nausea. He stays in his own room and reads a great deal.

The therapist describes the boy as one who "lives in a dream world." He has few friends and mingles very little with other people. His superficial behavioral adjustment is excellent in that he complies with the rules and regulations of the house. However, he refuses to participate in sports, dances, or group life of any kind. He feels that his mother has abandoned him and that he has no support from his stepfather. In his view, no one person has a particular interest in him. He has a poor image of himself and feels inadequate. He clings to the maternal image of love and affection, while at the same time he deeply grieves for the grandmother, who recently died. This grandmother overindulged him and granted every request. Disappointment in the maternal image and mourning for the grandmother (a maternal image) are compounded by a feeling of abandonment by his father and an extreme resentment of his dependent alcoholic stepfather. He shows an almost feminine personal identification problem and has little in his environment to provide an adequate masculine role model.

The following is the summary of a boy who lives with both parents but exhibits outright aggression in the community and appears to behave in similar fashion to the Italian-American disturbed boy.

Boy in Delinquent-Like Episodes

Summary

This boy lives at home with both parents. His intelligence quotient is "bright normal." He shows constrictive defenses in the Rorschach test through intellectual and compulsive defenses against the conflict of anxiety. This boy has depressive episodes and verbalizes feelings of rejection by his father. He is bitter, avoids people, and feels that all people are against him. He feels defiant, and he has a tendency to act out his conflicts of anxiety and hostility. The mother is overindulgent and compensates for the father's rejection. The father is a dependent person and has a tendency toward alcoholic episodes.

The poor father image leads to a confused sexual identity, so in an effort to achieve masculine identification, this boy follows gangs and delinquent crowds. These delinquent groups are disorderly and defiant toward authority. The therapist sees gang behavior as a drive for more material and masculine values. When not with the gang, this boy isolates himself at home in his own room. He fantasizes a better life and a happier existence. Impulsive escapades with delinquent gangs in petty misbehavior alternate with periods of good compliant behavior at home.

The central conflicts revolving around this boy include feelings of inadequacy in view of his father's expectations of masculinity. The father expects this boy to be an athlete and scholar and is, in general, somewhat critical of the boy's tendencies in other directions. He prefers his friends over his family. The father, outside of criticism, steers clear of managing the boy, leaving this to his mother. The mother is helpless and bribes the boy who, in turn, overcontrols the mother in the bid for attention. The boy becomes interested in groups that are against society. In an effort to find identity with a better value system and a less confusing one, this boy puts on a tough facade in the interest of masculinity. He displays poor superego development which shows scars of paternal neglect. There is also evidence that this boy has an inadequate ego-ideal related to poor parental encouragement. Overindulgence, combined with paternal neglect and criticism, encourages hostility and defiance of prohibitions in society.

Boy Living With One Parent

Summary

This boy lives alone with his mother and is the middle sibling. His father died in 1961. Tests indicate that the intelligence quotient is normal, although better intellectual performance was impaired by emotional disturbance. Clinical observation indicates that this boy is withdrawn in all social relations. He exhibits a lonely, defeatist attitude. He has few friends, and his personality is constricted. This boy is known to have acute anxiety reactions in which he overbreathes and becomes panicky. In addition, he has expressed feelings of inferiority. He utilizes fantasy easily and aggressively.

The therapist describes his central conflicts as generally sexual ones, especially his difficulty in making adequate male identifications. His tremendous interest in athletics is seen as an effort to adopt the male role. He shows a great deal of repressed hostility by isolating himself and avoiding association with people of his own age. His mother "nags" him to grow up and be independent, to which he reacts by isolating himself and retreating into a fantasy world. His mother, in despair over the boy's increased retreat to his own private world, voluntarily brought this boy to the clinic for therapy.

Boy Living At Home With One Parent

Summary

The mother died five years ago, and the father remains a widower. This boy's intelligence quotient is normal, but his performance is impaired by emotional disturbance. Clinically, he is observed to be inhibited, unperceptive, and guarded, and he denies any problems. He has expressed feelings of being misunderstood, of being punished unfairly, and of having thoughts of running away. The therapist describes this boy as making a tremendous effort to seek independence from his father.

The central discord in this boy is his tremendous conflict with his father and his younger brother. This boy feels rejected and unwanted. He feels his brother is the favorite son. He feels resentment toward his father and misses his close relationship with his mother. The mounting tension and anxiety, together with feelings of inadequacy and inferiority are covered over by guarded denial of problems, resentment, and hostile independence of the father. He achieves control of suppressed aggression by inhibition, seeming lack of perception to social events, and an asocial retreatism.

Boy Living in Residence

Summary

This boy's parents are separated. He was placed in residence because, in living with the mother who was employed, his adolescent adjustment reactions were seen as needing constructive group living. Psychological tests show this boy to be of superior intelligence. However, his school achievement has suffered because of reduced efficiency and "freezing" in the classroom. He is described as quiet, withdrawn, and detached. He has somatic symptoms which portrayed apprehension and uneasiness. Emotionally, this boy expresses himself as one who feels inferior and lonely. He feels depressed, likes to dream, and feels emotionally detached from the world around him. This boy likes a rigid schedule of activities organized and planned in advance. He likes to be orderly, and in his dreams he likes to be grandiose. Since this boy lived with one parent (the mother), he has a tremendous clinging to the maternal image, but he has a very poor and ill-defined relationship to the father. This is evident in his feelings that his father abandoned him and in his striving to hold the image of what he thinks the father should be, in spite of separation from and lack of affiliation with the father.

His impoverished method of coping with reality, coupled with withdrawal into grandiose fantasies of masculinity, leads to compulsive doubting. He has a compulsive need to think big and to organize things into orderly, complex wholes. He has a general feeling of responsibility for the parental separation which leads him to feel he must be superior to compensate for his guilt.

The dominant and somewhat authoritarian mother and the absent father promoted confusion of reality with fantasy. Maternal employment, lack of masculine figures for identification, excessive withdrawal from the peer group world, and introverted techniques of coping with reality led the therapeutic authorities to feel that constructive group therapy in outside residence was essential for the rehabilitation of this boy.

The majority of Irish-American disturbed boys generally reacted to stress in characteristic ways. Their attitudes toward authority were compliant; their behaviors were manifested by self isolation and fantasy formation. They used hypochondriacal complaints as attention-getting mechanisms. The adolescent adjustment reactions noted here are primarily problems in masculine identifications complicated by maternal domination and inadequate father role models. Exaggerated older female and sister attachments were evident in the Life-Space Drawing. Compliance and orderliness were found to predominate on the Edwards Personal Preference Schedule. Heterosexual attachments were found, on the Life-Space Drawing, to be more distant than relationships with peer groups.

In examining the reactions of these adolescents, it appears that familial and personal factors are just as important as social factors. It would be hard to separate the two. Where there are characteristic ego-ideals and superego formations, most of the boys react to stress in generally defined ways. Where three boys in this group did not have sufficient and consistent ego-ideal formation, their characteristic behavioral patterns were patterned after the parents themselves. In concluding the description of the Irish-American disturbed group, we may say that the symptomatology prevalent in this group of boys corroborates Opler's (84) description of the Irish Schizophrenic group.

The Italian-American Disturbed Group

This group of boys reacted to anxieties and hostilities in a more active and aggressive manner than did the Irish-American disturbed boys. Anxieties and hostilities are expressed in this group by hostile often sadistic, interpersonal relations, with conversion reactions used as controls for relationships. They manifest their interpersonal aggression in such independence-seeking devices as argumentativeness and challenge of authority, rebellion and belligerence, and feelings of persecution and desires to "get even" with the injuring party.

Generally, the Italian-American boys, like the Irish-American boys, feel inferior, unwanted, and abandoned by their fathers. However, in contrast to Irish-American sadness and melancholy, the Italian-American boys evidence feelings of persecution. They show another greater emotional liability in their euphoria and aggressive thoughts. It is conceivable that his feelings of persecution may stem from the Italian-American boy's ability to transform his anxiety and hostility into active-aggressive acts. This active aggression brings retaliation which can induce, in emotional disturbance, an exaggerated feeling of being persecuted by other people.

Table 8

Frequency of Behavioral Descriptions and Emotional Expressions
from the Clinical Records of the Italian-American Disturbed Group

Behavioral Descriptions	No.	Emotional Expression	No.
Argumentative	11	Feels persecuted	6
Destructive, hostile	10	Feels inferior	3
Rebellion, disobedience	8	Feels unwanted	3
Joins aggressive gangs	5	Euphoric	3
Low tolerance for authority	4	Feels abandoned by father	2
Aggressive	3	Aggressive thoughts	2
Impulsive	3	Guilt feelings	1
Stutters, conversion reaction	3	Feels infantile	1
Fights with peers	2	Dependent upon mother	1
Aggressive sexual tendencies	1		
Sadistic	1		
Daydreams	1		
Dreams of female role	1		
Total	53	Total	22
	N = 24		N = 24

On the Life-Space Drawing, we see this boy loses his anxieties in group participation with peers and in active attempted heterosexual engagements. Active aggression, as found on the Edwards Personal Preference Schedule, coupled with dominance and exhibitionism, enables this boy to join aggressive gangs and to make an attempt at identification with male companions, albeit with those who bring him into trouble with the law. Only one boy exhibits the phenomena of daydreaming and withdrawal, and dreams of playing the female role. In this group, conversion symptoms such as stuttering and other forms of somatic expressions may express conflicts around aggression and exhibitionism in their adolescent struggles for independence and masculinity. In stuttering, verbal defiance and aggression are spontaneously inhibited by underlying anxiety, and fear of disapproval and loss of love.

In this group only four overprotective mothers and grandmothers are blamed for poor male identification and feelings of inadequacy. In one case, the mother was perceived as threatening because of her own psychiatric disorder, which included delusions of persecution

Table 9
Central Conflicts Abstracted and Summarized
from the Clinical Records for the
Italian-American Disturbed Boys

CENTRAL CONFLICTS	No.
Confused sexual and male identification	6
Cannot fulfill father's expectations	2
Disappointment in father	2
Poor male identification	5
Inadequate male identification	3
Lack of masculine identification	5
Lack of a good authority figure	1
Afraid of father—stern, rigid	2
Female figure is hostile and threatening	1
Grandmother is overprotective	2
Extensive dependence upon the mother	1
Maternal overprotection	1
Total	31
	N = 24

and hostility. In contrast to the Irish-American boys, there are no outright parental desertions or parent-of-son rejections. There does, however, appear to be more direct conflict with fathers and confusions in the assumptions of masculinity. Sexual confusion exists for seven boys in their inability to fulfill paternal expectations and in their disappointment in the father who, they feel, does not understand them.

Thirteen boys had poor and inadequate male identifications due to the threat posed by rigid paternal figures. This confused male identification can lead to the utilization of aggressive and exhibitionistic conduct in efforts to prove masculinity. Activity in peer groups and heterosexual advances are potential modes of proving such powers. These potential patterns of conduct do not exist for the Irish-American disturbed group.

The following are compendiums of behavior, emotional expressions, and central conflicts of the Italian-American adolescent boy, again categorized according to parental and residential status.

Boy Living With Both Parents

Summary

The compendium of this boy reveals that his intelligence quotient is average. He shows, however, poor school adjustment with his relative aimlessness and confusion held responsible for low achievement.

Clinical observations indicate that he reacts impulsively, bringing about disorders in the schoolroom, the home, and the street through clownishness, fights, and petty mischievous acts. He is also defiant and disobedient in the classroom and in the home, especially with friends who are ruffians and nonconformists. This boy makes friends easily with peers who are sympathic to this behavior. He disobeys his mother's orders, stays out late with girls, and defies orders to return home at a certain hour. This boy is careless in appearance and resistant to direction; he puts on a bravado act in ingratiation, coupled with clownishness and cynicism. Conversion symptoms seem to appear in gastro-enterological complaints. These symptoms are in line with Fenichel's (31) description of the person who relies upon exhibitionism as an important mechanism in coping with the demands of reality. Throughout all this there is a masked determination to do as the boy wants to do.

The central conflicts of this boy reveal confusion in masculinity because of inconsistent parent-child relationships and parental roles. A glimpse into intrafamilial relationships reveals a very ingratiating mother. She does not give the boy time or the opportunity to assert himself and to express himself, since she is too anxious and concerned about him. Sometimes the mother shields the boy from the father and accedes to the demands of the boy without consultation with the father. As a result, the boy manipulates his mother to excuse him from everything he does not want to do. Contact with his father is usually poor, since the father works long hours.

The father is seen as rigid in his demands on the boy, often making a fuss over the daughters while making great deamnds of the son in athletics and scholastic work. The father, in a domineering and stern manner, often argues with the mother and openly conflicts with her over the boy's training. Because of these factors, the boy expresses deep feelings of anxiety and inferiority in relation to the father which he acts out partially in disobedience and partially in a psychosomatic manner. There is a strong hostile component, coupled with bitterness toward the male authority figure. Parental inconsistency results in ingratiation of the mother and avoidance of the father through peer group relations outside the family. Aggression and exhibitionism in peer groups helps to suppress feelings of inferiority and inadequacy.

The mother may smother the son with love to make up for a disappointed father's underlying rejection of imperfection in the abilities and behavior of the son. Overt parental conflict and overt ambiguity in an attempt to control the son produce ambiguity in the son himself. Open affective relationships are learned and imitated by the boy in assuming his own role. This overtness is manifested by active aggression in achieving some sense of masculine identity outside the home. There is an attempt to get away from mother ingratiation, which is, in a way, a form of maternal dominance, and there is an effort to deny the attempted dominance of the father. This denial is manifested by an attempt at identification with the actively aggressive male in outer society.

We can reiterate that active-aggressive thoughts and behavior without the qualities of succorance and nurturance produce a sullen, almost sadistic, approach to life's problems. As will be seen in the questionnaire, this type of emotionally disturbed boy acquires an aggressive shrewdness whereby he uses aggression to meet the requirements of authority, while at the same time using it to achieve private aims. It is evident that, in manifesting achievement and intraception, the aggressive drive for this group is a sociocentric one.

The following is a summary of a boy who lives with both parents but exhibits withdrawal mechanisms in similar fashion to the Irish-American disturbed boy.

Summary

This boy exhibits emotional disturbance more similar to that of the Irish-American boy than to that of the Italian-American boys noted above. He is withdrawn from social contact, is shy, and complains of an inability to concentrate. Emotionally, he is compliant and pursues a technique of isolation. Psychosomatic complaints are predominant, including headaches, fatigue, and assorted pains.

In contrast to the Irish-American boy, the daydreams of this boy are concrete dreams pertaining to reality problems and methods of coping with them. His thinking is concrete and pragmatically oriented. He exhibits dependent reactions through jealousy of siblings and complaints of illness to a much greater degree than the Irish-American boy. This boy thinks that all people are against him. His daydreams center on how to "get even" with certain people in the environment.

Where the Irish-American boy became delinquent under inadequate ego-ideals set down by the parents, the Italian-American boy in this case becomes withdrawn, isolated, and dependent when his father sets down too stern and rigid an ego-ideal. His father is described as a rigid and stern individual who discriminates between the children and places extremely high expectations upon the boy to be athletic, strong, and powerful in his achievement orientations. This results in extreme feelings of inadequacy on the boy's part to meet the perfectionistic designs of the father. He cannot achieve father identification when he is made to feel inadequate and inferior to the goal. However, even with this variation in conduct from the other Italian-American boy, this boy's social withdrawal is not as complete as that of the Irish-American boy who fantasizes self-glorification in a world apart from practical reality. The Italian-American boy dreams of concrete events and of concrete ways of retaliating against those who persecute him. In this way, he still manifests sociocentric mechanisms, even though these are made towards a seemingly malevolent world, while the Irish-American boy manifests egocentric mechanisms in a perceived benevolent world.

Boy Living With Stepfather and Mother

Summary

This boy was raised from the age of three by an Italian step-father. His father deserted the family when the patient was three years old. This boy exhibits certain sociopathic reactions by stealing candy and cigarettes and by giving these to other boys to secure their friendship. He requires constant attention from other people, directs attention to himself as a class clown, and joins aggressive groups that steal and commit legal misde-meanors.

The central conflicts of this boy indicate that, as with the other boys, he is ambiguous about identification with the fe-male or the male role model. The original father appeared never to have shown an interest in the boy. The stepfather in-dicates that he tries to be a good father and that he is being very "stern" with the boy. The grandmother in the home is very ingratiating. The boy is concerned with reasons for the de-sertion of his real father. As with the boys discussed above, his adolescent striving for independence has run into conflict with his stepfather's aims. This is coupled with female ingratiation and overprotection. He compensates for feelings of inadequacy and inferiority, with ambiguity of identification by aggres-sive acts in an attempt to receive friendship and personal atten-tion from other people. In his ambiguity, he has fled both fe-male and male authority figures as he identifies with aggres-sively oriented people in the community.

Boy Living With One Parent

Summary

The modal pattern for this boy is residence with the mother after the father separated and left the family. The mother was aided in her child rearing by the grandparent. The summary of psychological tests indicates a superior intelligence quotient. The Rorschach test reveals immature, poor emotional relations with others (weak superego development). There was a need for therapeutic measures that would enable the boy to develop his superego and consequent insight regarding "who he is" in relation to his mother and to authority figures.

Emotionally and behaviorally, this boy is restless, apprehensive, and has difficulty concentrating. He has temper outbursts, is rebellious, argumentative, and sullen in family and social relations. Emotionally, he directs these reactions to other people by impulsively lashing out at others and arguing with peers and those in authority. He appears indifferent to the wishes of other people and is defiant of authority figures. This boy engages in delinquent acts with friends and peer groups, of which he is often a leader. Anxieties and hostilities are directed overtly to family, father, and society.

The therapist interprets the central conflicts of this boy to be those of inadequate father identification and confusion between love for the father and love for the mother. The father, as an inadequate person, was unable to set proper examples, exert discipline, or command respect for the paternal role. His desertion produced an adolescent disappointment in the male image. (In an effort to control the situation, the boy defiantly defends the father.) On the other hand, the boy is surrounded by two female figures (mother and grandmother), whose ingratiation and overprotection negate desperate attempts to seek a male role model.

Emergence into adolescence with extreme dependence upon the mother and the grandmother produces an overreaction of overt, aggressive acts with peers in an effort to identify with the male sex. The combination of conversion symptoms and active aggression produced an affective upheaval in the home so that the mother despaired in her efforts to make the boy comply with authority and to keep him out of trouble with the law. This led to voluntary submission to therapeutic resources.

Boy Living With An Ill Parent

Summary

This boy lives at home with both parents, although the father is disabled with a chronic illness. We can see a variation from the pattern above in the following emotional and behavioral descriptions of this boy.

Clinical observation portrays this boy as agitated, anxious, pacing, and continually asking for reassurance. He expresses the urge to sneer at people and to hit them. Consciously, he is very constrained, and he appears to be overtrained in self-control. He is plagued by feelings that everyone is against him. He is obsessed by the fear of harming people and by the consequent guilt feelings of aggressive thoughts, which he directs to other boys in the neighborhood.

This patient was reared in an atmosphere of chronic illness and disability. He was considerably disturbed by the death of his grandparents, to whom he was very close. This boy was overly constrained emotionally because he had considerable responsibility for the care of his grandparents and of his chronically ill father. In earlier years his father pampered him; in later years this father demanded the boy's time and condemned the boy's own symptoms. The boy transferred the hostility directed toward his father to his friends and others in the neighborhood.

Boy Living in Residence

Summary

This boy is living in residence because the parents were separated and, in four cases, the mother was hospitalized for an acute mental disturbance. When the boy's mother was not hospitalized for mental disturbance, he was placed in residence because he had a severe behavior problem which forced the mother to a desperate, voluntary request for help.

This boy exhibits hypermanic activities of an expansive, euphoric, and aggressive nature. He proves to be loud, boisterous, unruly, and callous to authority.

The central conflicts of this boy indicate that there is a strong identification with the mother and the grandmother. These authority figures lavish gifts on the boy in an attempt to buy his love and to make up for the loss of his father. The boy is confused over the father's desertion and defends himself against further inroads of trauma by his family and society.

He has a strong need to be wanted and loved, but since his actions easily anger his mother and grandmother, he turns to peer groups to fulfill his rebellious needs and to gain some authority for his own self-image. His ego strength is strained when he finds that to get his way, his friendships outside the home must be both shallow and provocative. His inner restlessness and aggression are sometimes resented by his own peer groups. For purposes of treatment, the therapeutic authorities felt that a constructive group setting providing masculine role models would enable this adolescent more easily to decrease his expansiveness and defiance and to develop a more adequate ego structure.

The boys in the Italian-American disturbed group corroborates the research instruments in portraying a clinical picture of active aggression. As in the Life-Space Drawing, they show how they manipulate their social field to gain emotional comforts and prestige. These boys left confusing and inconsistent parent-child roles in order to prove to themselves that they are more significant with their peers and with the opposite sex than they are at home. To an adolescent, peer group success is important for self-esteem in a world where sophistication is admired.

The typical boy in this ethnic group was able to assume the dominant traits of his father, yet could not identify with him. Active aggression to fulfill narcissistic demands from the social field is a trait necessarily developed and nurtured in early childhood. When the boy feels inadequate and inferior in relation to the father, peer group status becomes even more important, and heterosexual accomplishments symbolize masculinity in spite of conflicts with the father. Where psychosomatic manifestations accompany emotional impulsivity, we can surmise that the conversion symptoms of the Italian-American boy symbolize hesitancy and feelings of inadequacy as inhibitory forces against impulsive behavior.

This pattern contrasts to the Irish-American boys, who develop hypochondriacal symptoms as attention-getting devices to gain succorance from kindly individuals. It appears that the Irish-American boy was not trained to utilize the forces of culture as exploratory tools for the maintenance of self-esteem. Instead, this boy develops idealistic ideas of good and evil, relying upon specific people to approve of his actions. When the world becomes too harsh and disapproval exceeds approval, this boy withdraws to a better world of fantasy. The ego deflation represented in the Life-Space-Drawings of both disturbed groups takes on different patterns of social relationships and behavioral manifestations.

Discussion

Two main questions have arisen in the presentation of the findings thus far. In studying the clinical record, we find that each ethnic group presented a couple of boys with problems in ego-ideals. In the Irish-American group we noted that the boys assumed the values of their own parents. When the boys in this group did not have sufficient and consistent ego-ideal patterns to follow in their parents, they showed scars of paternal neglect. Inadequate ego-ideals were, therefore, related to poor parental encouragement.

In the Italian-American group a couple of boys showed, in their clinical summary, problems similar to those of the Irish-American boys. In these cases, however, the clinical records illustrated the extremely high ego-ideal that the fathers set forth for them. Extremely high expectations resulted in extreme feelings of inadequacy because the boys could not meet the perfectionistic designs of their fathers. It seems that when parents set down extremely high ego-ideals which are beyond the youth's capabilities, they force unilateral respect in father-son relationships. Extremely high perfectionistic designs for a son lead to tremendous dependency coupled with aggression, so that there is not much left except to compulsively doubt one's own adequacy. Compulsive doubting of one's own abilities and adequacies may take the form of feeling persecuted by other people. On the other hand, like the Irish boy he introjects the rigid moral and ethical code of the dominant mother and develops a magical world where one is all-capable and omnipotent. Where dependency is fostered because of the demands of perfectionism, the ethnic groups express this dependency differently, if it is overwhelming, it leads one group to persecutory thinking and the other to magical thinking. This, then, is the contrast between pragmatic or sociocentric thinking and idealistic egocentric thinking. Excessive parental idealism in either form thwarts adolescent attempts gradually to gain independence in the assumption of life tasks.

Another point to be discussed from the viewpoint of adolescent maturation is the apparent inconsistency of parent-son relationships in the Italian-American groups. We assume that masculine identifications are consistent value orientations in a society where behavior is emphasized according to defined sex roles. Identification is, therefore, attempted with the parent of the same sex for social role behavior and for the formation of masculine self-concepts. The transition from childhood to adult autonomy is a period in which one's life changes from dependent childhood roles through independently formed adolescent roles into mature adult roles. Consistent patterns of relationships between parents and between parents and child become important for the security of the child in need of identification. Inconsistency in relationships leads to confusion and difficulty in identification. A boy's self-concept and his ideal image of masculinity are the product of a consistent self-image or of doubt in relation to his own parents. These boys scored high on abasement characteristics of the Edwards Personal Preference Schedule, yet they committed minor infringements of the law as they defied authority and tempted punishment.

If a boy's dependency, as a residual from childhood, is not reduced through decreasing authoritarian paternal pressure, he may seek independence by masculine identification coupled with hostility and aggression. The boy takes the father's dominance and aggression to express individuality for his own ends, which are not only hostile but also indicative of his desire for autonomy. Authoritarianism breeds excessive dependency and inferiority with resulting poor self-esteem. A boy whose father does not respect his maturational needs for increasing autonomy and who is quick to punish small infringements, hides his poor self-esteem by resolving his independent strivings into an apparent "don't care" attitude. This is a desperate effort to throw off authority.

If inconsistent parental values, such as the Italian-American pattern of dominant father and ingratiating mother, are exaggerated, they induce confusion. Dependency and hostility, love and hate, if unresolved, lead to callous acts of pleasure, with devious ways of self-retribution for induced guilt. Defiance of authority assumes, by dependence and identification, the same behavioral modes of the father. While punishing the father, one's behavior leads to self-punishment. This same pattern, perhaps to a greater extent, may be related to the problems of so called "psychopathic" youngsters. In either case, the boy feels he is being abandoned for the sake of ethics and buried for the sake of duty.

The disturbed boys in the two ethnic groups require contrasting kinds of therapy. The Italian-American boy needs help in redevel-

oping nurturance toward others and the ability to receive succorance from interested and significant others. He also needs assistance
in changing his attitude of malevolence in the outer world to a
more trusting benevolence. The Irish-American boy's egocentric activity needs to be concretely shared with others on a realistic basis.
In shared constructive activity with peers, he can more concretely
ventilate, counteract, and discuss his compulsive doubting of his
own concepts. Aggressive impulses and the need for change can be
directed to channels other than fantasizing. For therapeutic improvement he needs to desire things in real life, rather than in abstract life.

Adolescence is a period of breaking away from what is parental
and what is old. Extreme emotional immaturity registered as dependency prevents an individual from accepting what is new. Emotional immaturity represented as adolescent narcissism and rebellion may prevent one from accepting what is old. For both the
Italian-American and the Irish-American boys there is usually a
thrill in trying the new (within the limits of no danger to self or society) and motivation to see the value of the old and traditional
while they adjust to change because cultural innovations make this
necessary. If the personality is as much the result of its cultural pattern as it is of its own past life, then psychiatry must know that cultural pattern as it knows the patient's life.

The variations in disturbance between the two ethnic groups are
in keeping with Opler's (85) findings on Irish and Italian schizophrenic patients. These findings are especially relevant to his variables on behavior disorder, attitude to authority, and preoccupa-
tions.

It is interesting to note that the symptomatology found in
Roberts and Myers (90) with reference to social class III and social
class V may be somewhat influenced by the high percentage of
Irish-American patients in class III and by the high percentage of
Italian-American patients in class V. The somatic symptoms, overt
anxiety, and feelings of persecution, together with overt aggression
manifested in their social class V subjects, are in keeping with the
description of the Italian-American boys in this study. Their description of depressive reactions and psychological and interpersonal
symptoms with fantasies of superiority and grandiosity in social
class III are similar to the Irish-American group's display of symptoms in this study. Since social classes encompass many different
ethnic groups and religions, the findings of this study on ethnicity

may indicate a relatively large proportion of Irish-American people in class III and Italian-American people in social class V of their study.

Summary

Within the diagnostic schema of "Adolescent Adjustment Reactions," we analyzed clinical records for descriptive expressions of emotional disturbance. Ethnic group variations in behavioral and emotional manifestations are clearest in the content of their illnesses. These findings support the hypotheses that social and psychodynamic factors in the development of psychiatric disorders are associated with an indiviual's membership in an ethnic group, as manifested by the differential constellations of symptoms selected by adolescents to express their inner turmoil.

6

The Edwards Personal Preference
Schedule (EPPS)

The Edwards Personal Preference Schedule measures the relative dominance of fifteen enduring traits. In the following examination of the EPPS, I will examine each of the traits for each group by ethnicity and within-group class comparisons, and will also compare the ethnic groups with each other and with the high school and college normative samples. The subsequent analysis of the Life-Space Drawing and the perceptual life situation in the questionnaire should amplify those clusters of dominant traits for each group found in the EPPS. I will also compare self-concept measurements to the proposed ethnic group characteristics.

Murray (80) suggests describing the individual in terms of the patterns he exhibits frequently to reduce tension caused by internal stress of community press. If patterns of behavior are found in a single personality, patterns may be found among personalities with the contrast of a culture. A single individual or group of individuals may possess more of one trait than another group. This becomes a matter of relative dominance of personal and group traits in one person or group as opposed to traits in another person or group. Enduring traits of personalities, with consequent role patterns determined by value orientations, are therefore ordered into interlocking networks of dominance and emphasis. This is the variant synthesis in which dominant rank ordering of value orientation is the integrating thread.

This study assumes that the adolescent ego is a directive and judiciary power that develops from a particular social status and molds a sequence of experiences for present adjustment and an anticipated future. The ego presumably incorporates enduring traits of personality formation and an internal frame of reference for coping with reality. The study presumes that the subject of the project will encompass sub-cultural ethnic traits different from traits in the representative high school and college sample.

One can question the validity of the high school EPPS sample scores which Klett (65) examined in the extreme north-western part of the United States because it may exhibit regional and school differences in adolescent personality formation. However, unlike the representative college sample (23), Klett's sample is equivalent in sex, age, and grade to this study's sample which facilitates comparisons. Klett (65) did find certain trait differences between his high school sample and the college representative sample, so one should keep in mind whether these characterize adolescent personality or regional personality differences.

In the college representative sample studied by Edwards and associates almost 24 percent are male adolescents ranging from below fifteen years to nineteen years of age. Edwards indicates that the personality variables, as measured by inter-correlations, are independent.

Methodological Organization

We noted earlier that in this study we were combining social class categories into white-collar and blue-collar classes. In the EPPS, however, we have retained class V in order to compare it with class IV and classes I, II, III as upper-class aggregates. We did this originally because Hollingshead (55) stated that class V was a separate and distinct subculture. We did not find this distinctive class V subcultural factor among this study's subjects who rather more closely resembled class IV in occupation, education, trait analysis, and residence. Since *t* tests did not yield significant differences from class IV to warrant maintenance of class V, we grouped the two in the other research instruments to form the blue-collar class. This enabled us to use larger numbers for tests of significance, and we could make more precise divisions between upper and lower or white-collar and blue-collar classes in interpretations of statistical data. Tests of significance holding class V separate convinced us to incorporate classes IV and V into a blue-collar class.

We conducted analyses of variance between the ethnic groups for each of the traits examined. Essentially, we had a four-cell, two-way classification, split one way into control and disturbed groups and the other into Irish-American and Italian-American groups. Adjustments were made for unequal subclass frequencies.

Appendix II provides the definitions of the personal traits analyzed. We analyzed significant findings from the viewpoint of sociology and psychiatry with attention to the field of social psyhiatry.

EPPS Analysis

Achievement

There are no significant differences between the ethnic groups or between the disturbed and the control groups in mean value scores on achievement orientation. The social class scores do not emphasize differential achievement.

Both the high school sample scores (Klett, 65) and the scores of this study, however, are significantly different from representative

Table 10
Mean Value Scores on Achievement *

| Group | Social Class | | | | | | Class |
	I–II–III	IV	V	Mean	S.D.	N.	t
CONTROL							
Irish-American	14.81	13.35	—	14.45	3.46	35	N.S.
Italian-American	14.21	12.71	13.50	13.47	3.35	34	N.S.
DISTURBED							
Irish-American	11.33	13.23	12.66	13.72	2.98	25	N.S.
Italian-American	13.72	13.71	14.83	14.12	2.97	24	N.S.

High School: 13.88
College: 15.66

Overall Effect: $F_{3,114} = 0.66 \ p = N.S.$
Main Effect, Nationality: $F_{1,115} = 0.55 \ p = N.S.$
Main Effect, Disturbed-Control: $F_{1,115} = 0.00 \ p = N.S.$
Interaction Effect: $F_{1,114} = 1.52 \ p = N.S.$

* Due to the disproportionate numbers in social class groupings between the Irish-Italian and Control-Disturbed groups, these data were analyzed by "t" tests rather than incorporated in the analyses of variance. This applied to all tabular analyses.

college level achievement orientations. A series of t tests indicates the Irish-American control group's lower mean score for achievement is only suggestively lower than the score for the college sample group ($t = 1.95$, $p < .10$). Of all the groups, the Irish-American disturbed boys are most deviant in achievement orientation when achievement comparisons are made with college scores ($t = 3.10$, $p < .005$). Even so, this score is still not significantly different from the high school sample as shown by Klett (65).

Comparisons of the present sample with Klett's high school sample lead to the inference that the achievement values of the Irish-American and Italian-American control and disturbed groups closely approximate adolescent achievement normative values. These are consistently lower than those of the more mature college students.

Achievement involves a psychological need to excel, the desire to enter the competitive race for status, and the willingness to place high valuation upon personal achievement and success. Achievement orientation has its origins in early parent-child relations. The family and subculture that stress competition and high standards of excellence produce a child with high achievement motivation. It is for this reason that Rosen (96) studied six ethnic groups in achievement motivation while controlling for social class. His data show that in the United States, Protestants, Jews, and Greeks place greater emphasis upon achievement training than do Italians, French-Canadians, and American Negroes. The Italian group in his study is significantly lower in achievement motivation than the Greeks, but not significantly lower than the Jews and Protestants. According to Rosen, the Italians are in the middle of the ethnic groupings in achievement orientation which may account for the similarity of the Italian score in this study with the normative high school mean score. It also indicates that the Italian group helps to maintain the mean high school score more than other groups who tend to pull the achievement orientation average down. Strodbeck (108), in comparing upward mobility values of Jewish-Americans and Italian-Americans, found that the Jews were more oriented to upward mobility through education and occupation, while the Italian-Americans did not differ from the average for the rest of the sampled population.

McClelland and associates (77) studied parental achievement strivings and independence training in children of four subcultural groups. They found that Protestants and Jews favored earlier independence training than did the Irish and Italian groups. They equate independence training with achievement motivation by establishing a connection between the protestant ethnic of self-reliance in all aspects of life, as opposed to reliance upon the institution of the church. However, this study shows the Italian-American boys to display more self-reliance in the choice of occupation and in vocational aspirations than do Irish-American boys who show more dependence on authority. Parental aspirations for upward mobility are stronger in the Italian-American samples who stress better occupations and more education than in the Irish-American samples. This difference is evident in intrafamilial relationships, where freedom from clock-bound schedules allow the Italian-American boys to make more self-reliant choices within broader sanctioned limits. This is true despite the apparently greater authoritarian atmosphere of the Italian-American home.

In summary, the Irish-American and Italian-American boys, both control and disturbed, are not significantly different from the high school normative sample as Klett (65) presents it. Both the study sample and the high school sample do differ significantly from the college students' orientations. The lowest achievement orientation occurs in the Irish-American disturbed group. Social class differences do not appear to exist on vertical or horizontal levels. The questionnaire will illustrate how the ethnic groups differ in handling achievement motivation and how this relates to other ethnically different personality traits.

Deference

Statistical calculations summarized in Table 7 show Irish-American boys have suggestively higher scores in deference for authority, with significantly heightened deference in emotional disturbance ($t = 2.39$, $p < .02$). Deference for authority is lower in Italian-American boys.

Class IV of the Irish-American disturbed group has the highest deference for authority. This group also shows greater endurance which, combined with deference, leads to behavioral persistance in a passive-conforming way. This is especially true in a situation of conflict where the boy must respond.

Deference for authority entails compliant behavior and a tendency to depend upon the suggestion and direction of another person. The study hypothesized that the Irish-American boy, in his relationships to family and authority, would conform to direction and

Table 11
Mean Value Scores on Deference

Group	Social Class I–II–III	IV	V	Mean	S.D.	N	Class t
CONTROL							
Irish-American	11.42	11.35		11.40	2.96	35	N.S.
Italian-American	10.07	10.93	10.50	10.47	3.30	34	N.S.
DISTURBED							
Irish-American	11.22 *	14.92 *	13.00	13.36	3.10	25	3.03 *
Italian-American	10.57	13.00	12.34	11.95	2.67	24	N.S.

$t-$ * $p < .01$

High School: 11.38
College: 11.21

Overall Effect: $F_{3,114} = 3.42$ $p < .025$
Main Effect, Nationality: $F_{1,115} = 3.22$ $p < .10$
Main Effect, Disturbed-Control: $F_{1,115} = 7.09$ $p < .01$
Interaction Effect: $F_{1,114} = 0.00$ $p = $ N.S.

follow parental expectation in a passive-dependent manner. It also hypothesized that the Irish-American boy would seek approval and direction for his decisions and roles, and would make an effort to be concerned with idealistically good behavior. In contrast, the Italian-American boy would show more independent, outgoing action and would tend to question authority, behavior which would reveal his more freely expressed emotions.

The case history studies amplify the greater average deference paid authority among the disturbed Irish-American boys. They cope with their attitude of compliance by isolating themselves in the preservation of equanimity. The Italian-American boy shows superficial deference merely veils deeper hostility and challenge of authority. He says, in effect, "I will offer you respect and obedience if you can prove you are worth it." This attitude may decide his relationship to the therapist who may have to prove he deserves rapport.

We can infer that parental direction of achievement motivation will depend on the parents' ability to direct either the ego synthetic needs of the Irish-American boy or the broader challenging devices of the Italian-American boy. Opler (85) corroborated in general these attitudes toward authority, and therefore toward achievement motivation, in a study of Irish-American and Italian-American schizophrenic patients. He found that the two ethnic groups diverged in parallel fashion in their attitudes toward authority. The Italian-American male actively flouted authority while the Irish-American male was compliant but passively resistant.

Order

The only difference in organization and preference for detail and routine lies between the disturbed and control groups. In the manifestation of this trait there are no significant differences between social classes. Looking over the findings in general, the need for order correlates with the traits of aggression and heterosexuality and with personality deviations. The control groups did not show significantly different results from the high school normative group or the representative college sample.

The questionnaire showed the Irish-American boys to live under much more exacting and tightly run home schedules with their mothers ensuring that these schedules were obeyed. Since others made the rules, these boys had less inner need for self-regulation of daily activities. The Irish-American boys develop deference for authority which is reinforced on external levels.

In both control groups, the boys, although they showed somewhat more affection for their mothers, identified with their fathers

Table 12
Mean Value Scores on Need for Order

Group	Social Class I–II–III	IV	V	Mean	S.D.	N.	*t*
CONTROL							
Irish-American	11.27	9.40	—	9.65	4.65	35	N.S.
Italian-American	10.86	12.00	13.00	11.70	3.67	34	N.S.
Irish-American	13.22	13.66	12.33	13.32	4.20	25	N.S.
Italian-American	12.00	12.03	12.83	12.08	4.47	24	N.S.

High School: 10.47
College: 10.23

Overall Effect: $F_{3,114} = 1.50$ $p = $ N.S.
Main Effect, Nationality: $F_{3,114} = 0.04$ $p = $ N.S.
Main Effect, Disturbed-Control: $F_{1,115} = 3.01$ $p < .01$
Interaction Effect: $F_{1,114} = 1.47$ $p = $ N.S.

much more than did the disturbed boys. The control boys felt both parents accorded them preferential treatment so lack of masculine identification did not appear to influence as a defense mechanism the need for orderliness.

However, strict imposition of rules of conduct can lead to reactions of guilt and shame if these rules are broken. Severe penalties for transgressions evoke more intense compliance to avoid feelings of hostility and consequent guilt toward the parent whose disciplinary action causes frustration. Such is the case with the Irish-American disturbed group in whom deference and conformity dominate. In disturbance, their need for order increased significantly, ($t = 2.912$, $p < .01$ — almost $p = .005$, 2.915), while that of Italian-American boys was not significantly different from their control group. With changes in Irish-American group orderliness came disturbances in masculine identification with consequent changes in heterosexuality and aggression. Comparison between the Irish-American control group class IV mean score and the Irish-American disturbed group class IV mean ($t = 2.39$, $p < .025$) shows the greatly increased need for order of the Irish-American disturbed group. Here the blue-collar boys have higher compulsive, enduring, and compliant needs.

With the intensification of their need for order, the Irish-American boys become more passively dependent on their mothers in order to cope with life, and this in turn reduces aggressive feeling and heterosexuality. In disturbance their need for order exceeds significantly the representative normative groups ($t = 3.523$, $p < .001$).

The average Italian-American disturbed boy maintains order in routine as a provisional check upon his impulsive tendency. In maintaining the security of order, he organizes his rebellion and defiance to create a sense of effective control and success. This boy precariously walks a tight rope between conformity and non-conformity.

The attitudes of the two control groups to order show interesting differences from each other. The Italian-American boys scored higher on desire for order which reflects their problems with impulse control. In disturbance, they are less consistent and, in later analyses, they were found to possess less perseverance in the pursuit of a task. The Italian-American control boys appear to dislike change and to desire prearranged designs of behavior and organization of work. They apparently prefer the consistency of pragmatic prediction in ordering their daily lives, and they acknowledge their easy distraction from work programs and attraction toward pleasurable substitute pursuits.

The Italian-American boys have less clock-bound home schedules and must share more in housework duties. Greater self-reliance in everyday affairs without intensive close supervision drives the Italian-American boys to seek approval through more self-regulated activities in daily schedules of work and play. These boys seek routine order as a form of impulse control.

Gans (42) calls these boys "Action Seekers" of thrills and challenges when they defer their needs to the needs of social groups. They later mature to be "Routine Seekers." Higher levels of aggression and need for organization combine to make the Italian-American adolescent boys seek both independence and dominant control of their lives.

Aggression

Aggression can be overtly manifested in the form of self-assertion and/or hostile acts, or fantasy while conformity is maintained. If we grant that the overt behavioral manifestation is a function of preconditioned familial patterns, then the enduring style of aggression will show differently in combination with other aspects of personal traits.

Table 13
Mean Value Scores on Aggression

| Group | Social Class | | | | | | Class |
	I–II–III	IV	V	Mean	S.D.	N	t
CONTROL							
Irish-American	16.28	15.68	—	16.31	3.47	35	N.S.
Italian-American	13.21	15.71	14.50	14.47	3.26	34	N.S.
DISTURBED							
Irish-American	11.78	13.48	14.00	12.88	5.20	25	N.S.
Italian-American	16.00	13.57	13.33	15.00	3.05	24	N.S.

High School: 13.88
College: 12.79

Overall Effect: $F_{3,114} = 4.040 \; p < .01$
Main Effect, Nationality: $F_{1,114} = 0.050 \; p = N.S.$
Main Effect, Disturbed-Control: $F_{1,114} = 4.110 \; p < .05$
Interaction Effect: $F_{1,114} = 8.037 \; p < .01$

In this study there is an interaction effect where scores reverse on an ethnic basis between the disturbed and control groups. The Irish-American control boys have more aggressive desires than the Italian-American control boys ($t = 2.30$, $p < .05$). They also exhibit more aggressive feeling than both normative groups ($t = 4.05$, $p < .001$). On the other hand, although the Italian-American control group is significantly higher in aggressive feelings than the college group ($t = 2.823$, $p < .005$), it is similar to the high school score. The relatively high level of aggression in the Irish-American control group appears to balance a heterosexuality score lower than the normative groups. The Italian-American control boys present an ethnic contrast for their lower aggression balances with higher heterosexuality scores.

The decrease, in disturbance, of Irish-American aggressive feeling strikingly demonstrates the interaction effect ($t = 2.67$, $p < .01$), for at the same time, the Italian-American group maintains its aggressive score which is higher in disturbance than that of the Irish-American group. A check of the class structure shows more aggression in the Italian-American disturbed upper class than in the Irish-American disturbed upper class ($t = 2.758$, $p < .02$).

Here, there are two contrasting pictures in disturbance. On the one hand, the Irish-American disturbed group significantly increases its deference for authority and its need for order while significantly decreasing aggression. On the other hand, the disturbed Italian-American boy maintains the need for order, which he uses to support increased aggression and open hostility. Impulse control in defense against hostility and disorganization appears to be a major problem in the Irish-American boy who distrusts his own ability to rebel against extreme compliance. The Irish-American boy increases his dependence, while the Italian-American boy increases his efforts at independence.

Heterosexuality

Heterosexuality is a trait dependent upon physical, chronological, and psychological maturity. Aside from physical attraction and biological readiness for the opposite sex, the social environment can either encourage heterosexual shyness and constraint or heterosexual initiative. A major adolescent problem consists of difficulty in masculine identification and subsequent unreadiness for mature heterosexual relationships.

The main variance on heterosexuality is between control and disturbed groups. Both control groups exhibit more sexuality than the disturbed groups. The Italian-American group is considerably more heterosexually inclined than the Irish-American control group ($p < .05$), which is significantly lower in sexuality than the normative groups ($t = 3.22$, $p < .005$). The Italian blue-collar class has the most heterosexual interest. Since this group has the same mean value as the normative representative groups, there are indications of normative male scores for the Italian-American control boys, with the lower classes contributing heavily to Italian-American heterosexuality.

Table 14
Mean Value Scores on Heterosexuality

Group	Social Class I–II–III	IV	V	Mean	S.D.	N	Class t
CONTROL							
Irish-American	13.67	16.27	—	13.80	6.34	35	N.S.
Italian-American	12.43 *	19.14 *	17.00	16.00	5.95	34	3.55 *
DISTURBED							
Irish-American	14.89	10.46	8.67	11.84	6.04	25	N.S.
Italian-American	11.18	14.57	13.00	13.16	6.27	24	N.S.

$t - * p < .005$

High School: 17.31
College: 17.65

Overall Effect: $F_{3,114} = 1.61$ $p = $ N.S.
Main Effect, Nationality: $F_{1,115} = 1.77$ $p = $ N.S.
Main Effect, Disturbed-Control: $F_{1,115} = 2.90$ $p < .10$
Interaction Effect: $F_{1,114} = 0.07$ $p = $ N.S.

In disturbance, both Italian-American and Irish-American groups reduce their heterosexual drives, although the Irish-American heterosexual drive remains consistently lower both in control and in disturbance.

In addition to lower heterosexual drive, the Irish-American groups have higher aggressive values than the Italian-American groups, but both heterosexual drive and aggressiveness decline in the disturbed state. Deference to authority and desire for orderliness rise among the Irish-American boys who have poor male identification and maternal domination at home. Obedience to authority appeases the parent of preferential choice. Aggression in the Italian-American disturbed group, however, increases and becomes more open with simultaneous higher demands for order. The latter represents a possible defense against distressing hostility to authority figures: guilt can be appeased through excessive conformity to authority figures.

We saw that relative disorder (or less care for order) was characteristic of the Irish-American control group in contrast to the Italian-American control group. The Irish-American disturbed individual, however, exaggerates a need for order and scored significantly higher than the high school normative groups and their own control group. Such need for orderliness is described in psychiatric literature as a defense reaction against the repressed demands of disorder. Fenichel (31) describes these mechanisms of defense as reaction formations, the aims of which are opposite to the original drive; that is, the strength of the drive for order holds the original drive in its repressed place. Those who use this mechanism may react with compliance and passive-dependence to hold aggression in place. Orderliness, therefore, becomes an elaboration of obedience to environmental requirements. Emphasis on order increased beyond the normative degree enables the disturbed boy to feel protected against his own hostility and guilt as long as he behaves in an orderly manner. Everything is done according to a pre-arranged plan and timetable to ensure against dangerous spontaneity. This is why, as a later section will show, the Irish-American disturbed boy does not welcome blind dates with girls or events not planned for in advance. These mechanisms are particularly illustrated in adolescents who suffer from adjustment problems in masculine role identifications.

Guilt arises more readily in a democratic atmosphere because of the goodwill that envelopes interpersonal relationships. The average Irish-American boy has freer choice of self-defensive argument in the home than the Italian-American boy, who, feeling hostile to offending parents, reacts with guilt and inferiority. To compensate for this, daydreaming allows behavioral compliance while simultaneously granting a measure of self-glorification. One attains high esteem in daydreams through the fancied admiration of many people, and the omnipotence possible in a daydream repudiates reality. The ego, however, consciously recognizes realistic demands. The questionnaire reveals daydreaming to be a predominantly Irish-American trait. The temporary creation of a world of magic and omnipotence leads tó feelings of omnipotence.

The Italian-American boys are less intensely regulated in time and activity and are given freer choice within the confines of sanctioned good behavior. Efforts at male identification are more freely diverted into various social activities. Among the Italian-Americans the father shows greater authority which blunts aggressive retaliation—although partial identification with the aggressive father is still possible. The son carries overt aggression into interpersonal community relations instead, and he has higher requirements for order to control fearful aggressive impulses toward the dominant authoritative father. The Italian-American boys in disturbance defer to authority with suppression rather than repression of aggressive impulses.

Aggression can also be utilized to serve heterosexual drives, and the Italian-American disturbed boy often plays Don Juan in order to prove to himself that he is sexually adequate.

The Italian-American boys take on the same dominant and aggressive traits as their fathers and use them to penetrate the social field as we will show later. In the questionnaire, the Irish-American boys require prearranged dating schedules and foreknowledge of social events, but the Italian-American boys welcome spontaneous pleasurable events, and in fact indicate difficulty in sticking to jobs. For this reason, they require routine as a control against disorder and their own aggressive impulses in order to take care of daily responsibilities. These boys will not be as concerned with ideal behavior as they will with emotionally secure pragmatic solutions.

In contrast to the Irish-American boys, the Italian-Americans daydream of "concrete" action events, reflect inner needs to solve problems of concrete reality.

Affiliation

Table 15 on affiliation indicates no ethnic differences in participative tendencies or social intercourse. All groups are similar to high school and college normative groups in friendly attachments.

There are, however, social class differences in friendly group attachments. The Irish-American control boys become more affiliative with decreasing social class status. The questionnaire further illustrates increased socializing tendencies in the Irish-American lower classes. Disturbance lowered socialized scores for lower-class boys in both ethnic groups. This is most marked for the Irish-American disturbed boys, especially class V.

One reason for such low affiliation among lower class Irish-Amer-

Table 15
Mean Value Scores on Affiliation

Group	Social Class I–II–III	IV	V	Mean	S.D.	N	Class t
CONTROL							
Irish-American	12.62	15.00	—	14.02	3.90	35	2.069 ***
Italian-American	15.14	14.57	16.83	14.88	4.11	34	N.S.
DISTURBED							
Irish-American	15.33	14.31 *	9.00 *	14.80	3.89	25	2.12 **
Italian-American	15.36	15.71 *	12.00 *	14.46	3.13	24	1.99 **

$t-$ * $p<.10$, ** $p<.07$, *** $p<.05$

High School: 15.28
College: 15.00

Overall Effect: $F_{3,114}=.423 \ p=$ N.S.
Main Effect, Nationality: $F_{1,115}=.399 \ p=$ N.S.
Main Effect, Disturbed-Control: $F_{1,115}=.088 \ p=$ N.S.
Interaction Effect: $F_{1,114}=.843 \ p=$ N.S.

ican disturbed boys appears to be the economic and social pressures that conflict with socializing needs. Four of the five Irish-American boys in class V had difficulties forming sustained peer group contacts because of frequent residence change in childhood due to divorce and separation. This factor may have produced greater tendencies to autistic isolation in the disturbed state. This could also account for the low score among class V Italian-American disturbed boys as well, the mean score being tempered, however, by greater tendencies to join gangs and form delinquent associations.

Mathematical evidence of equivalence between the ethnic groups in affiliative drives does not indicate the ways in which they fulfill affiliative needs. When deference traits fuse with affiliative and nurturant traits in the Irish-American boy, there is respect for and a readiness to cooperate and comply with authority. When friendships are based upon compliance, the subjects follow friendship patterns marked out by others, are devoted to the authority of others, and are willing to follow the customary patterns of participation. Affiliation fused with nurturance produces the desire to help others, especially younger and less privileged people, or older people, or those under stress. Succorance fused with deference and affiliation suggests dependency upon another for affectionate consideration and love. These traits all increase in Irish-American disturbance.

On the other hand, affiliation fused with dominance, aggression, exhibitionism, and nurturance in the Italian-American boy shows up in helpful attitudes to peers and a desire to do things with others, self-assertion in the service of others, a refusal to be dominated coupled with retaliation against competing persons, frank expression of dominating viewpoints, defiance of authority, and leadership of friendship groups.

Change

The need for change means the desire to do new and different things, to meet new people, and to experience novelty in daily routine. It means that one is ready to experiment and to try new things. The need for change has a reciprocal relation with the need for order. Change may predominate as an active need in direct opposition to routine, or it may assume forms of compensatory fantasy or wishful thinking.

Table 16 shows a suggestion of ethnic difference in the need for change, which is especially evident when one compares the disturbed and control groups.

Although the Irish-American boys have the greatest need for change, they do not exceed the normative groups in this value.

Table 16
Mean Value Scores on Need for Change

Group	Social Class I–II–III	IV	V	Mean	S.D.	N	Class t
CONTROL							
Irish-American	14.04 *	16.36	—	15.29	3.50	35	1.917 *
Italian-American	13.36	14.64	12.17	13.67	3.24	34	N.S.
DISTURBED							
Irish-American	17.00	16.15	15.67	16.40	2.86	25	N.S.
Italian-American	16.91 *	17.86	13.87 *	16.37	3.31	24	2.338 **

$t-$ * $p<.10$ ** $p<.05$

High School: 17.12
College: 15.51

Overall Effect: $F_{3,114} = 3.72$ $p<.025$
Main Effect, Nationality: $F_{1,115} = 2.07$ $p<.10$
Main Effect, Disturbed-Control: $F_{1,115} = 8.67$ $p<.01$
Interaction Effect: $F_{1,114} = 0.567$ $p = $ N.S.

Class IV values in need for change again couple with generally increased tendencies to socialize and affiliate with peer groups. In contrast, the Italian-American boys show greater ethnic differences in disturbance than they show in social class when comparisons are made with the ethnic control group ($t - 2.81$, $p < .01$).

The Italian-American control group's need for change is suggestively lower than its contrasting Irish-American group ($p < .10$). These boys favor routine and seek less change in life than the high school sample ($t = 6.05$, $p < .001$). The Italian-Americans have at the same time generally greater inconsistency in self-perception (as a measured trait). When he combines need for order and desire for change with aggression, inconsistency, and heterosexuality, the Italian-American boy has the problem of control of disorder and impulses. Inconsistencies between these areas and defensive maneuvers to provide for self-regulation in the interest of conformity are evidence of this.

The higher level scores in disturbance, significantly increased for the Italian-American boys, are a function of discontent with the usual and discomfort in the present. Combination of traits, however, define behavioral modalities more completely. Reviewing the traits analyzed thus far, the Irish-American and Italian-American disturbed boys utilize the desire for change with different behavioral modalities. The Italian-American disturbed boys show more overt aggression in seeking the new and novel, while the Irish-American boys seek new experiences as conforming members of adventurous groups and with fantasy formations of great adventures. Normative levels of desire for change in disturbance may be subject to adolescent discontents that are weighted by ethnic class and other social factors. Nevertheless, the Italian-American disturbed boys significantly increase their need for change and their exhibitionistic tendencies, while they defy familial authority and run into trouble with the law.

Dominance

Italian-American boys have a consistent pattern of emphasis upon dominance in social relations. Again, along with need for order, heterosexuality, exhibitionism, and desires for change, the sons of skilled workmen (class IV) consistently tend toward greater overt sociability and selectively tend toward dominance in group roles.

Dominance means that one is ready to argue for one's own point of view and to be a leader in groups to which one belongs. It requires that one be able to exert the initiative to persuade or influence others in order to do what one wants.

Although the Irish-American control boys maintain normative scores, the disturbed Irish-American boys value dominance significantly less than both Italian-American groups ($t = 1.97$, p almost .05). They incorporate greater dependency and passivity into their reaction pattern in contrast to the dominance and aggression Ital-

Table 17
Mean Value Scores on Dominance

Group	Social Class I–II–III	IV	V	Mean	S.D.	N.	Class t
CONTROL							
Irish-American	15.06	13.41	—	14.00	3.83	35	N.S.
Italian-American	13.87 *	16.14 *	12.33	14.79	3.25	34	2.086
DISTURBED							
Irish-American	12.78	11.69	13.67	12.32	3.11	25	N.S.
Italian-American	14.82	14.43	13.83	14.33	3.69	24	N.S.

$t - ^* p$ .05

High School: 13.96
College: 17.44

Overall Effect: $F_{3,114} = 2.10\ p < .10$
Main Effect, Nationality: $F_{1,115} = 3.33\ p < .10$
Main Effect, Disturbed-Control: $F_{1,115} = 2.18\ p < .10$
Interaction Effect: $F_{1,114} = .66\ p = $ N.S.

ian-American boys manifest. The Irish-American disturbed boys achieve the lowest scores in dominance, which associated with low aggressive values amplifies the tendency toward passive aggression and conformity. In contrast, the Italian-American disturbed group has higher mean values on dominance and aggression. Where all high school adolescents suffer dependent-independent conflicts in maturing, the Italian-American boys border on higher level adolescent dominance scores. Higher college normative levels in dominance are probably associated with maturity, where dependent-independent conflicts in relation to authority are greatly reduced.

Exhibitionism

The term exhibitionism designates the wish to have others take notice of you. It means that one may try to be the center of attention and that one tries to be admired for the ability to tell amusing and adventurous stories.

Statistical evidence again indicates ethnic differences.

In the Irish-American control group the need for succorance increases along with affiliation and the desire for change ($p < .10$ to

Table 18
Mean Value Scores on Exhibitionism

Group	Social Class			Mean	S.D.	N.	Class t
	I–II–III	IV	V				
CONTROL							
Irish-American	15.70 *	14.05	—	14.88	3.58	35	N.S.
Italian-American	17.07 *	15.05	14.00 *	15.88	2.75	34	2.07 *
DISTURBED							
Irish-American	15.56 *	13.00 *	14.67	14.12	3.52	25	1.718 **
Italian-American	14.45	15.86	16.17	15.54	2.67	24	N.S.

$t -$ * $p < .10$ ** $p < .05$

High School: 15.40
College: 14.40

Overall Effect: $F_{3,114} = 1.52$ $p =$ N.S.
Main Effect, Nationality: $F_{1,115} = 3.65$ $p < .10$
Main Effect, Disturbed-Control: $F_{1,115} = 0.80$ $p =$ N.S.
Interaction Effect: $F_{1,114} = 0.09$ $p =$ N.S.

$p < .05$) as status decreases. Consequently, aggression in this group is less self-assertive as social status decreases. These needs illustrate passive-dependent patterns in the poorer socioeconomic classes which arise because these people value kindness and attention from others. Heterosexuality and aggression are overruled by the more dependent traits of succorance and deference. In accordance with this pattern, increasing desire for change more often leads to discontented wishful thinking than to self-assertion. As passivity increases with decreasing social status, aggression converts at least partially into narcissistic succorance. Heterosexuality and affiliative mechanisms in social intercourse appear as closer but fewer intense and trustworthy attachments where succorance is received in return for deference.

The Irish-American disturbed boy in the lower classes has even more reduced exhibitionistic tendencies than his own control group and tends even more to defer to authority ($p<.001$). In view of the fact that this boy already shows reduced aggression and heterosexual impulses, as well as less need for succorance, there is some withdrawal from social intercourse and an exaggerated compliance with authority to gain social approval. This is perhaps why the desire for change appears in the construction of a self-glorifying dream world.

The Italian-American groups maintain mean values on exhibitionism in line with the higher scores of the high school normative sample. These scores show adolescents to have higher exhibitionistic values than more mature people, and the Italian-American boys achieve this mean level more than do the Irish-American adolescents. Suggestively greater tendencies toward exhibitionism exist in the upper classes of the Italian-American group. In disturbance, their exhibitionism rises with declining socioeconomic status and it is in accord with higher heterosexual scores among lower-class Italian-American adolescents.

The summarizing tables on social class contain interesting phenomena. Here exhibitionism, heterosexuality, and aggression show curious alignments with each other. In the Italian-American control group, exhibitionism declines with declining socioeconomic status, while heterosexuality, aggression, and dominance increase with lowering social status. The significant lowering of abasement and intraception with decline in status ($p<.02$) indicates overt aggression and heterosexuality in the service of self-esteem with less moral and intellectual conflict.

In contrast to the Irish-American disturbed boy, the Italian-American disturbed boy, in addition to having more heterosexual, aggressive, and exhibitionistic tendencies in the lower socioeconomic classes, exhibits greater consistency and endurance. This boy shows less need for succorance and desires to give nurturance to other people. In this respect exhibitionism helps to supply narcissistic needs to compensate for decreased self-esteem and heterosexuality. With the maintenance of dominance in his self-structure, he guarantees his aggressive self-assertion.

Psychoanalytically, one reveals exhibitionism in the public demonstration of one's talents and in the enjoyment of manifesting one's powers. This trait can take the place of succorance in that it seeks public approval and appreciation in order to enhance narcissistic supplies for self-esteem and respect. Hopes of winning praise, prestige, and commendation promote such behavior. Those who emphasize this trait differ from more orderly submissive people in their lack of reaction against openly aggressive behavior, and by their flight into reality when faced with their own fears. Exhibitionism, when associated with sexuality, has an aggressive overtone. These people force their audience to give compensatory reassurances against anxieties and inferiority feelings. The demonstration of the self and its talents compensates for aggression and reassures a boy who is confused about his masculinity. One can thus equate striving for heterosexual satisfaction with immature striving for fulfillment of narcissistic needs. Don Juanism is just such an effort to prove sexual adequacy and maintain self-esteem. If this exhibitionism fails to attain its goals, the repressed aggressive impulse explodes against the object audience.

Conversely, aggression combined with deference for authority and order is an attempt to overcome hostility by kindness, politeness, and conformity to community mores. One can see this behavior as an attempt to conceal disorganization by order and hostility. These people may collect things systematically and retain and perfect such organized collections as a reassurance against loss of self-esteem and feelings of inferiority. In psychoanalytic terms, the super-ego formation, as a result of parental discipline, is held in check by the ego through dependent-passive constructions of conformity with nostalgic longing for independence (Erikson, 26). Adolescents develop such reaction formations as a shield against their own sexuality. Passive sexuality results from ambivalence to a masculine role model; the ego protects the boy against both the environment and the self when poorly formed masculine role models are assumed.

Different combinations of personality traits and different emphases upon these combinations as modes of handling reality indicate variations in subcultural personalities within the dominant cultural entity. Both the Irish-American and the Italian-American boys have a dire need to prove to themselves and others that they are not really "bad" and inadequate, but "good" and self-sufficient, yet the devices used to achieve this self-concept are polar opposites.

Autonomy

The need for autonomy is apparently felt by most as a manifest life process, since there are no differences between the ethnic, high school, or college groups in emphasis upon this trait.

The need for change can be associated with the desire for autonomy in the conflicting adolescent swings between childhood dependency and adult autonomy, and the need for change is greater in the disturbed groups.

Table 19
Mean Value Scores on Autonomy

Group	Social Class			Mean	S.D.	N	Class t
	I–II–III	IV	V				
CONTROL							
Irish-American	13.71	14.91	—	14.22	3.91	35	N.S.
Italian-American	14.41	14.64	13.50	14.21	4.17	34	N.S.
DISTURBED							
Irish-American	12.78	12.31	16.33	12.96	4.83	25	N.S.
Italian-American	13.36	11.29	13.83	13.41	3.28	24	N.S.

High School: 14.57
College: 14.34

Overall Effect: $F_{3,114} = .731\ p = \text{N.S.}$
Main Effect, Nationality: $F_{1,115} = .133\ p = \text{N.S.}$
Main Effect, Disturbed-Control: $F_{1,115} = 2.030\ p < .10$
Interaction Effect: $F_{1,114} = .030\ p = \text{N.S.}$

The Italian-American groups have less deference needs and more aggression and exhibitionism than the Irish-American groups. Thus, the kind of changes desired vary according to the potential behavior modalities of the groups and the intrafamilial environments from which these sprang. An aggressive drive for autonomous action can be overt or covert. The need for autonomy that hides behind a barrier of restraint can convert to an inner defence mechanism against anxieties of a perceived reality. When autonomy is compounded with aggression, exhibitionism, and dominance in the Italian-American disturbed group, we have self-assertion for the control of others, histrionic displays in rebellion, defiant challenge of authority, and an active attempt to free oneself from restrictive prohibitions and existing rules. Verbal autonomy cannot be only ideological independence, but it can exist to serve the aggressive impulse as a forceful and verbal attack upon others.

Autonomy, compounded with deference, succorance, and the need for order and nurturance, makes the Irish-American disturbed group desire for change less self-assertive, less defiant, and more dependency-oriented in order to achieve self reliance. The conflict between hostility and the desire for independence and change combined with the guilt feelings that follow hostile wishes directed against a particular individual, allows deference to gain control. Conflict is resolved covertly.

Succorance

The need for succorance is a measure of emotional support needed from others to resolve insecurity and anxiety. The measurement of this trait indicates a significant ratio between the disturbed and the control groups. There are no differences between the Irish-American and the Italian-American control groups in the need for succorance as an adaptive phenomenon, however (as seen in Table 20), these ethnic control groups are significantly above the normative groups in the need for a nurturing object (College-Irish $=t=3.05$, $p<.005$; Italian, $t=4.61$, $p<.001$).

The study discussed Italian-American need for succorance previously as a measure meeting narcissistic demands for self-esteem and social prestige, without which anxiety prevails. The Irish-American control group's need for succorance increases significantly with decreasing social class status, while exhibitionism and aggression decrease with social class. When people who are important to them cheerfully meet the adolescent needs for kindness and understanding they have, it appeases Irish-American aggression and Italian-American exhibitionism.

Alternation of exhibitionism with succorance needs is evident in the Italian-American disturbed group, where exhibitionism rises gradually on insignificant levels and need for succorance declines steadily with socioeconomic status ($p<.20$). It rises again in class V, where affiliation drops below the level of the previous classes. This is less true of the Irish-American disturbed group, where non-significant lower needs for exhibitionism and aggression are associated with lower needs for succorance throughout the ethnic class struc-

Table 20
Mean Value Scores on Succorance

Group	Social Class			Mean	S.D.	N	Class t
	I–II–III	IV	V				
CONTROL							
Irish-American	11.14	14.27	—	12.91	4.01	35	3.26 **
Italian-American	13.21	13.14 *	15.17 *	13.52	3.38	34	N.S.
DISTURBED							
Irish-American	13.56 *	10.83 *	10.33	11.52	4.15	25	1.859 *
Italian-American	12.91 *	9.71 *	11.00	11.61	3.66	24	N.S.

$t-$ * $p<.10$ ** $p<.005$ High School: 11.03
College: 10.74

Overall Effect: $F_{3,114} = 2.83 \ p<.05$
Main Effect, Nationality: $F_{1,115} = 0.48 \ p = $ N.S.
Main Effect, Disturbed-Control: $F_{1,115} = 7.87 \ p<.01$
Interaction Effect: $F_{1,114} = 0.12 \ p = $ N.S.

ture. Where flight "into" reality is not apparent, flight "away" from reality enforces reality self-made in isolation. Since the Italian-American disturbed group requires significantly less overt succorance than the control group ($t = 2.65$, $p<.01$), exhibitionism appears to be a method of obtaining desired succorance. When succorance cannot easily be obtained indirectly, it is sought directly.

The question arises as to why the disturbed groups' succorance needs approximate the level of the normative groups, when the control groups require significantly more succorance than the normative groups. Psychiatric therapy conceivably reduces this need because the disturbed subject receives kindly and considerate personal attention during the therapeutic session. However, such rapport and treatment require much time in establishing more permanent effects upon the patient. It is therefore more likely that succorance needs fuse with other personality traits in the dynamic reaction to stress.

In the Irish-American disturbed group, deference for authority and the development of relationships with stronger and wiser nurturant figures at least partially satiates the need for succorance and emotional sustenance. Suppression of sexuality and aggression by conformity and orderliness receives the disciplinarian's praise and prevents the rise of impulsive behavior. Projections of blame upon someone other than the self are additional manifestations of the tendency for sameness and avoidance of censure. Without this conforming base, the subjects cannot entertain projections of future achievement and autonomy because they feel helpless and despairing. Identification with others often allows one to bask in another's achievements and to see oneself in the future as the other person.

In contrast to the Italian-American disturbed group, the Irish-American disturbed group shows exaggerated maternal domination and affection toward sisters. The Irish-American disturbed group achieved succorance partially through identifications and praise in conformity, while fantasies of self-glorification compensated for all of the things one wanted to be and to achieve. When faced with insatiable needs, reduction of succorance in reaction to stress intensifies the flight from reality. The greater endurance of the Irish-American youth in stress spells out this ability to live in one's own world if the actual world becomes frustrating. The Italian-American disturbed group rejects succorance because the intrafamilial identification process is blunted and confused. In rebellion and defiance, their social aggression and exhibitionism compensates for their sense of helplessness and despair.

In summary, the Irish-American and Italian-American disturbed groups react to stress, like others, with needs for sympathetic emotional understanding and emotional sustenance. However, like other people they often feel significant others will not offer succorance. They are disappointed in the amount and kinds of succorance they receive and consequently they partly deny they want succorance and partly make up for this lack of emotional sustenance and sympathetic understanding through compensatory mechanisms. The Irish-American disturbed boys withdraw from reality and conform passively while the Italian-American disturbed boys project themselves forcibly into reality in efforts to gain the attention of other people.

Nurturance

Nurturance designates the ability to forego narcissistic needs in order to aid another who demands succorance or exhibits weakness and distress. Condoning another's actions is equivalent to compassion and empathy.

Examination of Table 21 shows an interaction effect between ethnicity and the disturbed-control variables, which influence the mean

Table 21
Mean Value Scores on Nurturance

Group	Social Class I–II–III	IV	V	Mean	S.D.	N	Class t
CONTROL							
Irish-American	13.63	14.32	—	14.22	4.07	35	1.98 *
Italian-American	16.29	15.14	15.33	15.55	2.68	34	N.S.
DISTURBED							
Irish-American	16.59	13.85	15.00	14.96	3.83	25	N.S.
Italian-American	14.36	13.43	11.67	13.37	3.08	24	N.S.

$t-$* $p<.10$ High School: 14.04
College: 14.12

Overall Effect: $F_{3,114} = 1.94$ $p>.10$
Main Effect, Nationality: $F_{1,114} = 0.02$ $p = $ N.S.
Main Effect, Disturbed-Control: $F_{1,114} = 1.08$ $p = $ N.S.
Interaction Effect: $F_{1,114} = 4.72$ $p<.05$

value scores of the ethnic groups in an inverse direction. The Italian-American control boys have higher nonsignificant values in the performance of nurturance. This group in all social classes places considerably more emphasis upon the development of this characteristic than do the normative groups ($t = 2.877$, $p<.005$). On the other hand, the Irish-American upper-class adolescents value nurturance somewhat less than do the lower-class ones. This characteristic harmonizes into a picture of the upper-class Irish-American boy who is less affiliative, demands less succorance, gives less nurturance, but leads a more ordered life in the interests of self-esteem.

In contrast to the control groups, the mean values reverse in the disturbed groups. The Italian-American disturbed boys place less value upon nurturance than do those in the control group ($t = 2.84$, $p<.01$) or the Irish-American disturbed boys ($t = 1.72$, $p<.10$). In effect, the Italian-American disturbed adolescents have a greatly reduced ability to nurture other people, while the Irish-American disturbed boys are able to give affection and care in keeping with normative values.

Fenichel (31) states that those who utilize nurturance as a means of atonement and self-sacrifice can condone moral masochism. Blame-avoiding measures serve to ward off selfish, guilty feelings. One can offer nurturance and kindness in order to receive them in turn. In this case, such behavior rewards through reciprocity and proof to the giver that he is good.

It appears that both Irish-American and Italian-American boys are capable of nurturance as subsidiary to succorance, aggression, and other emotions. All people need succorance and narcissistic supplies of love and consideration. The ability to be compassionate with the needs and problems of another is consonant with the adaptive requirements of a healthy personality. The ability to empathize with and to help others is the test of maturity.

The significance of this interaction mechanism is illustrated in disturbance. The Italian-American disturbed adolescents become subtly more dominant and aggressive with the display of more exhibitionism in the lower classes. Both as a disturbed group and an ethnic one, lower-class Italian-American disturbed boys harbor more of these mechanisms. This group refuses to accept succorance or to give nurturance. Behavior of this kind manifests a lack of trust in people and a shrewd and flaunting defiance of custom and conformity. Such people display an "apparent" lack of guilt feeling out of keeping with reality. This lack of abasement was not revealed, however, by the Italian-American boys in their scores on the abasement trait.

Incomplete and unsatisfactory interpersonal relationships with rebellious and abortive masculine identifications is conducive to ambivalence and conflict, producing defiance and the refusal to trust people. The Italian-American disturbed boys manifested delinquent behavior. In the clinical situation and on the questionnaire these boys appeared to be sly in their social contacts. They showed overt respect for authority but were restrained in discussing affiliative social groups. These boys were wary of ordinary constructive group activities enjoyed by other adolescents in the community. They traveled alone more often, or with those from whom they could receive symbiotic satisfaction because these people nurtured their own more exhibitionistic and aggressive needs. These boys appeared on guard against criticisms and blame. They traveled with a "chip on their shoulder," and they desired uncommunicative autonomy from those who told them "they were wrong."

Abasement

The study scores on abasement (or production of guilt and self-criticism) align most closely with the high school representative abasement parameter. As with the high school youths, the adolescents in all groups have higher abasement values than the college group ($t = 2.735$, $p < .01$). We can assume the significance of this trait lies in the group age, not ethnicity or disturbance.

Social class analyses on horizontal levels show greater between-class variations. Both control groups have significantly decreasing abasement scores with decreasing socioeconomic status. These scores are in reverse to heterosexual and succorance values. In both control groups, significant decreases in abasement are associated with significant to suggestive increases in heterosexuality—especially in

Table 22
Mean Value Scores on Abasement

Group	Social Class I–II–III	IV	V	Mean	S.D.	N	Class t
CONTROL							
Irish-American	16.30 *	13.77 *	—	14.65	4.00	35	2.22 **
Italian-American	17.07 *	12.36 *	14.00	14.26	3.93	34	3.92 ***
DISTURBED							
Irish-American	13.67	14.85	16.35	14.68	4.20	25	N.S.
Italian-American	13.55 *	14.29	16.33 *	14.10	3.14	24	2.00 *

$t —$ * $p < .10$ ** $p < .05$ *** $p < .001$ High School: 14.35
College: 12.24

Overall Effect: $F_{3,114} = .105$ $p = $ N.S.
Main Effect, Nationality: $F_{1,115} = .315$ $p = $ N.S.
Main Effect, Disturbed-Control: $F_{1,115} = .007$ $p = $ N.S.
Interaction Effect: $F_{1,114} = .021$ $p = $ N.S.

the Italian-American group. The only group in which this does not occur is in the Italian-American disturbed group. Here abasement scores increase with decreasing class position while heterosexuality and succorance do not. However, in disturbance heterosexuality and succorance are significantly reduced. It is difficult to analyze and to interpret the singular rise in lower-class abasement in disturbed Italian-American boys, except to say that the more confining aspects of lower social position (where achievement orientations and heterosexual adequacies are not so easily listened to by those in other social class position) threaten their needs for omnipotence and autonomy.

Shame is an emotion easily absorbed by guilt, a sense of inferiority, and despair. Shame, according to Erikson (29), involves a self-consciousness. One is visible and not ready to be visible. If this is the case, shame exploits the sense of being small and inferior, and this excites self-blame. The voice of the super-ego, therefore, deflates the sense of omnipotence and power. As adolescents, these boys are concerned with who they are and what they are in the eyes of themselves and of significant other people. The increased voice of the super-ego in adolescence exploits the sense of being not only inferior, but also dependent upon more experienced superiors to show them the way. A sense of guilt and introjected hostility become heightened aspects of selfhood until such time as a resynthesis of ego identity realigns judiciary strength. Where abasement occurs with decreased heterosexuality and succorance, problems in masculine identification tend to produce psychic deflation, guilt, and remorse.

Intraception

Inner conceptualizations, images, and analyses of one's feelings are said by Murray (80) to be basic to strong inner feelings, sentiments, and inclinations where thinking is dominated by imaginative reconstructions. This is opposed to extraception, which is characterized by a tendency to see facts as concrete, clearly observable conditions with an emphasis upon overt behavior and observable traits. Relative emphasis upon intraception or extraception thus leads to a general description of personality tendencies.

Dominance of thinking and imaginative reconstructions of both ethnic groups are equivalent to the normative high school sample, and have significantly lower parameters than the normative college group (t with Irish-American control group $= 2.90$, $p < .005$). This difference can be looked upon as an adolescent phenomenon since abstract conceptualizations of life and imaginative innovations achieve their height of encouragement in college and come to fruition in successful college careers.

The white-collar classes of both Italian-American groups approach the intraceptive degree of college representatives more than do the Irish-American white-collar classes. In a later section, we will see that more Italian-American boys are encouraged to attend college and more of these boys fraternize with others in serious discussions.

These scores do not significantly differentiate the Irish-American from the Italian-American boys in ethnic terms.

Table 23
Mean Value Scores on Intraception

Group	Social Class			Mean	S.D.	N	Class t
	I–II–III	IV	V				
CONTROL							
Irish-American	13.04	14.55	—	14.02	4.12	35	N.S.
Italian-American	15.07 *	12.29 *	13.00	13.56	3.46	34	2.396 *
DISTURBED							
Irish-American	13.89	14.92	13.67	14.41	3.50	25	N.S.
Italian-American	15.00	13.57	15.00	14.37	4.37	24	N.S.

$t-$ * $p<.025$

High School: 13.13
College: 16.12

Overall Effect: $F_{3,114}=.282$ $p=$N.S.
Main Effect, Nationality: $F_{1,115}=.133$ $p=$N.S.
Main Effect, Disturbed-Control: $F_{1,115}=.654$ $p=$N.S.
Interaction Effect: $F_{1,114}=.040$ $p=$N.S.

Endurance

How long an individual remains at a task as a measure of the persistence of effort can depend upon achievement motivation, the philosophy of work, and devotion to the enterprise. Endurance also is a factor in illness and emotional disturbance, for these abnormal states affect the ability to concentrate and produce easy fatigue, undirected fantasy, and irritability. Endurance may mask indifference to surroundings and withdrawal from reality, and in such instances this apparent endurance is merely apathy.

The significance of this trait lies in the disturbed-control variable. Here, the Irish-American disturbed boys deviate from the normative scores ($t=2.46$, $p<.02$). This group is significantly higher in endurance to the task than is the more mature college group ($t=2.978$, $p<.005$).

In Irish-American disturbance we have found a rise in deference and in the desire for order and organization coupled with a decrease in aggression and dominance. The tendency to meet stress by retiring into autistic fantasies of self-glorification and omnipotence may produce endurance as a compensatory quality. Such fantasies characterize the Irish-American disturbed group. Endurance can appear as conformity to please authority and, in addition, to effect change and new experience by withdrawal into fantasy. Idealistic

Table 24
Mean Value Scores on Endurance

Group	Social Class I–II–III	IV	V	Mean	S.D.	N	Class t
CONTROL							
Irish-American	15.19 *	11.18 *	—	12.86	3.60	35	2.311 **
Italian-American	13.36	11.50	14.17	12.73	4.29	34	N.S.
DISTURBED							
Irish-American	12.22 *	17.31 *	16.67	15.40	4.46	25	4.20 ***
Italian-American	13.18 *	15.71	16.50 *	13.91	3.79	24	1.756 *

$t -$ * $p < .10$ ** $p < .05$ *** $p < .001$ High School: 13.81
                                                                      College: 12.66

Overall Effect: $F_{3,114} = 2.127$ $p < .10$
Main Effect, Nationality: $F_{1,115} = 0.701$ $p =$ N.S.
Main Effect, Disturbed-Control: $F_{1,115} = 5.000$ $p < .05$
Interaction Effect: $F_{1,114} = 0.632$ $p =$ N.S.

fantasies of self-glorification also motivate achievement orientation.

When we examine social classes for endurance, we again must examine it in combinations. Significant decreases of endurance in the Irish-American control blue-collar classes occur with significant decreases in abasement. On the other hand, the blue-collar classes increase in succorance and affiliative values. When these lower-class boys become disturbed, their endurance rises, but their needs for succorance and affiliation decrease. Decreases in needs for interpersonal communication accompany increase in endurance and abasement in the Irish-American groups. The blue-collar Irish-American control boys tend to be somewhat more affiliation-oriented than the white-collar classes. The Irish-American disturbed boys appear to have lower succorance and affiliation needs and a greater sense of shame and self-criticism. This pattern can be called an apparent endurance set against a harsh reality, and it is especially emphasized in sons of skilled and semiskilled workers. On the questionnaire, the disturbed Irish-American boys engage in more autistic fantasies of self-glorification, thus framing a not-so-harsh reality.

In the Italian-American disturbed group, the non-significant increased mean value in endurance, as compared to the control group, joins with increased aggression, dominance, exhibitionism, and reduced deference to authority. This combination copes with reality by such behavior as lability in emotional interaction, greater rest-lessness in coping with tasks, and defiance of authority. It is difficult to maintain achievement motivation because of easy distraction from the task at hand.

It could be argued that endurance is a motivation aligned with maturity and utilized as an endeavor to overcome narcissistic succorance needs. If this is the case, then we can align endurance with aggression, achievement orientation, and dominance for the attainment of success.

Consistency

Consistency is the persistence, firmness, and coherence with which one sees and describes the self and with which one meets the task at hand. In this regard there is an ethnic difference. The Irish-American groups and the high school sample are significantly lower in consistency than the college sample ($p < .01$). These groups, however, have considerably more consistency than the Italian-American groups ($p < .05$).

The only Italian-American class meeting the consistency standard of the Irish-American groups is the blue-collar class. This is the class where father-son conflicts are most evident.

Table 25
Mean Value Scores on Consistency

Group	Social Class I–II–III	IV	V	Mean	S.D.	N	Class t
CONTROL							
Irish-American	10.50	11.10	—	10.74	1.98	35	N.S.
Italian-American	9.78 *	11.45 *	8.66	9.85	2.42	34	1.798 *
DISTURBED							
Irish-American	10.44	10.00	11.00	10.48	2.04	25	N.S.
Italian-American	8.90 *	11.00 *	10.10	9.90	2.01	24	2.386 **

$t - $ * $p < .10$ ** $p < .05$ 　　　　　　　　High School: 10.81
　　　　　　　　　　　　　　　　　　　　　　College: 11.53

Overall Effect: $F_{3,114} = 1.32$ $p = $ N.S.
Main Effect, Nationality: $F_{1,115} = 3.78$ $p < .05$
Main Effect, Disturbed-Control: $F_{1,115} = 0.09$ $p = $ N.S.
Interaction Effect: $F_{1,114} = 0.12$ $p = $ N.S.

In an effort to determine if younger boys were less consistent in their self-perception than older boys, and if ethnic differences existed in this regard, a Kruskal-Wallis one-way analysis of variance by rank age was developed for the three age groups in each ethnic group. This test revealed that a higher level of consistency is attained by older boys in the Irish-American group.

Table 26
One-Way Analysis of Variance on the Distribution
of Consistency Scores by Ranked Age Groups
in Each Ethnic Group

Group	Item	Age Groups 13–15.9	16–16.11	17–19.11
CONTROL				
Irish-American	Sum of Ranks	68	344.50	394.00
	Mean	10	10.11	11.00
	N	5	17	18
$H = 14, df = 2, p < .001$				
Italian-American	Sum of Ranks	152.50	227.00	220.50
	Mean	8.9	10.16	10.45
	N	11	12	11
$H = 4.62, df = 2, p = N.S.$				
DISTURBED				
Irish-American	Sum of Ranks	260.00	39.00	92.00
	Mean	10.66	11.00	11.60
	N	18	2	5
$H = 33.77, df = 2, p < .001$				
Italian-American	Sum of Ranks	191.50	37.50	71.00
	Mean	9.52	9.66	11.50
	N	17	3	4
$H = 3.64, df = 2, p = N.S.$				

Analysis of this table shows that age, not social class, determines consistency on an Irish-American basis. Chronological maturity is not a factor among the Italian-American boys. In the Irish-American control group the more mature the adolescent the greater his consistency in application to the task at hand. In direct contrast, the Italian-American groups make consistency determinations by social position (Table 27). In this group, social class factors appear to be of more fundamental importance in self-awareness and introspection. The blue-collar classes are oriented pragmatically to themselves and their own self-honesty.

Socio-economic Review

Exaggeration and diminution of ethnic traits in disturbance influence the distribution of social class scores. These social class factors are necessary considerations, subject to the influence of one ethnic group's variant values in contrast to those of another.

On horizontal levels for each ethnic group, we compared the low-

Table 27
Significant and Suggestive Social Class Differences
in Personality Trait Mean Values Expressed as Class IV
or Class V Ascendance or Decline from Upper Class Levels

Group	Trait	Class IV	Class V	Less than p
Irish-American	Change	Higher	——	.10
Control	Affiliation	Higher	——	.05
	Abasement	Lower	——	.05
	Endurance	Lower	——	.05
	Succorance	Higher	——	.005
Italian-American	Exhibiton	——	Lower	.10
Control	Consistency	Higher	——	.10
	Dominance	Higher	——	.05
	Intraception	Lower	——	.025
	Sexuality	Higher	Higher	.005
	Abasement	Lower	——	.001
Irish-American	Succorance	Lower	Lower	.10
Disturbed	Exhibition	Lower	——	.10
	Affiliation	——	Lower	.10
	Deference	Higher	——	.01
	Endurance	Higher	——	.001
Italian-American	Abasement	——	Higher	.10
Disturbed	Endurance	——	Higher	.10
	Change	——	Lower	.05
	Consistency	Higher	——	.05

est and highest social class scores. This involved utilizing most of the *t* tests of significance between the upper-class mean values and the class IV mean values. On examination of Table 27, the reader will find most *t* tests with class V were only suggestive of difference. In view of the small numbers and the consequent increased variance in class V, the combination of this social class with class IV would decrease the variation, and the *t* tests of significance between the upper and the lower classes would be sharper.

The data indicate that the Irish-American and the Italian-American control groups have greater need for socializing in class IV. The preferred social intercourse differs on an ethnic basis. The Italian-American group is more dominant in social intercourse while the Irish-American group desires succorance from important others.

In disturbance, the Irish-American boys increase their compliant behavior while the Italian-American boys become more consistent in their self-projections. Disturbances in the ethnic groups tend to fuse the mean trait scores in the social classes. Behavioral modalities in disturbance become more solidified into combinations of peculiar ethnic clusters.

The Irish-American Control Group and the Normative Groups

Table 24 is a composite picture of the Irish-American control group as it varies from the normative groups. The Irish-American control group shows significantly less need for change than does the high school normative group, and less need for order or punctilious organization of details than do both normative groups. These adolescents require novelty and change in significant excess from the Italian-American control adolescents, suggesting that, with a lower score or need for order, they vacillate in their behavior and deviate some from imposed routine schedules. Deference for authority, however, is on a level with the normative groups and submission to authority keeps these boys from deviating far from schedule. Externally imposed pressure for submission is easily turned into internally imposed restriction when they superimpose guilt and anxiety upon a search for the new and different.

The Irish-American control boys emphasize a need for succorance from others and simultaneously elevate aggression.

Their scores on dominance and abasement suggest drives in line with high school teenagers and appear to represent adolescent dependent-independent conflicts. When low need for change and nor mative deference values are combined with the need for succorance, a group personality emerges in which heterosexuality and aggression are repressed for submission to authority. Submission with frustration in interpersonal drives converts aggressive drives into fantasies of self-glorification as compensation for social and sexual inadequacies.

Table 28
EPPS Group Means and Significance of Difference
(*t*) Between the Irish-American Control and the High School
and College Normative Groups

Trait	High School	College	Irish-American Control	*t*
Achievement	13.88	15.66 *	14.49	1.95 *
Deference	11.38	11.21	11.40	N.S.
Order	10.47 *	10.23	9.65	N.S.
Exhibitionism	15.40	14.40	14.88	N.S.
Autonomy	14.57	14.34	14.22	N.S.
Affiliation	15.28 *	15.00	14.02	N.S.
Intraception	13.13	16.12 *	14.02	2.90 ***
Succorance	11.03	10.74 *	12.91	3.05 ***
Dominance	13.96	17.44 *	14.00	4.47 ****
Abasement	14.35	12.24 *	14.65	3.39 ****
Nurturance	14.04	14.12	14.22	N.S.
Change	17.12 *	15.51	15.29	3.039 ***
Endurance	13.81	12.66	12.86	N.S.
Heterosexuality	17.31 *	17.65	13.80	3.223 ***
Aggression	13.88 *	12.79	16.81	4.05 ****
Consistency	10.81	11.53	10.74	N.S.
	N=799	N=760	N=35	

t—* *p*<.10** *p*<.05 *** *p*<.01 **** *p*<.001

These repressions and compensations describe the Irish-American control group as passive-aggressive in nature. In this adaptation, aggression is socially inhibited and converted into an introjective cognitive system that reaches heroic proportions in fantasy and daydreams.

The Italian-American Control Group
and the Normative Groups

The Italian-American control group as a variant from the normative groups has a greater need for succorance and a greater drive to give nurturance to those in distress. Thus, although there is a narcissistic need for supplies of kindness, there is at the same time a need to be compassionate with others. One could call this a state of empathy with another person, which is often a need as well for social approval. The Italian-American control boy is slightly higher than average in organization and order, utilizing this in his preference for social conformity. One might say that in preferring the pre-

Table 29

EPPS Group Means and Significance of Difference
(*t*) Between the Italian-American Control Group and the High School
and College Normative Groups

Trait	High School	College	Italian-American Control	*t*
Achievement	13.88	15.66 *	13.47	2.70 ***
Deference	11.38	11.21	10.47	N.S.
Order	10.47	10.23	11.70	N.S.
Exhibitionism	15.40	14.40 *	15.88	3.08 ***
Autonomy	14.57	14.34	14.21	N.S.
Affiliation	15.28	15.00	14.88	N.S.
Intraception	13.13	16.12 *	13.56	4.12 ****
Succorance	11.03	10.74 *	13.52	4.61 ****
Dominance	13.96	17.44 *	14.79	4.47 ****
Abasement	14.35	12.24 *	14.26	2.93 ****
Nurturance	14.04 *	14.12	15.55	2.88 ***
Change	17.12 *	15.51	13.67	1.05 ****
Endurance	13.81 *	12.66	12.73	N.S.
Heterosexuality	17.31	17.65	16.00	N.S.
Aggression	13.88	12.79	14.47	2.82 ***
Consistency	10.81 *	11.53	9.85	2.29 **
	N = 799	N = 760	N = 34	

t — * *p* < .10 ** *p* < .05 *** *p* < .01 **** *p* < .001

vailing social order, the Italian-American control boy seeks social conformity to the moral order by giving nurturance for social approval.

In achieving a suggestively lower score on endurance than the high school group, the Italian-American control boy would seem to prefer to get things done more quickly than the usual high school adolescent, and he finds it easier to abandon a task if it bores him.

The Italian-American control boys emphasize aggression and exhibitionism when compared to the normative college sample. The possession of these attributes, together with significantly lower scores on consistency, indicate greater impatience, responsiveness, and impulsiveness in actions. The slightly higher than average score on dominance reinforces the above inference in signifying initiative in social action and the tendency to convert aggression into affectionate relationships.

The above combination of traits suggests that the Italian-American control boy resolves adolescent dependent-independent conflict in gregarious peer group activity. Nurturance in sublimating social aggression receives social approval, which thereby gratifies succorance. The description of the Italian-American control group suggests active aggression with the social field which serves as a stage for the resolution of conflicts.

The Irish-American and the Italian-American Control Groups

The Irish-American control group predominates in deference, desire for change and novelty, and aggressive needs. They do not direct their aggressive impulses particularly into affiliative or other social forms of behavior, nor is the achievement orientation greater than that held by the Italian-American group. From the data in Table 28, we can infer that aggression represses heterosexuality with compensatory, reactive comforming behavior. The desire for change is thus relegated to fantasy. The higher need for change and lower need for order complement each other as they stand for changing modes of purpose and work. Adolescent dependent-independent conflicts cause these boys to defer to authority while fantasizing and daydreaming new experiences. Resistance for the sake of autonomy is passive resistance.

The Italian-American control group personality requires less change in habits and routine and less novelty and experimentation. The mean score on order correlates with that of change through a

Table 30
EPPS Group Means and Significance of Difference
(*t*) Between the Means of the Irish-American
and Italian-American Control Groups

Trait	Irish-American Control Group	Italian-American Control Group	*t*
Achievement	14.49	13.47	N.S.
Deference	11.40	10.47	1.60 *
Order	9.65	11.70	2.69 ***
Exhibitionism	14.88	15.88	N.S.
Autonomy	14.22	14.21	N.S.
Affiliation	14.02	14.88	N.S.
Intraception	14.02	13.56	N.S.
Succorance	12.91	13.52	N.S.
Dominance	14.00	14.79	N.S.
Abasement	14.65	14.26	N.S.
Nurturance	14.22	15.55	N.S.
Change	15.29	13.67	1.84 **
Endurance	12.86	12.73	N.S.
Heterosexuality	13.80	16.00	2.11 ***
Aggression	16.31	14.47	2.30 ***
Consistency	10.74	9.85	2.27 ***
	N = 35	N = 34	

t −* *p* <.10 ** *p* <.05 *** *p* <.01

felt desire for prearranged designs of behavior and organization of work patterns. The significantly higher score on heterosexuality in the representative Italian-American control boy is associated with less aggression than in the Irish-American control boy, but with significantly more exhibitionism and nurturance in social intercourse. There is less consistency in this boy, indicating an impulsive quality in contrast to the Irish-American control boy. Ordered activities and organization of daily routine insures against dangerous spontaneity of aggressive impulses and the powers of disorganizing inconsistency.

Adolescents gain autonomy through social experience in affiliative pursuits. Participation in the social scene coupled with compassion and social approval can bring them tangible results in the form of power, status and prestige. Active aggressive characteristics differentiate the average Italian-American boy from the representative Irish-American control boy.

Deviation of the Disturbed Groups from the Control Groups

Disturbance leads to the exaggeration of some traits and the minimization of others in an ethnic fashion.

The representative Irish-American disturbed boy significantly exaggerates deference and subordination to counsel and direction. This boy significantly rigidifies order as an important way of life. Organization and conformity to detail not only place this boy in a dependent position, but also appear to serve as a reaction formation against hostility and feelings of guilt. This is manifested by significantly fewer aggressive impulses and by less heterosexuality than are characteristic of the control group. Attention to order and detail not only suppresses sexual and hostile impulses, but also diverts them to conforming and, therefore, approved channels.

The desire for change, existing to the same degree as in the control group, is suppressed for order and deference to authority. Exaggerated decrease in dominance further confirms dependency as a personality trait. The increased dependent position of a passive-aggressive person means that the desire for change and aggression requires compensatory mechanisms for defense against these drives.

Since succorance declines and socially extroverted traits are no more apparent than in the control group, passivity necessarily includes the discharge of aggressive energy through the fantasy of change, variety, and the idealization of selfhood. Introjected self-glorification compensates for feelings of social and sexual inferiority. It compensates for uncomfortably suppressed reactions to the world of reality.

The representative Italian-American disturbed boy has significantly lower scores on heterosexuality, succorance, and nurturance in social intercourse than the control boy. As a consequence, the exhibitionistic, domineering, and aggressive drives become free from the need for social approval or for ingratiation for self-esteem and prestige. If these drives become disassociated from harmonious interpersonal communication, then they can be used for personal power and defiance of authority. Coupled with the above, the increased desire for change initiates the desire for new affiliations and

Table 31
EPPS Group Means and Significant Differences (*t*)
Between Each Control Group and
its Disturbed Group

Trait	Italian-American			Irish-American		
	Control	Dis-turbed	*t*	Control	Dis-turbed	*t*
Achievement	14.49	13.72	N.S.	13.47	14.12	N.S.
Deference	11.40	13.36	2.39 **	10.47	11.95	N.S.
Order	9.65	13.32	2.91 ***	11.70	12.08	N.S.
Exhibitionism	14.88	14.12	N.S.	15.88	15.54	N.S.
Autonomy	14.22	12.96	N.S.	14.21	13.41	N.S.
Affiliation	14.02	14.80	N.S.	14.88	14.46	N.S.
Intraception	14.02	14.41	N.S.	13.56	14.37	N.S.
Succorance	12.91	11.52	N.S.	13.52	11.61	2.65 ***
Dominance	14.00	12.32	N.S.	14.79	14.33	N.S.
Abasement	14.65	14.68	N.S.	14.26	14.10	N.S.
Nurturance	14.22	14.96	N.S.	15.55	13.37	2.84 ***
Change	15.29	16.40	N.S.	13.67	16.37	2.81 ***
Endurance	12.86	15.40	2.46 **	12.73	13.91	N.S.
Heterosexuality	13.80	11.84	1.64 *	16.00	13.16	1.74 *
Aggression	16.31	12.88	2.67 ***	14.47	15.00	N.S.
Consistency	10.74	10.48	N.S.	9.85	9.90	N.S.
N	35	25		34	24	

t − * *p* <.10 ** *p* <.05 *** *p* <.01

interpersonal conquests. Dominance and aggression compensate for resentments and feelings of inadequacy in relation to important figures.

As discussed in a previous section, exhibitionism can replace succorance by forcing attention upon the subject and his talents. This attention compensates for feelings of masculine and social inadequacy. Audiences, therefore, must be carefully selected and affiliative members chosen for their appreciative qualities. Action orientation with peers who appreciate this special kind of autonomous striving leads to sociopathic escapades and conflicts with the law. Since the mean score on abasement approximates the high school normative score, the conscience of this boy usually enforces egoistic judiciary control. The adolescent-authoritarian conflict usually remains on the level of legal misdemeanors when this boy has problems with impulse control and engages in rebellious escapades.

Summary

The Edwards Personal Preference Schedule, in measuring sixteen personality traits, differentiated between the two ethnic groups and between control and disturbed groups, as variants from the normative groups. The use of this instrument indicates that adolescents show a style of behavior in keeping with that of their ethnic culture. Ethnic subcultures, more than social class, determine styles of emotional disturbance. The EPPS begins to clarify and validate the frames of reference pointing to ethnicity as a foundation for pattern modalities in emotional expression. Analysis of the succeeding instruments amplifies, explains and validates these findings.

7

Life-Space Drawing

This chapter describes pictorially produced illustrations of the adolescents' perceptual field of social relations in the previous chapter, and amplifies the characteristic Irish-American passive aggression and Italian-American active aggression. These pictorial representations show how the variant predispositions in personality adjustments determine personal relationships in the social world of adolescence. The adolescents draw representations of orientations and directions in their social world, which indicate their concepts of the social world and their place within it. This includes the family as the primary social group and the community outside the family.

The drawings symbolize not only personal frames of reference in relation to self but also in relation to other people. Proximity choice patterns indicate the degree others satisfy personal needs and indicate how large a social field is chosen for the resolution of needs and emotional stress, and how selective the choice may be. By use of the Life-Space Drawing, we can make useful inferences about the adolescent's sense of ego adequacy. Such explorations can reveal to social workers and others in community organizations the types of treatments best suited to the various types of responses.

Focused Projective Interpersonalization

The procedure described in this chapter could well be given the convenient but perhaps ambiguous term, "projective method." A projective method tries to confront the subject with an unstructured situation—a piece of paper and a pencil—and asks him to draw something. Since little external aid is provided to help him structure the situation, the subject must give expression to the most readily available forces within himself. In addition, the subject does not know what the experimenter intends to make of the subject's response, so his attention focuses on the task at hand, thus providing a picture of the individual as close to his usual social environment as possible.

The projective technique originated with Freud's method of free association, which was aptly termed the "royal road of the unconscious." In adopting this method, Freud hoped to elude the defensive, socially patterned personality in order to learn about the subject's less rational private world. Freud recognized that what a person says or writes about himself by no means completes the account of his personality, for there are things that a person cannot tell about himself on a conscious level not only because they are repugnant to him, but also because they will escape his notice.

Psychologists in recent years have noted that even in his perception of the people and objects about him a person possesses personality traits that he cannot perceive as characteristics distinguishing him from others. The Rorschach test is a good example of a projective test that displays certain outlines of the whole personality.

The Life-Space Drawing is not meant to bring out the deeply repressed elements of the personality, but rather to secure an expression of feelings and sentiments not available to direct questioning. This test is meant to be used as a tool in examining selective perceptions and attitudinal formations on interpersonal levels. In this drawing, the adolescent structures his own social world with no help from the examiner. The drawing's validity and reliability are difficult to assess because there are no normative representative groups with which to compare. However, some measure of validity and reliability can be made as follows:

> Perceptual and conduct disturbance will reveal singular perceptual differences of the social field, in line with the kind of disturbance exhibited and in line with the personality attributes on the Edwards Personal Preference Schedule on ethnic group bases.

The Life-Space Drawing: Pattern of Choice

The initial instructions for the Life-Space Drawing asked the boys to draw a circle in the center of the page and label it "Me." Around this "Me," the boys were asked to draw circles to represent various people in their lives and to indicate social proximity and social distance. The boys were told that they could relate to anybody in various degrees of social distance. They were to draw circles representing those people to whom they felt closest in closer alignment with the "Me" circle, while those people to whom they felt increasingly more distant should be drawn increasingly further from the "Me" circle. They were to label the circles in terms of relationship, such as mother, friend, sister, and "other."

We drew Life-Space graphs from tabulations of the individuals' Life-Space Drawings in terms of eight choices of social proximity and three major collective groupings. First choices indicate perceptual proximity, and each succeeding choice indicates less perceptual proximity or greater social distance. The major groupings are: nuclear family, extended family, and extrafamilial relations. We then placed specifically defined relationships under major headings for relative sociometrically perceived choice in terms of degree of attachment (closest choice) or social distance (more distant choice). The social field for each individual in the ethnic group thus contributed to the ethnic group's Life-Space Drawing as a modal pattern of ethnically perceived social proximity and social distance. These modal patterns are pictorially reproduced and described for each group. We measured the sizes of the "Me" circles and discuss them here. We treated by correlation analyses adolescent relationships with working mothers.

Range of Interpersonal Choice

The following discussion is a summary of the detailed social choice in the interpersonal field under the major collective headings. Work tables and graphs that illustrate the direction of and orientation to intimacies and association with important figures in the adolescents' world accompany discussions for the ethnic groups. The graphs illustrate the range and pattern of response to the seven choices, while the work table indicates the detailed choice within each major collective grouping.

The Control Groups

Maternal and paternal attachments rank first and second respectively on the table for both control groups. More Irish-American boys show maternal attachments than do Italian-American boys.

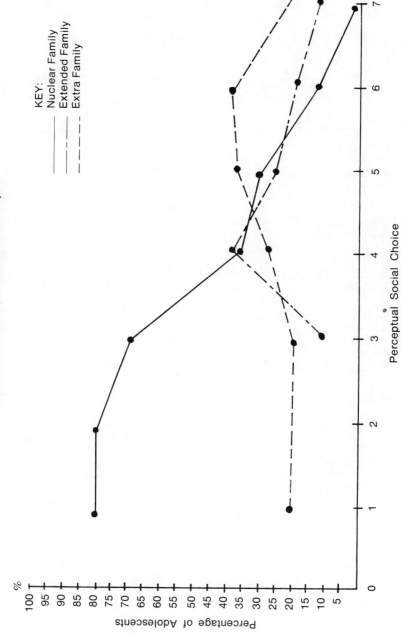

FIGURE 3

**The Irish-American Control Group's Choice Pattern
by Percentage for Major Collective Groups**

KEY:
——— Nuclear Family
—·—·— Extended Family
— — — Extra Family

Perceptual Social Choice

Percentage of Adolescents

FIGURE 4

The Italian-American Control Group's Choice Pattern by Percentage for Major Collective Groups

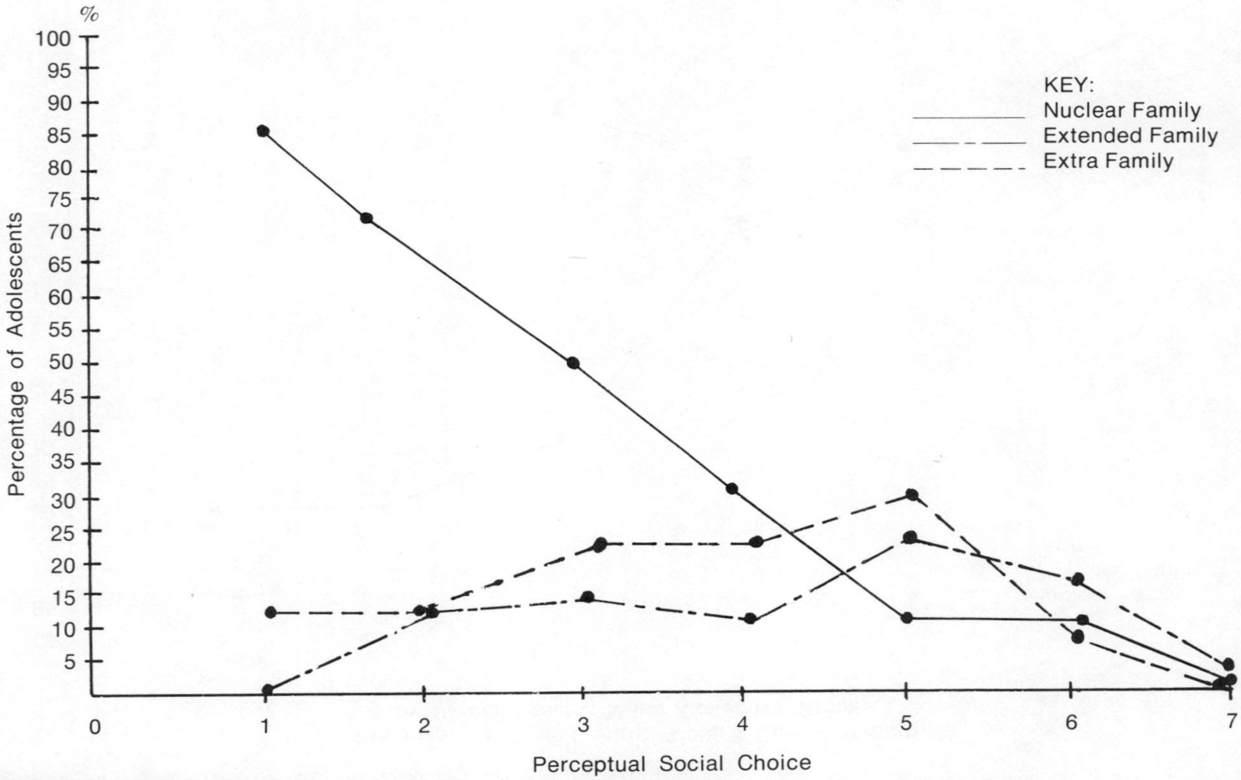
%
100
95
90
85
80
75
70
65
60
55
50
45
40
35
30
25
20
15
10
5
Percentage of Adolescents
0
1
2
3
4
5
6
7
Perceptual Social Choice
KEY:
Nuclear Family
Extended Family
Extra Family

Table 32

Perceptual Proximity by Control Groups (C1 = Irish, C2 = Italian) by Percentage, Each Choice in Rounded Figures

| Choice: | 1 | | 2 | | 3 | | 4 | | 5 | | 6 | | 7 | |
| Weight: | 8 | | 7 | | 6 | | 5 | | 4 | | 3 | | 2 | |
Group:	C1	C2	C1	C2	C1	C2	C1	C2	C1	C2	C1	C2	C1	C2
Nuclear Family: Total	80	85	80	73	68	50	35	32	30	15	13	17	5	00
Parents	3	24	00	6	00	3	00	00	00	00	00	00	00	00
Mother	52	47	25	15	10	00	3	6	00	00	00	00	00	00
Father	20	15	43	29	13	6	5	15	00	00	00	00	00	00
Brother	5	00	10	9	23	18	15	15	5	6	8	12	00	00
Sister	00	00	3	15	23	15	13	12	25	9	5	4	5	00
Siblings	00	00	00	00	00	9	00	00	00	00	00	00	00	00
Extended Family: Total	00	00	00	15	13	18	38	15	25	26	23	21	15	6
Grandmother	00	00	00	00	5	9	5	00	00	9	00	00	00	00
Grandfather	00	00	00	9	3	00	00	00	3	00	00	00	00	00
Grandparents	00	00	00	00	00	00	5	00	3	00	3	00	3	00
Aunt	00	00	00	00	3	6	13	00	5	00	5	6	5	3
Uncle	00	00	00	00	3	00	10	00	13	00	5	00	00	00
Cousins	00	00	00	3	00	00	3	00	00	9	5	3	3	00
Relatives	00	00	00	3	00	00	3	15	3	9	5	6	5	00
Nieces	00	00	00	00	00	3	00	00	00	00	00	3	00	00
Nephews	00	00	00	00	00	00	00	00	00	3	00	3	00	3
Extra-Family: Total	20	15	20	12	20	27	28	27	38	32	40	12	20	12
God	5	3	00	6	00	6	3	00	00	00	00	00	00	00
Girlfriend	10	00	3	3	8	6	3	3	18	12	10	00	3	3
Friends	00	12	13	00	8	15	8	12	13	15	13	3	8	3
Dog	3	00	5	3	3	00	8	3	3	3	00	6	3	3
Teacher	3	00	00	00	00	00	3	9	3	3	10	3	3	3
Priest	00	00	00	00	3	00	3	00	00	00	5	00	5	00
Total Percent	100	100	100	100	100	95	100	74	93	73	76	50	40	18
X^2 test =	N.S.		$p. <.10$		N.S.		N.S.		N.S.		N.S.		N.S.	

From the second choice onward the Irish-Americans select extrafamilial attachments in preference to the extended family attachments of the Italian-American boys. In the Italian-American control group, extended family attachments, beginning with the grandparents, range throughout all choices on the social attachment scale. This extended family attachment has close competition in extrafamilial choices, especially the categories of girl friends and friends.

Figures 3 and 4 portray the relationships between the three major categories for each group. In these graphs one can see that, aside from nuclear family choice, the Irish-American control boys' extended family attachments start one sociometric choice beyond those of the Italian-American boys, peak quickly, and quickly subside. At the same time there is a higher extrafamilial choice from the beginning that gradually rises to a peak by the sixth social distance category. The Irish-American boys make extra familial choices not only with friends and girl friends but with a variety of older, authoritarian figures such as teacher, preacher, coach, boss, and God.

The Italian-American control boys' graph indicates that they choose extrafamilial friendships more frequently and authoritarian figures less frequently than the Irish-American boys. The only authoritarian figure the Italian-American control group presents to any degree is God. This choice is less predominant than with the Irish-American group and occurs mainly in the first three choices as a substitution for nuclear and extended families. God may possibly be substituted as the masculine role model rather than the father. The Irish-American boys have stronger brother relations compared to stronger sister attachments of the Italian-American boys. We will discuss the possible significance of these choice patterns in the section on the modal Life-Space Drawings.

From the foregoing we could surmise that of the two ethnic groups, the Italian-Americans have greater social attachment to nuclear and extended families, for, unlike the Irish-American group, the Italian-American boys apparently perceive extrafamilial choices at a greater distance from their extended families.

The Disturbed Groups

Table 33 and the graphs illustrate that neither disturbed group differs from its own control group in first choice of mother as closest relation. In both disturbed groups there is an equivalent extension of parental substitution on first attachments to siblings, extended

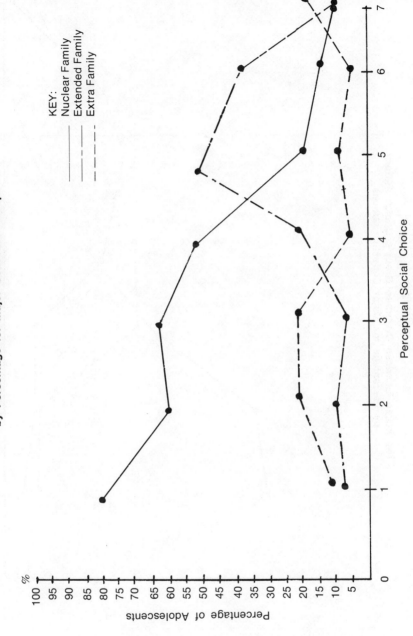

FIGURE 5

**The Irish-American Disturbed Group's Choice Pattern
by Percentage for Major Collective Groups**

KEY:
Nuclear Family
Extended Family
Extra Family

Percentage of Adolescents

Perceptual Social Choice

FIGURE 6

The Italian-American Disturbed Group's Choice Pattern
by Percentage for Major Collective Groups

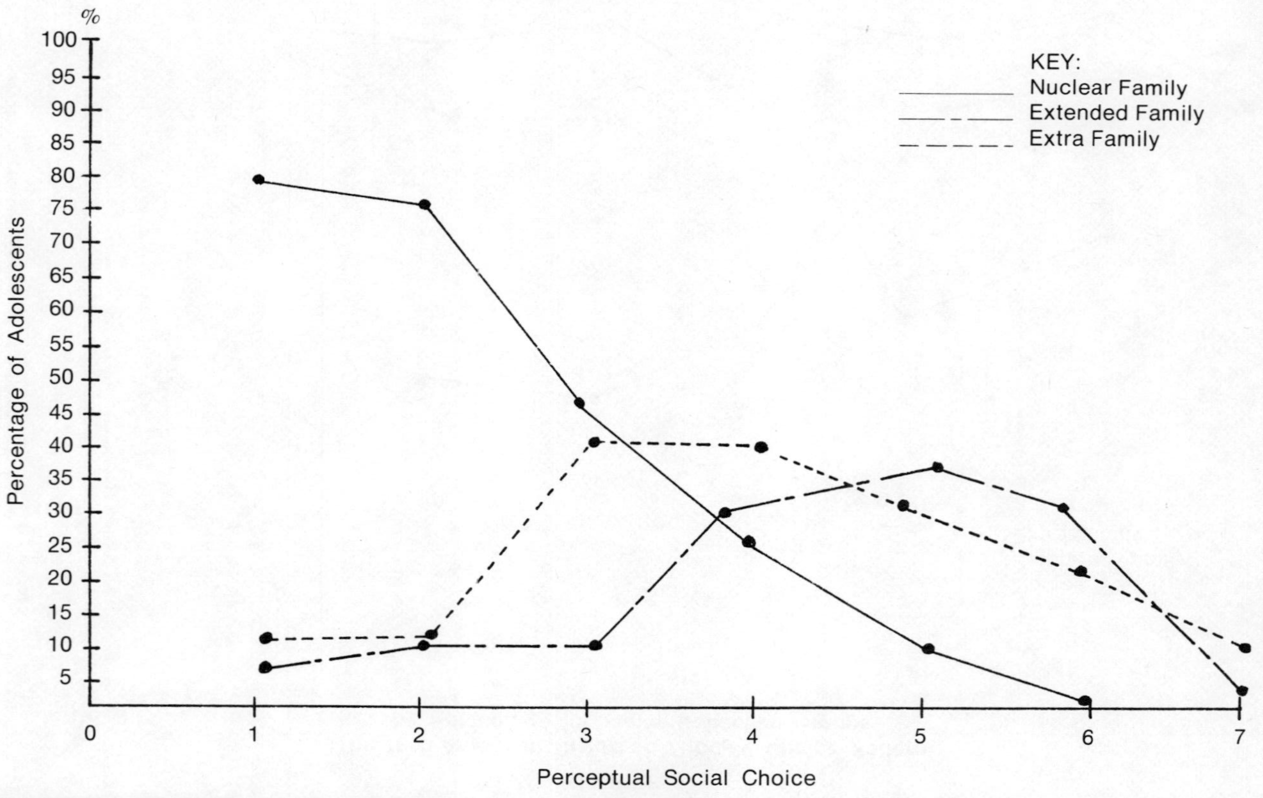

KEY:
Nuclear Family
Extended Family
Extra Family

Percentage of Adolescents

Perceptual Social Choice

Table 33

Perceptual Proximity by Disturbed Groups (C1 = Irish, C2 = Italian) by Percentage, Each Choice in Rounded Figures

Choice:	1		2		3		4		5		6		7	
Weight:	8		7		6		5		4		3		2	
Group:	C_1	C_2	C_1	C_2	C_1	C_2	C_1	C_2	C_1	C_2	C_1	C_2	C_1	C_2
Nuclear Family: Total	80	79	60	75	64	46	52	25	20	13	16	00	12	00
Parents	4	4	00	4	00	4	00	00	00	00	00	00	00	00
Mother	60	50	4	21	4	00	00	00	8	4	00	00	4	00
Father	8	16	32	21	00	9	00	4	8	4	00	00	4	00
Brother	8	8	12	4	24	8	20	8	00	00	4	00	4	00
Sister	00	00	12	25	36	25	28	13	4	4	12	00	00	00
Siblings	00	00	00	00	00	00	4	00	00	00	00	00	00	00
Extended Family: Total	8	8	16	13	12	13	24	29	52	36	40	29	12	4
Grandmother	4	8	8	4	8	00	00	4	00	16	00	00	00	00
Grandfather	00	00	4	00	00	4	12	8	12	4	16	00	00	00
Uncle	00	00	00	4	4	00	20	4	20	00	4	4	4	4
Aunt	4	00	4	4	00	4	00	13	16	8	8	13	4	4
Cousins	00	00	00	00	00	4	00	13	00	4	12	9	4	00
Nieces, Nephews	00	00	00	00	00	00	00	00	4	4	00	4	00	00
Extra-Family: Total	12	13	24	13	24	41	8	41	12	33	8	21	20	16
God	00	4	00	00	00	00	4	00	4	00	00	00	4	00
Girlfriend	00	00	4	00	00	8	00	13	4	4	00	4	00	00
Friends	8	4	16	00	16	25	00	17	4	13	8	9	12	12
Teacher	00	4	4	8	4	4	4	8	00	00	00	00	4	4
Dog	00	00	00	4	4	00	00	00	00	00	00	4	00	00
Therapist	00	00	00	00	4	4	00	00	00	4	00	00	00	00
Priest	00	00	00	00	00	00	00	00	00	8	00	00	00	00
Foster Parents	4	00	00	00	00	00	00	00	00	4	4	00	00	00
Policeman	00	00	00	00	00	00	00	00	00	00	00	4	00	00
Total Percent	100	100	100	100	100	100	84	95	84	82	64	50	44	20
X^2 test =	N.S.		N.S.		$p < .10$		$p < .05$		$p < .05$		$p < .05$			

family, and extrafamilial persons. There is more first choice of grandparents as substitution for nuclear family choice than in the control groups. As one views the range of social distance choices for each group, they give parental proximity less emphasis throughout the whole range of social choices.

In addition, the graphs illustrate that the Italian-American disturbed group gives extrafamilial relationships greater qualities of friendship than the extended family, unlike its control group. On the other hand, the Irish-American disturbed group, in contrast to the control group, holds on to familial attachments through half of its choice range. This is particularly in evidence in the choice of sisters. In this group also, friends of the same sex take the place of the girl friend attachments evident in the control group.

In general, the ethnic disturbed groups reverse their interpersonal preference patterns as compared to the control groups and to each other. Indications of sister identification, identification with friends of the same sex, and less parental identification from the second choice on leads to a picture of parent-child conflict and identification disturbance.

The Irish-American disturbed groups substitute high proximal choice and feelings of close attachment for members of the extended family when nuclear family orientations are reduced. Throughout the range of choice this group exhibits an intensive and vigorous clinging, first to nuclear family orientation, and then to extended family relationships. This orientation in personal needs may be due to a deprivation of close family ties and possible submission to authority relations. Many of the Irish-American boys have lost their nuclear family due to separation and broken homes. These boys may consequently hope for a sense of unity in both nuclear and extended family relationships. The ideal of a family that supplies love, self-esteem, and social approval appears to be a deeply important emotional element in the Irish-American boys. Family unity provides one with a feeling of belonging which in turn furnishes a sense of identity and security. On the Edwards Personal Preference Schedule these boys revealed deference for authority and need for succorance by a kindly individual. Their nurturance to meet social approval is understandable, especially when a boy whose internal balance relies upon social approval possibly feels guilty about a broken home.

In a statistical analysis, a series of chi-squares indicates certain departures in personal relationships between the ethnically differentiated disturbed groups. These groups differ significantly in third, fourth, and fifth choice preferences. Although neither of the disturbed groups have primary parental choices in the manner of their control groups (due to separation, broken homes, and illnesses), in the third choice level the Italian-American disturbed group still has more parental preference, especially for the father, than does the Irish-American group. The Irish-American group shows more sibling preference, especially for the sister. The Italian-American disturbed boys begin to have more extrafamilial choices rather than choices of extended family. This accentuates in the level of fourth choice (p <.05) where the Irish-American boys maintain sister attachments and the Italian-American boys show extrafamilial attachments. In the fifth choice level the two disturbed groups again differ (p <.05). Here, the Irish-American groups give parents as more socially distant choices to a much greater extent. The straggling of parental choice throughout the social distance categories is greater among the Irish-American boys. The extended family begins to substitute for the nuclear family, while extrafamilial relationships remain on a lower level. This reverses for the Italian-American disturbed boys with whom, from the third choice onward, extrafamilial relationships compete closely with the extended family.

There are significant differences in attachments to specific relations and in social perceptions of the *Environment*. In the second-level choice, the Irish-American disturbed boys do not choose the parents in close relationships the way the control group chooses them (p <.02). As a consequence, they choose sisters, grandparents, teachers, foster parents, and friends more often as parental substitutes. Since the Italian-American disturbed group makes similar choices, at the same time relating to older, helpful figures, we feel that the Irish-American choice may reflect disturbance due to parental discord and establishment of the boys in residence, for these things aggravate adolescent reaction patterns and maladjustment situations. On the level of third choice in social distance, the Irish-American disturbed group again differs from its control group (p <.10) in giving greater weight to siblings, grandfathers, and uncles. At this point particularly one can see the Irish-American disturbed boy's preference for the extended family as an alternative to the nuclear family. Within the nuclear family, though, sister preference seems to predominate. The Irish-American fifth choice level exaggerates these factors (p <.05). Here, the disturbed boys value extended family relationships, and some of them have placed their parents in this more distant category of personal intimacy.

The disturbed groups reversed their sociometric choice for intimacy, friendships, and identifications in the social world. The Irish-American group reversed from its control group, which had a nuclear family orientation by relating vigorously to the extended family. This type of reaction formation is in keeping with the theory that disturbance increases compliance with authority, deference for authority, and passive-aggressive characteristics.

The Italian-American boys show higher personal preferences for extrafamilial choices rather than extended kin ones. These boys appear to have little trust in their family relationships, rebel against the domineering authority and disapproval of extended kin, and prefer people of their own age among whom they can express their personal needs of dominance, exhibitionism, and aggression. We should reiterate that the Italian-American disturbed boys grew up in families with more overtly expressed emotions and more authoritarian fathers as will be seen in the section on the questionnaire. To achieve some emotional security and freedom from emotional conflict within the family, these boys turn to outside people who they feel understand them better. We will investigate these passive-aggressive and active-aggressive contrasts further in the section on the modal Life-Space Drawing.

Modal Life-Space Drawing

We calculated the modal Life-Space Drawings for each ethnic group in the following manner. In an effort to determine the field of social relations for each ethnic group, we calculated the percentage of boys making particular choices from first to eighth on the Life-Space pattern-choice chart. We then weighted these choices by an eight to one consecutive weighting (reversed numerically) after we obtained an average percentage for each choice. Thus, the one to whom the boy felt closest received the greatest weight (eight) and the largest average index percentage rating. By weighting the percentage of each choice by the weight given to the choice, we computed and graphed these modal choices of identifiable groups as shown in Table 33. Those groupings around the "Me" circle with the highest index ratings are perceived as the closest relations (eight), those with lowest average percent index numbers are perceived as the most distant (one) to the self in the social field.

Before proceeding into an analysis of the modal Life-Space Drawing itself, we will compare and discuss the characteristics of the "Me" circles. In addition, we will search maternal choice characteristics for factors associated with ethnicity.

We found no significant differences between the social classes in each group for any of the characteristics in the Life-Space Drawing.

Diameter Measurement of "Me" Circle

The initial instruction in making the Life-Space Drawing was to draw a circle in the center of the page and label it "Me." This represents the self. We measured the diameters of the "Me" circles for each group and found them to range from .5 inch to 6.5 inches. After establishing the percentage of boys in each group who drew each size circle, we then sought significant differences in diameter measurement for the ethnic groups.

Statistical evaluation supports the impression that the Italian-American control boys drew significantly larger figures than the Irish-American control boys. Seventy percent of these boys made cir-

Table 34
Measurement of Circle Diameters of "Me"
by Percentage of Boys in Two Ethnic Groups

	Circle Inches .50–1.15	Circle Inches 2.00–3.15	Circle Inches 4.00–5.24	Circle Inches 5.25–6.50	Total	N
Irish-American Control %	22.50	47.50	10.00	20.00	100.00	40
Italian-American Control %	2.94	26.48	50.00	20.58	100.00	34
Irish-American Disturbed %	36.00	52.00	8.00	4.00	100.00	25
Italian-American Disturbed %	12.50	62.51	8.30	16.00	100.00	24

$x^2 - 16.27$, 3 d.f. $x^2 = .86$, 1 d.f. $p < .50$
$p < .01$

cles between 4 inches and 6.5 inches in diameter. In contrast, 70 percent of the Irish-American boys drew "Me" circles from .5 inch to 3.11 inches in diameter.

We must remember that these boys, in drawing their circles, were signifying their selves and how they fit into their social scheme. They may only dimly perceive their schema, but its projection objectively pictorializes the way they see themselves in relation to other people.

We can develop crude categories of differentiation between feelings of inadequacy and those of self-sufficiency. These categories also describe relative feelings of insignificance or significance and feelings of deference as opposed to feelings of influence over other people. If we grant the above, then the significantly different-sized circles point to different modes of social perception in the Irish-American and Italian-American boys. We can thus infer ethnic ideational schemes from the size of the circles as well as those arrived at through the Edwards Personal Preference Schedule.

The Irish-American Group

The Irish-American boys, in drawing smaller circles, apparently see themselves as smaller in the eyes of others. Their self-image emerges from certain dependencies upon the goodwill of the generalized others and from appeals to specific people for rewarding relationships. It's this way that others influence their outlook on the nature of life. They maintain idealistic, moral, and religious values in order to hold friends. The representative Irish-American boy's relationship to specific people rather than generalities makes his smaller "Me" circle understandable. This configuration of the self in the social world amplifies the Edwards Personal Preference Schedule and is further reinforced by the Tennessee Department of Mental Health Self-Concept in a later section.

If we can say that a key aspect of the adolescent's self-image is his masculine identification, then the differences in circle size not only reflect differences in the self-image, but also in the masculine role. The study suggested in the previous section on personality traits that the Irish-American boy had somewhat greater identification with the father through a more democratic and permissive atmosphere in the home. The passive-aggressive characteristics revealed in his personality tend to make the Irish-American boy grant the father omnipotence in the social situation. In so doing he converts any feeling of guilt into fantasies of being a similar omnipotent character himself, and later sections corroborate these postulated fantasies of self-glorification.

Social anxiety in masculine identification and in assumption of the masculine role in adolescence often necessitates an energetic suppression of aggressive strivings and a development of submissiveness in order to make the environment will disposed toward oneself. Specific people in the environment fulfill the narcissistic demands for love and for the alleviation of guilt feelings toward oneself. The conception of the self as a smaller entity dependent upon the goodness of other people within one's environment and upon social identification for the relief of social anxiety provides a Gestalt pattern that is different in certain aspects from that of the Italian-American boys.

The Italian-American Group

The boys in this group drew significantly larger "Me" circles which suggest that the self-image is seen as a unique, total entity surrounded by less significant people who can fulfill the actively aggressive narcissistic demands. Accordingly, these boys would tend to see themselves as dominant and influential personalities in relation to other people, and as significant beings, adequate in autonomous acts and in the ability to obtain approval from others. Other people in the environment exist to enhance the boys' own self-esteem and their own self-image. It is as if these boys utilize the social field as a tool for action. They identify with and introject cultural objects as a part of the self. Self-sufficiency thus joins with the participative use of the social field in the interests of culture as an extension of the self. The exhibitionistic, domineering, and aggressive drives that appeared as part of the Italian-American personality culture support this ideation.

In view of the above, we can surmise that these boys, if frustrated, are aggressive toward others in their environment. Since they depend upon others for the maintenance of their own self-esteem, their sources for narcissistic self-satisfaction are external. One might also say that they are dependent in a very real social sense, while appearing to be independent. They exhibit extremely active social and masculine behavior in compensation for frustrated needs. In contrast to the Irish-American boys, the Italian-American boys exhibit greater confusion in father identification as well as a defiance of authority that create a greater need for substitute sources from the social environment in order to enhance self-esteem. Such needs encourage greater and more diverse social and heterosexual activities.

Compared to its control group, the Italian-American disturbed group drew smaller circles which merge in size with the Irish-American disturbed group at the 2.0 to 3.9 inch level. This significant difference in size indicates certain dimensions in disturbance and in the perception of the social field. These boys have exaggerated tendencies toward exhibitionism, dominance, and aggression, while the need for succorance from kindly people and the need to be kind to other people decline to low levels, yet social punishment for aggressive acts tends to make the Italian-American boys show somewhat less ego inflation.

Poor identification with the father and imitation of his dominant behavior in social relations appear to be a form of social aggression and adventure that wards off a sense of helplessness and fear in social anxiety. Increased aggression and domineering actions comsate for heterosexual and social insecurity, but they often lead to conflicts with the law. The adolescent is thus forced to see himself as a smaller part of the social field and is forced to face society's judgment that his social functioning is inadequate. He is humbled and his ego is deflated. Resisting this threat to ego deflation and society's moral judgment, he leaves his family's succorance and protection, declines to give nurturance, and seeks to compensate for these deflated social feelings. His defiance of society and flouting of its rules is directed not only against those who punish illegal behavior but also against his own deflated selfhood and increasing sense of smallness.

In summary, the ethnic groups show personality differences as a further dimension of ethnicity through an analysis of "Me" circle diameters. The Irish-American boys drew circles that support the picture of a boy who is dependent upon other people for self-esteem. Possibly for this reason the disturbed Irish-American boy vigorously attaches himself to nuclear and extended family for a sense of belonging and of adequacy. We will see in succeeding chapters that this boy employs idealism and more rigid moral-ethical codes in the construction his own self-image, for his self-image depends on the kindliness and approval of other people.

The modal Italian-American boy continues to illustrate the active-aggressive fulfillment of narcissistic demands from other people. In drawing larger circles, this boy shows he feels more influential and self-sufficient in his utilization of the generalized others for his self-enhancement. He relates more to general others, whereas the Irish-American boy relates more to specific people. The Italian-American control boy is in good standing with his nuclear and extended family, but the disturbed Italian-American boy runs into conflicts with the law and receives social punishment for his acts. His ego deflates and resisting this threat he reacts not only against the social authority but also against his greater sense of smallness.

Maternal Choice

Since first choice of the mother predominated for both the control and disturbed groups, we tried to analyze associations between the mother as first choice of the parents, and such other factors as working mothers and separation of parents. In addition to this, we tried to determine if there were significant differences between the social classes in each group in first choice of the mother.

Table 35
Distribution of Maternal Choice by Maternal Employment
in the Irish-American Control Boys

Choice	Non-working Mothers	Working Mothers	Total
	%	%	%
Positive	17	33	50
Negative	25	25	50
Total	42	58	100

rt. $= +.25$
"Q" $= +.30$

The Control Groups

In the Irish-American control group, both measures of degree of association indicate a low positive association between choice of mother as first relation and maternal employment. In this group the employment of mothers does not appear to be detrimental to the choice of mother as the closest and most important interpersonal relationship. There are no social class differences in this respect.

In the Italian-American control group there is some social class difference in choice of mother as primary attachment figure, with the lower classes preferring this choice more. This does not appear to relate to maternal employment. Looking ahead to the questionnaire data, maternal choice for the Italian-American control group appears to coincide in the lower classes with some evidence of conflict with fathers.

We can interpret the correlation coefficients in both ethnic groups as signifying that employed mothers may still be the favored choice even though they are out of the home during working hours. Qualitatively, we can state that the presence of the mother at home does not ensure the presence of a positive maternal relationship. We

Table 36
Distribution of Maternal Choice by Social Class
and by Maternal Employment in Italian-American Control Group

| Maternal Choice | Social Class | | Non-working Mother | Working Mother | Total |
	I–III	IV–V			
	%	%	%	%	%
Positive	42.85	75.00	35.00	21.00	56.00
Negative	57.15	25.00	35.00	9.00	44.00
Total	100.00	100.00	70.00	30.00	100.00

$x^2 =$ (corr. for cont.)   rt. $= +.30$
$\quad = 2.78$ "Q" $= +.40$
1 d.f., $p < .10$

can state that working mothers do not necessarily pay less attention to their sons' emotional needs.

The Disturbed Groups

Both disturbed groups made equivalent first choice of mothers, however, we noted that both disturbed groups had poorer relationships to the parents. Second choices were not equivalent to the control group choices, and parental choices straggled throughout the choice levels. We also saw that from the first choice onward there were substitutions for parents with members of the extended families (particularly grandparents). Such substitutions were not evident in the control groups. In analyzing maternal choice in the disturbed groups, we must remember that several boys in each group were living away from home at the time of study. Of the Irish-American disturbed group 50 percent of the upper-class boys and 65 percent of the lower-class boys were living away from home. In this group all boys in residence also lived with separated parents, mainly the mother, before going into residence. In neither disturbed group does social class make a difference in the number of boys having separated parents. Of the Italian-American disturbed group 33 percent of the upper-class boys and 39 percent of the lower-class boys were living away from home. In addition, due to death and parental desertion, three of the Italian-American boys lived at home with only one parent. The grandparents assisted in child-rearing, thus accounting for some influence in the substitution for maternal choice.

Table 37
Distribution of Maternal Choice by Maternal
Employment in the Italian-American
Disturbed Group

Maternal Choice	Non-working Mother	Working Mother	Total
	%	%	%
Positive	50	21	71
Negative	25	4	29
Total	75	25	100

rt. $= +.30$
"Q"$= +.428$

The boys in the Italian-American disturbed group, like those in the control groups, are not affected by working mothers. However, the correlation coefficients indicate that there is an inverse relation between separation and the choice of mother. Forty-two percent of the boys made positive maternal choices in those cases where the parents were not separated compared to 21 percent who made maternal choices where parents were separated.

In contrast to the Irish-American disturbed boys, the Italian-American disturbed boys were cared for more frequently in the home by parental substitutes who attempted to hold the family together, and the findings show that these parental substitutes are frequently first choices, especially when they are extended family members. Desertion and separation are not particularly condoned which may encourage negative attitudes toward the parent who deserted.

Table 38
Distribution of Maternal Choice by Parental
Separation in the Italian-American
Disturbed Group

Maternal Choice	Non-separated Parents	Separated Parents	Total
	%	%	%
Positive	42	21	63
Negative	8	29	37
Total	50	50	100

rt. $= -.72$
"Q" $= -.75$

In beginning the discussion of the Irish-American disturbed boys' maternal choice, we can state that social class makes no difference in the percentage of boys who choose the mother as the most important relation.

The coefficient correlations found in tables 39 and 40 indicate that separation of parents makes no difference in the number of Irish-American disturbed boys relating to the mother. Although the correlations are somewhat negative in both tables, the findings are so slight that one can safely state that these adolescents choose mothers as closest relations much more than the Italian-American

Table 39
Distribution of Maternal Choice by Maternal
Employment in the Irish-American
Disturbed Group

Maternal Choice	Non-working Mother	Working Mother	Total
	%	%	%
Positive	44	16	60
Negative	28	12	40
Total	72	28	100

rt. $=$ .00
"Q" $= -.08$

boys do, whether or not the parents are separated or the mother is working. In contrast to the Italian-American disturbed group, we can see that despite maternal employment and greater divorce and separation in this group, the mother identification patterns are much more marked for the Irish-American disturbed boys.

Parental disunity and discord often characterizes the nuclear family of the Irish-American disturbed boy. In addition he has less contact with the extended family than is typical for the Italian-American disturbed boy. We also saw that this modal boy shows more interest in the extended family unit. There is further evidence of a melancholic longing for family unity and for inner cohesion with the maternal image for psychological security. The mother repre-

Table 40
Distribution of Maternal Choice by Parental
Separation in the Irish-American
Disturbed Group

Maternal Choice	Non-separated Parents	Separated Parents	Total
	%	%	%
Positive	32	28	60
Negative	20	20	40
Total	52	48	100

rt. $= -.10$
"Q" $= -.06$

sents home and leadership in spite of separation. The extended family represents fortification against further potential separation from parents and loss of love.

In contrast, the Italian-American boy relates pragmatically to the parent or the parental substitute who fulfills his narcissistic demands and who assures him of a close relationship. The presence and helpfulness of extended family relations make this practical approach possible.

Life-Space Models

We will now analyze and discuss the pictorial representations of the indexed social fields for each ethnic group. These social fields are modal patterns tabulated and weighted by social distance choices, which results in what may be termed a self-structured field of affinity with other human beings.

The Control Groups

An examination of Figures 7 and 8 leads to the following observations. The Irish-American control boys give greater weight to parental attachment as second to the mother. This is in keeping with the greater democracy evident in his home which eases the identification processes.

In comparison with the Italian-American control boy, the representative Irish-American control boy perceives a nuclear family relation of parents, brothers, and sisters, and places somewhat greater emphasis on brotherly affection. They prefer specifically chosen kinship relatives to the more general "relative" choice statements of the Italian-American boy, and they give these specific extended family relationships greater social distance than friends and girlfriends. One may reasonably infer here that peer group relations and girl friends are more important than the extended family for emotional security and adolescent empathy. This contrasts with the representative Italian-American boy who chooses his kin before extrafamilial possibilities. The more intense girl friend attachments of the Irish-American boy may conceivably relate to greater father identification, indicated by a heavier average index. If this is the case, greater masculine identification results in more ability to relate to girls and to cope with heterosexual attractions. The Irish-American boys acknowledge specific attachments to uncles, as well as to brothers; such attachments enhance masculine role model identifications. The Italian-American boys do not include these specific role models but give "relatives" in general greater weight. However, this does not preclude their having role models.

The representative Italian-American control boy appears to form a cluster of nuclear and extended kinship systems in an intensely perceived social field that is high in its relations to the boy's perception of social intimacy. His world appears to be ordered by and through his large-family pattern. This boy's high valuation of sister relationships may be due to the emphasis on masculine protection of women in the Italian-American culture. According to Ware (113) and Handlin (49), the Sicilian male is deemed superior to the woman, but he serves as her mentor and protector. Most of the Italian-American boys in this study are older siblings who may well be protecting their younger sisters in the Italian tradition. In accordance with Florence Kluckhohn (66), this ethnic group asserts the basic values of collaterality in relational patterns. However, the other findings of her study are not evident in this representative third-generation Italian-American boy. These findings are the man-nature-subjectivity relations, concern with the present in time, and with "being" in activity.

In both the Irish-American and Italian-American control groups, male peers stand out as a testing ground for social relations. According to Fenichel (31), adolescents often prefer peer groups of the same sex in order to avoid the excitement caused by the other sex and, at the same time, to have the social reassurance of others who have fears and anxieties about sex. Thus they can congregate for the purpose of exchanging stories about sexuality. Many relationships at this age may be used as instruments to relieve tensions, as proof of one's abilities, or as reassurances against anxieties.

If we can assume that the nature of the ethnic personality conforms to the nature of early identifications, then masculine identifications assume a large role in differentiating the Irish-American and Italian-American boys. If the adolescent adopts as the masculine ideal in his own generation the ideal of his parents, the principal identification will be made with the parent who is the most dominant in giving decisive permissions and prohibitions. This dominant figure may not necessarily be the father. Alternative identifications may be made with a male relative or older brother if the father is found to be a dependent or inadequate masculine role model for adolescent idealization.

An examination of Figure 7 allows one to infer that the Irish-American boy may find in uncles and older brothers alternatives to his father as ideals of masculinity. A younger brother regarding his older brother's successes as his own may enter the hero-worship stage of adolescent identification and avoid sibling rivalry. The brother toward whom he behaves thus altruistically may simultaneously represent the boy's own ideal image of manhood. Identification with a dominant mother does not necessarily preclude identification with a brother or uncle on another level of relationship.

The Irish-American control group suppresses aggressive tendencies in favor of submission to a particular authority so they may fulfill ideal demands. Submission to authority confirms and reinforces their ethical code. Submission to the loving protection of an omnipotent God in an idealization of social behavior is enhanced

FIGURE 7

**Modal Life-Space Drawing by Weighted
Index of Perceptual Proximity**

Irish-American Control Group

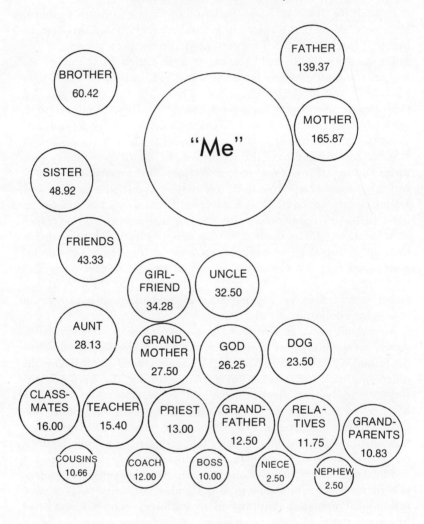

FIGURE 8

Modal Life-Space Drawing by Weighted
Index of Perceptual Proximity

Italian-American Control Group

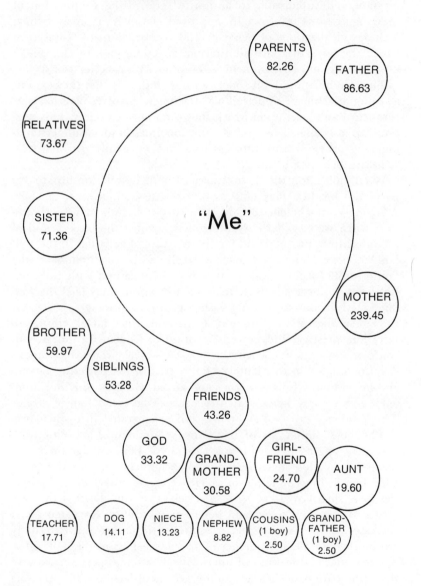

by the attachment to the clergy, who represent the prohibitions and sanctions of this omnipotent power. These boys, having adequate male identification, can find in the opposite sex an appropriate love object as society demands they should. Suppressed aggression and submission to authority require the sublimation of these aggressions into socially approved channels, a process which includes idealizations of behavior and constructions of fantasies in which the boy can attain admiration, affection, love, or changes in his existence and environment in keeping with a better world.

The graph for the Irish-American boys indicates that they exhibit a strong attachment to pets. This attachment involves paternal nurturance of an object upon which they can appease desires. This relationship also offers some relief from loneliness and misunderstandings and provides substitute gratifications when interpersonal relationships become difficult.

What holds for the Irish-American boy in relationship to his peers and brothers may hold as well for the Italian-American boy. A stronger attachment to God than to girl friends may be significant when we consider this attachment against the background of relationship to parental and family structure. The father in the Italian-American family is a harsh disciplinarian who dominates the family unit. Intimidation by an omnipotent father, with little opportunity to form substitute male identifications, may lead the Italian-American boy to identify with a greater omnipotent power for the reassurance of affection and, at the same time, for obtaining admiration, prestige, and power. Devotion to God may connect with compensatory fantasy when the boy feels weak under his father's domination, for in this fantasy he is a part of the powerful partner and he no longer feels powerless and afraid. He then convinces himself he can enjoy heterosexuality because he is no longer afraid. This tendency can be heightened and exaggerated in disturbance.

The boys' imitations of the father's dominance, exhibitionism, and social aggression are often exaggerated. They assuage their consciences by various heterosexual and social achievements that mitigate their feelings of helplessness. However, unassuaged social anxieties force such boys to reassure themselves continually that they are a success and have social and heterosexual ability. Repeated social successes of an assertive and exhibitionistic nature can externally symbolize heterosexual potency. This same behavior wards off internal anxieties and feelings of inferiority by forcing spectators to give the approbation needed to counteract these feelings. If spectators do not fulfill these narcissistic demands, aggression can be directed against them. These personality characteristics may find reassurance and protection in identification with a divine, omnipotent power. Thus, the Italian-American boy who states he wants to feel close to God "to avoid the wickedness of this world" is compensating for his own feelings of guilt and fear.

Thus far, the Edwards Personal Preference Scale and the modal Life-Space Drawing corroborate and bring into focus the passive-aggressive personality of the Irish-American boy and the active-aggressive personality of the Italian-American boy.

The Disturbed Groups

We noted that in disturbances the range of choices in major collective groupings were in reverse to those of the control groups. Figures 9 and 10 present the relationship models for each disturbed group. In these figures the "Me" circles, from an ethnic viewpoint, are similar. However, the configurations of interpersonal relationships have changes.

In both disturbed groups there is a strong emphasis on sister relationships which are second only to the primary maternal relationships. This is most apparent in the Irish-American disturbed group, who place fathers at lower choice levels than the control groups. We can infer that closer relationships with sisters in preference to fathers, in conjunction with prominent maternal identifications, leave little room for adequate authoritative masculine role model identification.

The Irish-American disturbed boys may possibly hero worship their brothers, for they prize the relationship to brothers more than to friends. These boys are middle siblings, and older brothers offer convenient models in life experience. This is not so for the Italian-American boy, who prefers selective peer group friendships over extended kin.

The Irish-American disturbed boy continues to have male friends in his usual basic pattern, but he prefers specific extended family relationships to the girl friends he formerly favored. Extensive maternal and sister relationships, combined with male peer group attachments, extended family preferences, and placement of girlfriends at greater distance, leads to the supposition of poor masculine identifications.

Reliance on the omnipotent power of God and the relationship to the authoritarian power of the priest diminish in favor of kin

FIGURE 9

Modal Life-Space Drawing by Weighted
Index of Perceptual Proximity

Irish-American Disturbed Group

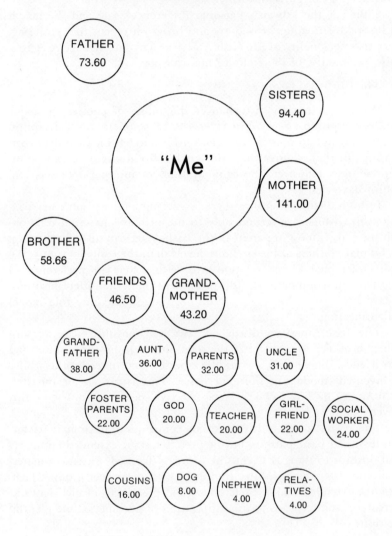

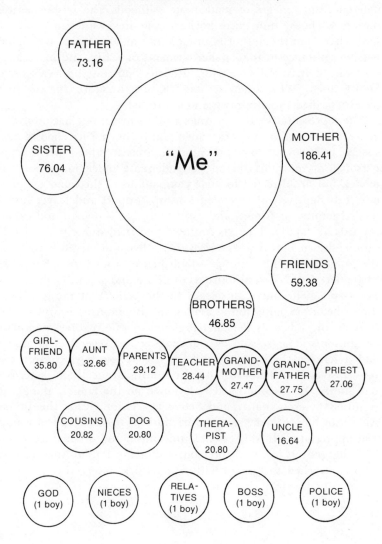

FIGURE 10

**Modal Life-Space Drawing by Weighted
Index of Perceptual Proximity**

Italian-American Disturbed Group

FATHER
73.16

"Me"

MOTHER
186.41

SISTER
76.04

FRIENDS
59.38

BROTHERS
46.85

GIRL-
FRIEND
35.80

AUNT
32.66

PARENTS
29.12

TEACHER
28.44

GRAND-
MOTHER
27.47

GRAND-
FATHER
27.75

PRIEST
27.06

COUSINS
20.82

DOG
20.80

THERA-
PIST
20.80

UNCLE
16.64

GOD
(1 boy)

NIECES
(1 boy)

RELA-
TIVES
(1 boy)

BOSS
(1 boy)

POLICE
(1 boy)

group choices. Clinically, these boys withdrew from the difficult world of reality and reverted to fantasies of self-glorification. These fantasies focused upon the self as the omnipotent hero whom everyone admired. This reversion to familial choice, coupled with the clinical picture of withdrawal, suggests a boy who has feelings of deference and images of inadequate selfhood. The Irish-American boys now choose human authoritarian figures, while turning away somewhat from the authority of God and his representatives. Their passive resistance to the harsher elements of reality and maturation shows in their compliance with authority and clinging to a sense of family unity. While they accomplish this, they are, for the most part, described as withdrawn and depressed.

The representative Italian-American disturbed boy has no overall general orientation to his extended family, but rather chooses more specific relatives in closer proximity to himself. These specific interpersonal orientations include no adequate older masculine role model, but are directed to male companions of the same age. This boy feels deprived of extended kinship support and leaves his extended family for friends and girlfriends. He is defiant and cynical towards his family. There is confused and inadequate male identification, shown by third choice of the father and eleventh choice of the grandfather. The aunt is established as a nurturant figure. He surrenders God as an authoritarian figure and socializes more with peers and girlfriends. This leads to the belief that the greatly reduced heterosexuality found among the Italian-American disturbed boys on the Edwards Personal Preference Scale involves dominant, exhibitionistic aggression as a defense against severe social anxiety and a sense of helplessness and despair. These boys continuously need to reassure themselves of their continued social and heterosexual ability. His self-imposed isolation from the family, along with confused heterosexuality and active aggression, leads the Italian-American boy to make selective friendships in order to feel wanted and appreciated. In this case, exhibitionism and dominance accompany aggression in social intercourse. For the Italian-American boy who is attached to his kin with collateral leanings, this action appears to be particularly radical in its beginnings.

Summary

An examination of the projected social process for each ethnic group indicated that the Irish-American control group orients toward the nuclear family while the Italian-American control group places high value upon the extended family. Both control groups seek peer group associations vigorously in the process of maturation.

In disturbance, the ethnic groups reverse their social orientations. The Irish-American disturbed boys relate more vigorously to extended family relationships. They choose the mother first despite separation or employment. The Italian-American disturbed boys reduce their primary relationships to extended family while activating more peer group relationships. They give first choice to mothers who are not separated or to maternal substitutes. These boys show confusion in assuming the masculine role by their vigorous relating to peers while endeavoring to detach from the authority figures of their families.

Analysis of the "Me" circles indicates ethnic differences in the self-image. The sense of inadequacy in the Irish-American boys contrasts with the self-sufficiency of the Italian-American boys. These findings coincide with those of the Edwards Preference Schedule. The value patterns for Irish-American boys provide them with egocentric orientations in terms of an internal sense of good and evil, while the value patterns for Italian-American boys provide them with sociocentric orientations, in terms of greater impulsivity and social spontaneity.

The exploratory Life-Space Drawings give further illustration of the underlying mechanisms in social perception and interpersonal relationships that this study proposed. The self-images in social contexts accord with the passive-aggressive personality of the Irish-American boy and the active-aggressive personality of the Italian-American boy. Each disturbed group exaggerates predominant ethnic traits of role and behavior found in its control group.

8

Tennessee Department of Mental Health
Self Concept (TDMH)

The demands of this study made the self-concept, as an index of self-evaluation and self-satisfaction, a necessary test to compare with the previous research instruments. We have formulated from the data that the two ethnic groups operate differently regarding self-evaluation and approach to significant others in the environment. In addition to the overall propositions of difference, the self-concept tested for differences in attitudes toward the physical, psychological, and social selves. We have proposed that if ethnic differences do exist in self-concept formations, then these are handed down through intergenerational communication at home which has been the adolescent's principal environment.

Fitts (35) indicated in a personal communication to the author that he found no differences in the self-concept between adolescents and adults or between Negroes and whites. He wrote or said, however, that ethnic groups were neither tested in purity nor compared with each other. In his abstract of research findings (86), comparative analyses of differentially diagnosed patient groups did not include adolescents with the diagnostic schema in this study. We will compare the self-concept scores for the two ethnic groups to the normative groups and total patient group scores validated by Fitts (86).

We can assume that areas of learning, motivation, and perception influence the idea one has about one's self in relation to others and in relation to the qualities one deems desirable in one's self. With these considerations, we anticipated that the Italian-American boys, in contrast to the Irish-American boys, would have more positive feeling toward themselves and toward other people in secondary community groups. Also in contrast to the Irish-American boys, these adolescents would stereotype themselves less, in the interest of adapting more easily to the various social groupings in the community. The Italian-American boy would not only show more satisfaction with himself and his associations, but he would also be able to criticize himself more openly or to recognize parts of himself from a negative frame of reference.

Tennessee Department of Mental Health Self-Concept Scale

The Tennessee Department of Mental Health Self-Concept Scale is broken up into a five-by-three category analysis. The five horizontal categories represent the external frames of reference regarding the concept about one's self and one's primary and secondary group memberships. These externals are answered by three measures of internal frames of reference. The consistency scores, distribution scores, and the positive-negative continuum provide measures for the analysis of personality adjustment, for the clarity of the self-concept, and for the certainty of the self-concept.

The data on the eight areas of investigation were statistically approached with the use of F-ratio. Essentially, we maintained a four-cell two-way classification, split one way into the control and the disturbed groups and the other way into the Irish-American and Italian-American groups. The Irish-American control group was reduced in number to achieve proportionality with the other three groups on the basis of a two-way classification system. The following formula was applied:

$$X : 34 \text{ as } 25 : 23$$
$$\text{and}$$
$$X : 25 \text{ as } 34 : 23$$

The formula indicated that the number of Irish-American control boys required for analysis of variance in a two-way classification table for the use of this instrument is thirty-seven. We withdrew by random selection three self-concept score sheets from the total of forty Irish-American control subjects.

Where F-ratios were shown to be significant, we performed t distribution analyses for measures of significant differences between the mean value scores. The mean scores of the ethnic groups were compared to the mean values of the normative representative groups, of the total patient group, and of the diagnostically differentiated psychiatric patients studied by Fitts (35). Significant tables are in Appendix I.

Self-Criticism

The self-criticism scale is composed of ten items taken from the Minnesota Multiphasic Personality Inventory. These are all mildly derogatory statements that most people admit as being true for themselves. Individuals who deny most of these statements by labelling them false or mostly false are interpreted as being defensive and making deliberate efforts to present a favorable picture of themselves. High scores generally indicate normal, healthy, open response and a capacity for self-criticism. Extremely high deviant scores indicate that the individual lacks defenses and indeed may be pathologically undefended. Extremely low scores indicate extreme defensiveness.

Table 41 shows that the control subjects are quite frank and honest in responding to the self-criticism statements and that they make little effort to present a deceptively good picture of themselves. Although the scores for these groups are somewhat higher than those for the normative group, they fall within the normative group's limits, indicating a normal, healthy openness and capacity for self-criticism.

Analyses of variance (Appendix I) statistically demonstrate a significant difference between the control and the disturbed groups in self-criticism ability. For both disturbed groups, the mean scores on defensiveness are significantly higher than those of the control groups. Although these scores are not significantly reduced from the patient and normative groups, the reduction *per se,* coupled with significant deviant directions away from the control groups, give evidence of defensive distortions in conscious self-evaluation. It can be said that the Irish-American and the Italian-American control groups are less defensive than the disturbed groups.

Total Positive Score

This score reflects the overall level of self-esteem. Persons with high scores tend to like themselves and to feel that they are persons of worth. People with low positive scores are doubtful about their

Table 41

Mean Values—TDMH Self-Concept by Ethnicity and Comparisons with Patient and Normative Groups

Self-Concept Score	Irish-American		Italian-American		Patient Group	Normative Group	Exact p
	Control	Disturbed	Control	Disturbed			
Self-criticism	39.00 ***	33.16 ***	37.29 **	33.16 **	36.00	35.54	*** .001
							** .02
True-false	1.16	1.16	1.33	1.16	1.17	1.03	
Total positive	67.13	66.00	69.90	70.00	53.00	75.57	
Physical self	19.22	18.80	17.17	16.00	13.30	17.78	
Moral-Ethical self	n12.07 **	11.64	n13.70 *	12.17	11.20	16.33 **	** = .02
Psychological self	n12.67 *	10.16	n12.22 *	11.69	6.90	10.55 *	
Family self	n13.21 **	12.72	n14.45 **	15.52	10.80	16.83 **	(Irish)
							.025
Social self	13.32	10.84 *	14.05	14.86 *	11.00	14.07	
Abstract self	33.81 *	n26.84 **	35.47	31.48	26.20	37.10 *	.02
Behavior	19.35	19.32	n21.00 **	19.69	18.00	25.00 **	
Self-satisfaction	16.27	17.72	14.47	17.78	9.10	13.67	
Total consistency	n43.62 **	40.64	*49.26 **	*43.17	51.60	49.03 **	Footnote
Internal consistency	24.32 ***	20.76 **	30.73 ***	26.82 **	28.60	29.50 ***	*** .001
External consistency	20.29	20.72	18.47 **	21.95 **	23.00	19.60	** .02

t— * $p < .10$ ** $p < .05$ *** $p < .001$

NOTE: Columns with equal number of stars are given "t" distribution analyses and probability values for two compared groups.

Example: Self Criticism = Italian-American Control **, Italian-American Disturbed ** = $p < .05$

** Where (n) appears in upper left of mean value, this value is compared to the normative group and (*) symbol to upper right indicates p value.

NOTE: Total Consistency: Left lower star with mean value indicates the Irish-American control group and the Italian-American disturbed group differs from the Italian-American control group at $p < .10$.

own worth, feel depressed and unhappy, and have little confidence in themselves.

There are no significant differences between the ethnic groups and between the control and disturbed groups in total positive feelings (Appendix I). The standard deviations are large in both ethnic and normative groups, leading to non-significant comparisons. In line with Fitts's (86) patient groups, there are greater variations around the mean scores in the disturbed groups.

Some very mild distortion in the self-concept by the disturbed groups might be indicated in the greater defensiveness on the self-criticism scale. It is, of course, apparent that to perceive one's self in a totally negative light is an extremely threatening and traumatic state of affairs, and it is not surprising to find that these boys artificially increase positive views of themselves. Fitts (35) indicates that even within the representative patient groups, specifically diagnosed patient groups show differences in total positive scores. He indicates that patients with anxiety reactions have the most normal profiles on the scores. He states that these total positive scores may be held at the expense of more than average inconsistency between the external social areas and the internal personal areas. The Italian-American groups have lowered internal consistency. The active-aggressive components of their personalities enable these boys to seek self-esteem from their social environment. Internal balance is thus subject to external interpersonal harmony. Fitts (35) indicates the correlation between total positive scores and these aggressive traits on the Edwards Personal Preference Schedule to be low, but positive.

The adaptational maneuvers employed by the Irish-American groups enable them to deny aggression, to restrict affectivity, and to utilize ingratiating and compliant behavior in their social aspirations. Positive self-concepts are moderately correlated by Fitts with the use of such traits as order, deference for authority, and nurturance. These groups maintain their positive feelings at the expense of greater rigidity in the maintenance of internal balance. This is done especially for social approval, as is shown by a poorer "social" self-concept or by feelings of inadequacy in the realm of generalized others. This is associated with poorer positive feeling in the area of identity,—who he is in relation to other people. In contrast to the normative group, the Irish-American boys are dissatisfied with their moral-ethical behavior and with their sense of family self.

In both the control and the disturbed Irish-American groups,

Table 42

Mean Value Scores of Self-Concept (TDMH) by Social Class

Self-Concept Score	Irish-American Control			Irish-American Disturbed			Italian-American Control			Italian-American Disturbed		
	I–III	IV–V	"t"	I–III	IV–V	"t"	I–III	IV–V	"t"	I–III	IV	"t"
Total positive	45.00	75.78	*** 3.59 (p<.001)	42.22	70.63	1.80*		NS			NS	
Physical self	7.00	NS		12.98	20.58	2.32**		NS		12.81	19.75	3.00**
Moral-ethical self		13.04	1.91*		NS			NS			NS	
Psychological self	10.27	14.31	1.43*		NS			NS			NS	
Family self	NS	NS			NS			NS			NS	
Social self	10.50	15.85	1.83*		NS			NS			NS	
Abstract self		NS			NS			NS			NS	
Behavior		NS			NS			NS			NS	
Self-satisfaction		NS			NS			NS			NS	
Total consistency		NS			NS			NS			NS	
Internal consistency	27.22	21.05	1.92*		NS		32.14	26.50	2.19**	29.54	24.16	1.40*
External consistency		NS			NS			NS			NS	
	N=37			N=25			N=34			N=24		

t—* p<.10 ** p<.05 *** p<.01

there is significantly more positive feeling in the lower social classes. This finding is confirmed by the questionnaire, which showed that the lower-class boys in the Irish-American groups tend to socialize more, have more affiliations, and in general appear to manipulate their environment in a relatively more overt manner than do the upper-class boys. This is accompanied by more positive feelings in the social, moral-ethical, and psychological areas of the self-concept. They accomplish this with greater internal consistency.

Association of internal unity with more positive feelings in the Italian-American lower-class boys means that these boys are more concerned with external standards as criteria for self-evaluation. Thus, socialization and environmental manipulations dictate inner balance and positive feeling. In essence, adequate inner balance requires successful socialization and relatively confident environmental manipulation. The mechanisms of socialization thus are different for the two ethnic groups.

The Physical Self

In this area, the individual presents his view of his body, his state of health, his attitude about his physical appearance, his physical coordination and dexterity, and his sexuality.

Analyses of variance demonstrate no significant differences between the ethnic groups in positive feelings toward their physical selves. There are no differences between the ethnic group's and the normative group's mean values. The mean scores for the ethnic groups, both disturbed and control, are well above the mean score for the patient representative group.

Of the two disturbed groups, the Italian-American group has the lowest positive feeling toward the physical self; their mean score is closer to that of the personality disorders found by Fitts (mean score 16.10). Fitts (35) also indicates a moderate negative correlation between aggression, exhibitionism, dominance, autonomy, and the physical self. He indicates that positive correlations are evident between positive physical self-concepts and heterosexual drives, so the slightly lower physical scores for the Italian-American disturbed group are in keeping with the higher scores on exhibitionism, dominance, and aggression, and the reduction of heterosexual drives. We will observe in a later chapter that these boys included in their active social strivings frequent heterosexual activities, which they began younger than the Irish-American boys. We interpreted Don Juanism among the Italian-American boys as an effort to display and prove heterosexual attitudes.

Normative positive feeling toward the physical self by the boys in the Irish-American disturbed group may be higher because of increased affiliation with male peers, as we will find in analysis of the questionnaire. Interaction with peer groups promotes a sense of self-esteem with regard to potential sexuality and the sublimation of sexuality through the exchange of sexual stories. The increased intraception in imaginative idealizations, which the Irish-American disturbed boys show, compensates for any depreciative attitudes that these boys might have toward their own physical prowess. Again, boys in the lower social classes have more positive feelings toward their physical selves. In view of the significantly lower heterosexual drive in this group of boys, the idealized image of the physical self differentiates this group from the more concrete, aggressive Italian-American group. An additional factor making for positive attitudes toward physique (power and prowess) emerges from the very active interest boys of all the ethnic groups have in athletics and in the development of the power of their own bodies.

The Moral-Ethical Self

This score measures the attitude toward one's moral worth, the relationship to God, and the feelings of being a good or a bad person.

There are no significant differences between the ethnic groups in moral and ethical self-image. There are, however, differences between the ethnic and the normative groups in moral-ethical satisfaction. In this respect, the Irish-American control adolescents deviate most significantly from the normative group ($p < .02$). The Italian-American control group is only suggestively lower in moral-ethical satisfaction. Both Irish-American groups and the Italian-American disturbed group appear to approximate the neurotic score more than they do the normative scores.

A review of the mean values by ethnicity (table 41) illustrates that for both Irish-American groups, lower moral-ethical satisfaction appears in the area of the abstract sense of selfhood. These boys concern themselves with who and what they are in the eyes of others and in relation to what they should be. They have less confidence in their self-image in relation to their family role. Aggressive feelings and guilt over transgressions couple with less adequate self-identification.

The Italian-American groups are not satisfied with their moral-ethical selves, but their problems appear to concern satisfaction with their actual behavior. This orientation implies concreteness in perceiving oneself and one's relationships with other people.

The Irish-American control group shows more positive orientation to its moral-ethical code in the lower classes, yet these classes have still less positive orientations to selfhood as family members than in the normative group.

Although Fitts (35) indicates that there are no differences in the self-concept between adolescents and adults, division of adolescents into ethnic groupings appears to produce more deviant scores from the normative in moral-ethical values. Comparisons with the normative group indicate that the Irish-American boys differentiate from the Italian-American boys on the basis of associations between moral-ethical values, identity, and values in other categories of selfhood. These differential components of the self-image that make one ethnic group different from another in its stylistic maneuvers, confirms our previous findings of passive aggression in the service of compliance, and active aggression in the service of defiance. These factors exaggerate in disturbance because of suppressed aggression in the Irish-American boys and the potential for impulsivity in the Italian-American boys.

The Psychological Self

The score on the psychological self reflects the individual's sense of personal worth and his feelings of adequacy. This part of the test permits him to evaluate his personality apart from his relationships to other people.

There are no overall differences in this area with regard to a sense of general personal worth. In this study, the boys in the disturbed groups appear to be more satisfied with their psychological selves than do those in the patient group. Difficulties over moral-ethical principles, identity, and behavior do not necessarily indicate inadequate feelings, but rather adolescent confusion.

In contrast to the representative patient scores, the boys in these ethnic groups, both control and disturbed, can admit both positive and negative things about themselves and maintain some semblance of personal adequacy. In terms of scores tabulated later, we can state that the boys in both ethnic groups are relatively more satisfied with themselves in terms of their own ideals and what they feel they want to be. They tend to rate themselves by what they are, as opposed to what they are not. These factors all indicate optimistic conceptions of selfhood in the interest of personal improvement. It appears that boys with adolescent adjustment reactions are not so anxious about feelings of worthlessness as they are about adequate masculine identifications and meeting adult roles in comfortable and socially approved ways.

The Family Self

This score reflects adolescent feelings of adequacy and worth as a family member. It refers to the adolescent's perception of himself in reference to his closest circle of associates.

There are no differences on F-ratio between the ethnic groups in primary group membership values. However, when the ethnic groups are compared to normative groups, they have less positive feeling for family membership. This is especially the case with the Irish-American control boys, while the disturbed boys exaggerate this difficulty. Resistance to maternal domination can indicate incipient rebellion in the cause of maturational autonomy.

The Irish-American values achieved on family group membership are in line with the findings on the questionnaire and on the Edwards Personal Preference Schedule. We found maternal domination in household affairs and a tight schedule of activities, which enforced dependence and decreased the sense of adequacy as a family member. The possibility of infringing rules and regulations is greater in the Irish-American group than in the Italian-American group, where such clock-bound activities do not exist.

The Irish-American disturbed group's mean score more closely approximates the neurotic score than it does the normative group score. In the questionnaire, we note that the Irish-American boys feel extremely dependent upon maternal domination, which broke their sense of personal worth within the family. The Irish-American boys endured domestic upheaval, during which they received little attention, and therefore they tended to feel that their families had little concern for them. They also suffered from weaker collateral kinship ties in contrast to the Italian-American boys.

The quality of family group membership for the representative

Italian-American boy shows in his ingratiation of his mother and greater obedience to his father. The Italian-American disturbed group maintains a sense of personal importance to the family even though it may leave the collateral family in search of self-esteem and personal adequacy in the community. In view of their greater impulsivity and dominance, family self-concepts suffer when these boys try to throw off the yoke of paternal authoritarianism. The clinical records illustrate concern and aid from the extended family in time of stress. These boys must realize that, despite their actions, they can go home again. Although they may object to paternal authoritarianism and defy what they consider to be irrational punishment, these boys feel that their mothers love them and forgive them. Although these boys love the members of their extended family, they feel it is time for them to prove to their fathers that they know better the ways of their own generation of men.

In summary, when the ethnic groups are compared to the normative group, differentiation of selves in terms of family images are apparent. The more compulsive home schedule of the Irish-American boy and the harsher discipline of the Italian-American boy tend to balance precariously feelings of adequacy as family members. In both ethnic groups, parental domination (maternal domination in the Irish-American groups and paternal domination in the Italian-American groups) exceeds participant functions. Participant functions and infringement of family regulations bring about different concepts of the self and one's place within the family.

The Social Self

The social self is described as the self as it is perceived in relation to other people. It reflects the person's sense of adequacy in social interaction with other people.

There is a distinct difference between the Irish-American and the Italian-American groups with regard to feelings of social adequacy (table 5 in Appendix I). This difference between the two ethnic groups heightens in disturbance (table 41). The Irish-American groups extend their feelings of inadequacy from primary group membership to general social relationships. We noted that the Irish-American control group's lower classes have more positive self-images with regard to the generalized others than do its upper classes. These social class findings do not appear in the disturbed group (table 42). The findings in disturbance, as with the Edwards

Personal Preference Schedule, appear to fuse in favor of ethnic findings. The Irish-American disturbed group projects its inadequacies of selfhood in relation to other people on a par with the patient group.

There is consistently less Irish-American positive feeling toward secondary groups than Italian-American, as we have inferred from the previous findings. On the Life-Space-Drawing, the Irish-American "Me" circles were smaller and these boys saw themselves as more insignificant socially, while the Italian-American boys contrasted with illustrations of greater participant and influential capacities in general social intercourse. The clinical records also illustrated the withdrawal pattern of the Irish-American boy and the projective pattern of the Italian-American boy.

It is understandable that these mechanisms of autistic thinking and withdrawal found in the Irish-American boys would accompany diminished relationships to primary and secondary groups. Cognitions and perceptions of the self in relationship to other people reveal why the Irish-American boys relate to specifically perceived significant people in the environment, while the Italian-American boys relate to others in a more all-inclusive way. The Irish-American boy would appear to have small potential for delinquency, for he scores high in self-criticism, and questions his moral-ethical ideal. Such a boy would find it rather difficult to engage in aggressive social acts, because he is busy with moral self-criticism and abstract meditations about himself and his significance in relation to other people. In disturbance, he retires to a better world of fantasy.

Abstract Self-Identity

This scale is an integral part of the internal frames of reference. These frames of reference take into consideration what the individual says about himself and how satisfied he is with himself and with his actual behavior. In the description of identity, the individual seeks primarily to describe what he is by evaluating his personal traits and characteristics. Fitts (35) considers this to be one of the most basic areas of the self-concept.

There are significant overall differences between the ethnic groups in identity values (table 6, Appendix I, table 41 in text), and differences are particularly evident between the disturbed and the control groups. In addition, there are interactions between ethnicity and the disturbed-control variables.

The boys in the Italian-American control group have the highest positive feelings of personal identity, and the group's mean value is equivalent to that of the normative group. The Irish-American control boys have lower positive feelings than do the Italian-American and the normative boys. This exaggerates in disturbance, where the Irish-American boys clearly approximate the patient group's mean value.

The representative Irish-American boy is more critical of himself, denies fewer negative statements about himself, and is more internally consistent in all of the areas of his self-image.

The typical adolescent view of American maleness presents the Irish-American boy with two difficulties. First, this boy has to find a way to escape maternal domination. Second, he has to learn an "I dare to discover" attitude. In contrast to the Italian-American boy, his greater dependency leaves him open to tremendous conflict between maternal domination and striving for masculine autonomy.

Behavior

This scale is made up of items that say "this is what I do" or "this is the way I actually act." This score measures the individual's perception of his own behavior or the way he functions.

The study adolescents' perceptions of their behavior are not statistically differentiated by the ethnic groups. However, tests of significance (table 41) indicate that the typical Italian-American control boy has significantly lower positive feelings toward his own behavior than do the normative subjects. Although the Irish-American control and disturbed group mean values resemble those of the patient group, the standard deviations are large and make no contribution to other than chance differences from the representative groups.

The representative Italian-American control boys are more satisfied with the perception of themselves in the abstract, but they do not appear to be so happy with their actual behavior. The representative boy perceives himself as an identifiable individual with sex, age, and cognitive-social roles. His greatest behavioral difficulties appear to be in the area of moral and ethical standards and orientation to his self-image as a family member. This boy may be eager to escape paternal control. In view of the Italian-American group's strong heterosexual drives and spontaneity in behavior, moral and ethical values are directed towards female dating patterns. These boys have relative internal inconsistency, since they rely upon group guidelines for social approval.

The Italian-American disturbed adolescents, however, do not show dissatisfaction with their actual behavior, when their mean values are compared to those of the normative group. Although their scores appear to approximate the patient group more, the standard deviation loosely clusters the group mean between the patient and the normative group. In view of their relative satisfaction, we can infer that in disturbance the Italian-American boys feel justified in their hostile behavior and their bold opposition to authority. When we study the consistency scores, we discover that the Italian-American disturbed boys are not as emotionally labile as the control boys. Internal consistency has tightened, and there is more variability between the different selves on external levels. Examination of the scores reveals that this boy has become more defensive and stereotyped in his self-concept.

Although stereotyping and defensiveness are apparent, the boys exhibit greater self-integration at the expense of significantly reduced self-criticism. Their mean values show satisfaction in abstract concepts of selfhood and satisfaction with their own adequacy and influence in the field of human relationships. In the questionnaire we will see that even the Italian-American boy's daydreams are pragmatic, especially when they concern how to get even with paternal authority. In addition, we saw, however, on the Edwards Personal Preference Schedule, that the Italian-American disturbed boy was capable of abasement and could feel pangs of conscience. Where the control boy is identifiable according to the role he plays in society, the disturbed boy restricts his imaginative faculty, defends his adequacy and sense of worth, justifies his behavior, and seeks adventure among those who appreciate him. The Italian-American disturbed pattern contrasts with that exhibited by the Irish-American disturbed boys. The Irish group is satisfied with its behavior in their relationships to significant other. Their foremost problems are "Who am I?" and "Am I good?"

Self-Satisfaction

The self-satisfaction score comes from those items wherein the individual describes how he feels about the self that he perceives. This score reflects the level of self-acceptance.

Self-satisfaction is high in both ethnic groups. Although these boys are able to accept negative statements about themselves and have scruples about their moral-ethical principles, they feel that they are persons of worth and esteem themselves accordingly. Despite problems with regard to becoming the kind of person they would like to be, they are able to accept themselves and to move forward in their characteristic ways.

Both disturbed groups have non-significantly higher scores on self-satisfaction. Two factors may be responsible for these higher scores. Fitts (86) described his patient group as being more negative in abstract descriptions of selfhood, but more positive than the normative groups in self-acceptance. He indicated that this may be due to defense and resistance in the justification of feelings. The disturbed boys' higher scores, then, may be false positive self-acceptance scores. On the other hand, the boys in both disturbed groups are receiving therapy, in which one hopes to gain as a by-product positive feelings toward the self and increased self-acceptance.

Variability Scores

The variability scores provide a measure of the amount of inconsistency from one area of self-perception to another. These scores are inverse in that high scores mean that the subject is quite variable and inconsistent from one area of self-perception to another, while low scores indicate higher consistency that might even approach rigidity in the extreme. The variation is divided into total consistency, internal consistency, and external consistency.

Total Consistency

Total consistency represents the total amount of consistency for the entire record of the individual. High scores mean that there is a poorly integrated self-concept. This person tends to compartmentalize certain areas of the self and to view these areas apart from the remainder of the self. Lower scores indicate greater self-integration, and extremely low scores suggest extreme rigidity and defensiveness.

Analyses of variance (table 7 in Appendix I) demonstrate overall ethnic differences that affect the disturbed-control variable. The Italian-American control group's variability in the different areas of the self-concept is no different from the rest of the population. Tests of significance, however, indicate that the Irish-American control group is significantly more consistent in self-perception than the Italian-American group or the normative group ($p < .05$). This ethnic pattern carries over into the disturbed groups (table 41). Here, the Irish-American group is suggestively more consistent than the control group, while the Italian-American boys rigidify overall consistency in the interest of defensive upheaval, even while their mean values remain higher than those of the Irish-American boys. The Irish-American control group and the two disturbed groups have variability values that are significantly below the normative scores and the Italian-American control scores. This relative invariability in the different areas of the self indicates rigidity, defensiveness, and guardedness.

Somewhat more hedging and guarding was described for these groups on the true-false task approach. In these tasks, they tended to employ more responses that indicated a statement was only "partly true." At the same time, there is rigidity shown in the weight given to certainty or "absolute truth" answers. On ethnic and adolescent levels, this means that they find it harder to deny negative characteristics about themselves. They tend to see things as "they are" rather than "what they are not." They conform more closely to the ideals of traditionalism, with greater conformity and stereotyping in reference to "what they should be." The Italian-American disturbed boys achieve the same invariability in scores with ego deflation, social punishment, and the necessity to sit back and look at themselves because their behavior has met with disapproval.

It is not so much the integration of the self-image that suffers in modal Italian-American disturbance as it is a defensive reinforcement of individuality and autonomy for the resolution of personal problems. The more highly integrated and rigidified consistency within the Irish-American groups is understandable when one considers that their personality shows more compulsive attention to detail, a greater sense of order and organization, and more suppression of aggression and the utilization of compliance in order to gain social approval. The Italian-American disturbed boys achieve self-image integration at the expense of lower self-criticism. This a defensive phenomenon allowing for justification of deviant attitudes.

Internal Consistency

Internal consistency measures and summarizes the variations stemming from the differences between the abstract conception of basic identity, self-satisfaction, and the perception of one's actual behavior.

There are differences in internal consistency, not only between the ethnic groups but also between the disturbed-control groups (table 8 in Appendix I). This is an important area in differentiating the way in which both the control and the disturbed boys in the ethnic groups see themselves. The Irish-American groups are significantly more unified and integrated in viewing themselves as individuals from an introspective frame of reference. They have more rigid internal frames of reference than have the Italian-American groups. Their self-integration is based upon introspective individuality in the realization of an ideal based upon "goodness and shouldness." Evidence of this phenomenon appears in dissatisfaction with the self in some of the external areas of selfhood. Difficulties in ego identity are coupled with difficulties in assuming the role of the social self. The development of ideal individuality is framed by the various "should be's" of self, from physical and psychological to family and social types. They rigidify the self as an abstract individual apart from the many social and psychological roles the self must play. Compartmentalizing the self to play several roles does not reduce the difficulty in realizing identity.

In the Italian-American groups, internal and external frames are brought into unity. There is evidence they restrict their imaginative faculty and identify the self-image according to the variable roles they play. The Italian-American boys' self-images are more loosely bound to several social selves and more integrated into a socially bound totality. Although the boys in the Italian-American disturbed group have greater internal consistency than the boys in the control groups, they are not more rigid in their stereotyping and defensiveness than the normative group. In addition, these boys are more completely integrated in terms of internal and external unity than are the Irish-American disturbed boys. We might say that these boys are more defensive in their independence and self-assertion; they defend their right to be themselves.

In both control groups the boys in the lower social classes are more internally consistent (table 42). Again, the Italian-American boys appear to make less use of stereotype, and are less rigid than the Irish-American boys. Interestingly, the lower-class Irish-American control boys have more positive feelings toward moral-ethical selves, psychological selves, and social selves. The more rigid internal unity may indicate a defensive distortion in positive feeling because they cannot accept dissatisfaction with the self, or more likely the explanation for this phenomenon lies in the fact that the Irish-American group's upper classes are somewhat more egocentric than are the lower classes. This means that the Irish-American control upper-class boys are more imaginative and self-critical in their introspection. They idealize the relative goodness of a concept in greater extreme. The adolescent does not outgrow, even for the sake of autonomy, the unilateral respect and maternal dominance characterizing the initial moral constraint imposed by the adult in the upper classes. The questionnaire shows that for the Irish-American boy in the lower social classes, moral restraint is coupled with more overt socialization and affiliation.

The Irish-American boy in the lower classes has greater opportunity to utilize the different selves and has greater freedom of movement in the community. Thus, in spite of a highly developed internal frame of reference in which good and evil are opposed, the lower-class Irish-American boy is given reinforcement for greater sociocentricity and endurance on a competitive basis. He is thus somewhat more pragmatically oriented than his upper-class counterpart. The Irish-American upper-class boy is given the reverse in the form of exaggerated concepts of good as opposed to evil. In disturbance, the social class factors fuse toward ethnic phenomena.

External Consistency

This score measures and summarizes inconsistencies or variabilities between the external frames of reference: the physical, psychological, moral-ethical, family, and social self.

The overall significance of the analysis of variance is only crudely suggestive of possible differences between the ethnic groups and between the disturbed and control groups (table 9 in Appendix I).

The Italian-American control group has suggestively greater consistency, in keeping with normative values, in mirroring the self in social-psychological roles. In disturbance, however, the Italian-American group is significantly more inconsistent than its control group ($t = 2.20$, $p < .05$). However, its value does not exceed the normative group value. Relatively greater stereotyping and rigidifying of the "internal" self is focused upon social punishment and social disapproval of delinquent acts, where attention is forcefully brought to oneself.

In the case of the Irish-American group, a boy's anxiety over counter-aggression by the parent, or over anticipated loss of parental love, may lead him to suppress his hostility and to incorporate his parent's prohibitions so that his behavior and self-judgment are modeled after that of the parent. Stereotyping of the self and self-criticism can be high in the interest of conformity and approval. He brings about defensive mechanisms to achieve approval, in consequence of inferiority feelings, by compliance to regulation and a high sense of order. He sees himself in his many social roles as something apart from his ideal self. This boy would like to be accepted for the individual that he is, rather than for the kinds of roles he is forced to play.

The Italian-American boy is geared for action, social approval, and self-assertion to prove masculinity. He is integrated for control, aggressive influence, and autonomy in the face of pressure for too much conformity. He becomes obsequious only in a state of trust, or to avoid further punishment. This boy has normal abasement qualities so it is a question whether his delinquent potentialities will become a reality. He is oriented to a sense of strength, as opposed to a sense of weakness, and to social maneuverability as opposed to conditioned action.

A Point of View

An ego identity is a set of strived-for goals in identification with a given social reality. Ego identity seeks a definition of selfhood that is internally and socially directed. The ego, as the judiciary power of the unconscious and conscious processes of the individual, permits a conscious self-awareness as an outgrowth of, and a reaction to, the familial background from which an individual grows.

The boys in the Irish-American homes and the boys in the Italian-American homes differ in their home conditioning. The Irish-American boy's personality evolves in a maternally dominated and compulsively ordered home, while the Italian-American boy is a product of a home which permits the development of overt affective relationships and spontaneity in the expression of emotional aggression.

The self-concepts of the Irish-American boys appear to focus more upon good-evil dimensions, while self-concepts of the Italian-American boys appear to focus more on strong-weak dimensions. A broad difference between the Irish-American and the Italian-American boys in disturbance lies in the ability to live under someone else's emotional constraint or to live under no one's emotional constraint. The Italian-American boy's search for a true identity is activistic and outgoing. Rather than seek identity in reflective quests for essence in life, he searches for it in social relationships and in the manipulation of social roles.

The Irish-American boy regards the norms of society as intrinsically significant and experiences them as desirable in and of themselves. He internalizes various general standards which determine his evaluations of the self and others. Divergence from normative standards of society is defined by the disturbed boy as "wrong," regardless of any other resultant gains to himself. He defines the self as the locus of responsibility, and feels guilty when he diverges from societal norms perceived as significant. This kind of person may be more concerned with the good opinion of those in their primary groups: close friends and relatives.

The Irish-American boy will not think of himself in terms of his potency or power. He will value opinions of significant other people who agree with his own idealistic conceptions of emotional selfhood and internal discipline. He feels overt aggression and hostility to be dangerous and disorderly traits, foreign to a desired selfhood. The Irish-American boy experiences aggression with guilt and counteracts it by sublimation with a set of acceptable ideals. In disturbance, the Irish-American boy withdraws from social support and finds it lacking. The Italian-American boy seeks new sources of social support until he finds appreciative groups who will accept his manipulations and aggressive acts.

The modalities of the ethnic groups seem to differentiate most significantly in terms of Irish-American egocentrism and Italian-American sociocentrism.

9

The Questionnaire

This chapter attempts to amplify and sharply focus the life experiences of the adolescents in the four groups under study. The psychological instruments have indicated contrasts in life styles and experiences on the basis of ethnic grouping. In this chapter, the data from these instruments will be enriched and colored by the narrative reports of the adolescents themselves. The questionnaire was formulated according to a conceptual scheme covering the following broad areas of investigation: intrafamilial relationships, attitudes concerning school, vocational aspirations, attitudes toward male and female peers, and leisure-time activities.

The chi-square test was used to determine whether significant differences existed between frequency distributions. We used actual numbers in the computations and employed correction for continuity if we expected less than ten cases in any one cell. Significance was defined at the 0.05 level; however, we considered levels of $p < .10$ suggestive of differences between the two ethnic groups. The Fisher-Yates (32) test of significance in two-by-two contingency tables was consulted for critical values in those disturbed groups where frequencies were very small. In all computations, we held the social classes for each group constant, and computed chi-square evaluations for significant differences.

Intrafamilial Relationships

Numerous studies indicate that the family environment is a critical force in personality development. Internal family patterns during an individual's childhood shape many of his crucial relationships with other people who influence his social and psychological adjustment. The study views the family as a structure of roles based upon age and sex. Generational role relationships help to form a picture of home and family that molds the ways in which the younger generation perceives the world and adds to its diversity.

The Control Groups

When the boys in both control groups were asked "which person they thought and acted like the most," the majority chose the father. The 25 percent who designated "other" people for identification specifically stated that they thought and acted like "no one." The great emphasis upon father identification is of real interest

Table 43
"Which person do you think and act like the most?"

Choice	Irish-American Control	Irish-American Disturbed	Italian-American Disturbed	Italian-American Control
	%	%	%	%
Mother	10.00	40.00	41.70	20.80
Father	67.50	40.00	37.50	52.90
Other	22.50	20.00	20.80	26.30
Total	100.00	100.00	100.00	100.00
	N=40	N=25	N=24	N=34

$$x^2 = 8.49, 2 \text{ d.f.}, \quad x^2 = \text{N.S.} \quad x^2 = 3.01, 2 \text{ d.f.};$$
$$p < .02 \qquad\qquad\qquad\qquad p < .20$$

when it is remembered that on the Life-Space Drawing the boys chose the mother as that person in closest proximity to them. This is further corroborated on the questionnaire when the boys were again asked which person they felt closest to. Again, in both ethnic groups, 65 to 78 percent of the boys chose the mother. There is no difference between the social classes in either group.

While strong masculine identifications exist, 45 to 50 percent of the boys in both ethnic groups turned to persons other than their own parents for discussion of their personal problems. The majority of these boys prefer to go to friends for help. Approximately 10 percent of the Irish-American boys chose priests as confidantes. In contrast, 9 percent of the Italian-American boys went to "no one."

Here, the Irish-American boys defer to authority when friendships do not provide solace for problem solving.

Most of the boys prefer to discuss personal difficulties with peer groups but revert to one or both parents 35 to 40 percent of the time in the case of serious problems. Although one-fifth of the boys still go to outside sources with problems of great personal concern, the Irish-American boys prefer priests and friends, while the Italian-American boys prefer counseling by uncles and friends.

Furthermore, in the Irish-American group there is a significant social class finding ($p<.01$). Fifty-four percent of the lower-class boys choose the mother as a confidante, while 50 percent of the upper-class boys prefer sources outside the family. This lower-class phenomenon is in line with maternal choice and mother domination in the Irish-American groups, and exaggerates in disturbance. Thirty percent of the middle-class boys go to a priest, and 40 percent go to a close friend. These boys stated that their mothers would not understand, and that their fathers were not "helpful."

Emotional attachment to both parents is evident, for the majority of the boys reported that they felt that their parents were interested in them, understood them, and were interested in helping them work out their problems. However, the majority of the boys in both ethnic groups indicated that they felt the mother was the more interested of the two parents. The Irish-American mother was the manager of the household, while the Italian-American mother was the ingratiating parent, in contrast to the more authoritarian father.

The Disturbed Groups

Both disturbed groups show greater patterns of maternal identification, indicated by more frequent choice of the mother for the resolution of personal problems. Also, table 43 indicates that these groups, as in previous findings, have lower masculine identification than the control groups, and this lack of masculine identification has been a consistent offending symbol. In corroboration of the Life-Space Drawing, over 60 percent of the disturbed boys feel closest to their mothers. The rest of the boys in both disturbed groups prefer female extended kin, again corroborating the Life-Space Drawing in which greater emphasis is placed upon female kin relationships. The Irish-American boys are stronger in this orientation than are the Italian-American boys.

The choices of "other" persons for identification are mainly choices made as "no one." When these boys do choose confidantes for aid in the resolution of problems, there is no significant difference from choices made by the control groups. Friendships and peer group relationships apparently hold strong attractions to adolescents in need of empathy and understanding.

The majority of the boys feel that their parents are interested in helping them work out their problems, attributing most interest to their mothers. Most Irish-American boys feel that their parents understand them, but approximately half of the Italian-American disturbed boys do not. When the Irish-American boys state that their parents are interested in them and try to help them in spite of parental separation, these boys deny hostility toward parents and hide behind facades of proper ritualistic behavior even though they feel rejected and abandoned. Many of these boys were placed in residence and saw their parents only occasionally, if at all, but on the Life-Space Drawing, we saw that these boys clung tenaciously to extended family members in efforts to have some feeling of belonging to a primary social unit. The Italian-American disturbed boys more openly express their closeness to the maternal bond. They are more pragmatic and openly admit that they do not think their parents understand them. As inferred from the Life-Space Drawing, these boys, in their own minds, give up extended family connections.

In the Italian-American upper-classes there are interesting findings consistent with previously discovered phenomena. Almost half of the boys in this social class prefer to confer with friends, while 36 percent go to their mothers. These preferences contrast with almost 70 percent of lower-class boys, who seek their fathers as confidantes ($p < .01$). These findings add to data that point out that the boys have fathers who are more authoritarian, who punish them more, who demand more honesty and more achievement orientation, and who appear to manage a more authoritarian home. Upper-class boys apparently do not feel that they can go to their fathers for understanding, and they therefore seek out either their mothers or their friends.

In summary, the control groups manifest masculine identifications, with equivalent needs for the other parent in the resolution of personal problems. These findings are in line with those of Brittain (9). He indicates that parent/peer alternatives in making certain choices direct the adolescents toward peer conformity in some situations and toward parent conformity in other situations. He states that adolescents are more disposed toward parent conformity when the emphasis is upon the problem of long-term decisions. He predicts that when choices are in line with a larger society and with status positions that one can aspire to as an adult, then choices are made with the parents, who are perceived to be the more competent guides.

In disturbance, maternal dominance appears less in Italian-American families than in Irish-American families. The Italian-American group also prefers succorance from peer-group friendships. Choice of the father for problem-solving appears more ritualistic than preferred. A large percentage of the Italian-American disturbed boys come to perceive their parents as those who do not understand them. In the upper classes, the boys especially prefer other friendships for problem-solving tasks. This is part of the complex that involves more vigorous paternal authority and a resulting lack of communication.

In the Irish-American disturbed group there are more choices of the mother in areas of parent-child communication. The Edwards Personal Preference Schedule shows that the heterosexual drive was lower among these boys, and throughout the four instruments, this consistently has been shown to be associated with greater maternal dominance.

These findings are in line with the generalizations of Barrabee and Von Mering (4), who, in their study of ethnic variations and mental stress, indicate that the Irish-American boy shows a sex-linked preferential solicitude for the mother. They point out that the son experiences little aggression and accepts subordination. They indicate that the Italian-American boy is the recipient of sex-linked preferential treatment from both parents. This is indicated by paternal dominance and maternal oversolicitous affection.

Pattern of Home Rule, Infringement, and Punishment

In maintaining itself, a family establishes modes of communication and shared cognitive orientations. Ritualistic patterns within the family structure help to solidify the ongoing family behavior and to keep it oriented toward certain goals. Analysis of intrafamilial and subordinate-authoritarian relationships indicates variations and differences between the Italian-American and the Irish-American groups. These differences appear to be more significant from an ethnic viewpoint than from a social class viewpoint. The pattern of home rule amplifies the findings produced by the Edwards Personal Preference Schedule. We hope that the picture of home and family here developed will aid the reader to visualize the relatively democratic Irish-American mode versus the relatively authoritarian Italian-American pattern of intrafamilial relationships.

The Control Groups

The boys in both ethnic groups were asked to state what kind of rules they had in their homes, how they were punished for disobeying the rules, and what freedom they felt to argue against enforcement of certain home rules and regulations they thought conflicted with their rights in the family.

There are interesting differences between the ethnic groups over home management and in the way parental control is achieved. The Irish-American boys enumerated rules for everything. There are times to eat, times to sleep, times to play, times to do homework, and times to dress in certain ways. A higher proportion of these boys had a clock-bound schedule that set a time for most routine daily activities. The Irish-American boys appear to be subjected to a high level of parental pressure "not to come home late." It is for the disobedience of this rule that the greatest percentage (50 percent) of punishment was administered. In contrast, only about one-third of the Italian-American control boys were bound to the clock for scheduling of routine patterns. In addition, church attendance was stressed far less in the Italian-American group, but help with the housework was stressed to a greater degree. In spite of the seemingly freer home regimes among the Italian-American boys, there are indications of harsher authority over the boys and less constructive participation in the rituals of the home.

In response to the question "Which parent or guardian makes sure you obey these rules?" the Irish-American boys stated that both parents were harmonious and cooperative in this respect. In contrast to this, 47 percent of the Italian-American control boys reported that the fathers enforced obedience. However, approximately 65 percent of the boys in both ethnic groups state that when rules were disobeyed and the home regime was upset, the father was the ultimate authority who exacted punishment for disobedience.

In response to the question "What kind of rules do they punish you for not obeying?" approximately 50 percent of the boys in both groups stated that they were punished for coming home late. Tabulation of other rules that are disobeyed yields results suggestive of

Table 44
Home Rule and Regulation Established by Parents

	Irish-American Control	Italian-American Control	Irish-American Disturbed	Italian-American Disturbed	Social Class Italian-American I–III	Disturbed IV–V
	%	%	%	%	%	%
Rules for						
Everything	50.00	32.35	32.14	20.93	9.00	18.00
Church	12.50	5.88	28.57	00.00	00.00	00.00
Home arrival	22.50	70.58	28.57	31.16	42.86	22.76
Homework	30.00	23.50	7.14	20.93	14.28	27.27
Housework	5.00	23.50	3.57	27.90	23.80	31.81
	N=40	N=34	N=25	N=24		

$x^2 = 24.49$, 3 d.f., $x^2 = 19.16$, 4 d.f., $x^2 = 16.92$, 3 d.f.,
$p < .001$. $p < .001$ $p < .001$

First 2 categories combined for chi-square

ethnic differences ($x^2 = 5.16$, 2 d.f.; $p < .10$). Forty percent of the Irish-American boys are punished for failing to obey the rules of the house and failing to carry out orders given them by their parents. Only 21 percent of the Italian-American boys are punished for such disobedience. At the same time, the Italian-American boys give a somewhat greater response for failure to do their homework (14.70 percent) in contrast to the Irish-American boys who are so punished (4.54 percent).

In answering the questionnaire on the frequency of punishments, the boys divided evenly between punishment more than once a month and punishment less frequently. One boy stated, in singular fashion, "I am to behave as if my mother were standing next to me." Significantly, more Italian-American boys were punished more than once a month for coming home late. There is some suggestion ($p < .10$) that the Italian-American group's upper classes punish more frequently than its lower classes. Sixty-four percent of the upper-class boys are punished at least once a month. Lower-class boys are punished once in two to six months. Although crudely suggestive, this finding does fall in line with the general findings of greater authoritarianism in the upper-class structure of this group.

Punishment for the infringement of rules takes on different forms in the control groups. Significantly, more Italian-American boys are physically punished for infringement of rules, while verbal punishment and removal of privileges are the forms chosen by the Irish-Americans.

In both groups, the mothers praise the boys for tasks well done more often than the fathers do. Although there is a tighter regime of order in the Irish-American group, the fathers take an active hand in praise and encouragement as well as in punishment. This is in line with Barrabee and Von Mering (4), who assert that the Italian-American boy is the recipient of little affection from both parents. Beyond this finding, other data in this study contradict the findings of Barrabee and Von Mering. The Italian-American boy in this study appears to receive affective displays not only through physical punishment but also through a concern of both parents individually who assume their particular roles in the care of the boy. Affectional overtones in preference for the mother is linked with a high potential for identification with the father.

Although there is greater order in the Irish-American household, there is more pronounced succorance from both parents. There is not only more parental harmony and active interest in the son, but also a greater sense of freedom to argue and to express a viewpoint, in spite of the greater restrictions in the Irish-American homes. Sig-

Table 45
Form of Punishment

Form	Irish-American Control	Italian-American Control	Irish-American Disturbed	Italian-American Disturbed	Social Class Italian-American I–III	Disturbed IV–V
	%	%	%	%	%	%
Scolded with privileges removed	90.00	73.62	88.00	54.16	18.18	76.92
Physical punishment	10.00	26.38	12.00	45.84	81.82	23.08
Total	100.00	100.00	100.00	100.00	100.00	100.00
	$N=40$	$N=34$	$N=25$	$N=24$		

$x^2=4.05$, 1 d.f., $p<.05$. $x^2=6.85$, 1 d.f., $p<.01$. Fisher-Yates $p<.042$.

nificantly, fewer Italian-American boys feel free to argue for or defend their point of view in family affairs (table 46). In the Italian-American home, succorance is mainly from the mother since she is the principal person who praises the boy. It is thus logical to assume that since the father is more harsh and exacting and since he is the ultimate punishment figure but not the ultimate figure in praise, succorance is a greater need among Italian-American adolescents, and they satisfy it outside the family. They handle deference for authority more by avoiding contact with discipline, especially when there is less freedom to defend oneself in the family.

Of the Italian-American group's lower classes, a significantly high majority (80 percent) state that they have the freedom to argue, as

Table 46
Freedom of Argument in the Home

Response	Irish-American Control	Italian-American Control	Irish-American Disturbed	Italian-American Disturbed
	%	%	%	%
Yes	90.00	61.76	68.00	41.66
No	10.00	38.24	32.00	58.34
	100.00	100.00	100.00	100.00
	N=40	N=34	N=25	N=24

$$x^2 = 8.24, 1 \text{ d.f.,} \qquad x^2 = 3.51, 1 \text{ d.f.,}$$
$$p < .01 \qquad\qquad p < .10$$

opposed to a minority of the upper classes (43 percent). Since frequency of punishment for home rule infraction was less for the lower classes (once every two to six months), and since they have greater freedom to argue for what they feel to be their rights, a straining toward more conforming behavior is evident in Italian-American upper classes.

The majority of boys in both groups make positive attempts to please their parents by submitting to parental direction and demands. In the Irish-American group, there is an effort to keep relationships intact by facades of pleasantness and by the maintenance of "be polite, don't damage relations" attitudes. These boys try to be neutral and placid.

In contrast, the Italian-American boys withdraw from conflicts with their parents. They handle authority-conforming relationships externally and avoid hostility-guilt relationships with parental figures. These boys say that they "obey" voluntarily and "do what their parents advise." This modal coping with parental authority exaggerates in disturbance and contrasts even more highly with the Irish-American group. The Italian-American boys must get succorance outside the family. Hostility-guilt conflict with parental authority is thus handled through relationships outside the family circle, and is evidenced by greater release of aggression in the outer community circle.

Since the Irish-American boys show higher need for release of aggression (on the Edwards Personal Preference Schedule), submission to authority and conformity with parental ideals results in overcompensation elsewhere. The release of aggression in this group is sublimated into heightened desires for change and inner-directed fantasies of change.

The Disturbed Groups

In disturbance, the two ethnic groups exaggerate ethnic traits concerning home rule. Strict rules in the home still differentiate the Irish-American disturbed boys from the Italian-American. The Irish-American boys more frequently cite their parents' demands for church attendance and religious affiliations. In addition, there is increased parental pressure to arrive home "on time." In contrast to the Irish-American clock-bound variety of home rules, the Italian American boys are expected to participate in housework and to complete their homework. In addition, the Italian-American boys are still expected to arrive home at certain hours, and this is particularly evident in the upper classes ($p <.001$).

Significant social class differences in the Italian-American group indicate that many more lower-class boys are expected to do their homework and to help with the housework, while more upper-class boys are expected to arrive home on time (table 44). There apparently is an attempt on the part of parents in the upper classes to discipline the boys by keeping them off the street at certain hours and out of mischief. In contrast, the lower-class adolescents have detailed roles of good behavior and family participation. Social mobility, exemplified in stress on homework, is highly valued in Italian-American disturbance. Stress on church attendance is nil in either social class.

In both disturbed groups, as in the control groups, the father is the one who ultimately punishes the boy for infringement of the rules. However, in the Irish-American groups the mother still predominates in enforcing the rules of the home, while this is less the case in the Italian-American group.

The boys in both disturbed groups, as in the control groups, receive punishment more than once a month in approximately 68 percent of the cases. The majority of the Italian-American disturbed boys receive physical punishment for breaking home rules ($p<.01$) to a greater extent than their control group (table 45). This is particularly evident in the upper social classes where 82 percent of the boys are physically punished, while 77 percent of the boys in the lower classes are punished by having their privileges removed. This analysis amplifies the differences in the class structure of the Italian-American groups by confirming the greater rigidity in behavioral demands by upper-class fathers as well as greater authoritarianism in seeking overt conformity for their sons.

In both disturbed groups there are increased positive attitudes toward mothers who show some increase in household management. In disturbance, the choice of the mother as the one who enforces home rules and the choice of the mother as the one who gives praise and encouragement more often are significantly confirmed by first choice of mother on the Life-Space Drawing. These findings amplify the confused sexual identifications among the boys in both groups. In the Irish-American group, lack of security concerning the father figure as a participative member of the family may be due to broken homes (the boys live with the natural mothers and see the fathers little). In the Italian-American disturbed group, paternal punishment and control by physical force is evidence of harsher home rule, to which the Italian-American boy responds by the formation of negative attitudes toward home and family.

Tests of significance for the question "Do you worry about what your parents think of you?" indicate that considerably more Irish-American disturbed boys worry about what their parents think of them (80 percent) than do Italian-American boys (42 percent; $x^2=4.64$, 1 d.f., $p<.05$). Hostility-parent-guilt complexes differentiate the two ethnic groups in disturbance. The desire for succorance and dependency in the Italian-American disturbed boy makes him avoid parent-child conflicts and turns him pessimistically away from difficult family situations if he cannot remedy the authoritarian parental relationship under his own power. In contrast, the

Irish-American disturbed boy reacts by deferring to authority with abasement. This allows him to conform to the norms of the family group in order to avoid conflict in subordinate-authority relationships and to avoid feelings of inadequacy in seeking approval from others.

We can see amplifications of the foregoing data on differences in home environment and discipline in analysis of the boys' efforts to please their parents. In contrast to the neutrality and placidity of the Irish-American control boys, who are negatively oriented in pleasing their parents, in disturbance there is a positive reconstruction of a subordinate position. These boys give no negative reactions and instead attempt to get good grades in school, help parents voluntarily with tasks, "do an especially good job in what I do," and go to church regularly. One might say that this is a positive function of psychotherapy and group therapy, but if this therapeutic function exists, it has affected the Irish-American boys differently from the Italian-American boys, who are less constructive and more conscious of pessimistic feelings about the child-parent relationship. While 50 percent of the Italian-American disturbed boys feel that they want to please their parents by getting good grades, 30 percent of the boys please their parents by "staying out of trouble and keeping out of the way." Another 8 to 12 percent state that they "worry about their own feelings," that "they don't think I do things well," and that "I try to make them proud of me but it's no use, I don't do anything right."

If therapeutic intervention affects the pattern of efforts to please parents, the Irish-American boys effect a more passive-dependent release of aggression. They appease the hostility-guilt complex in parent-child relationships by conformity and endurance in the face of obstacles. The Italian-American boys appear to make little effort to reconstruct themselves in order to please their parents; they simply attempt to cast themselves in a less damaging light. External control enforces fatalistic views, with less freedom to explain or to defend one's behavior. In this group, endurance in self-imposed tasks in order to please the parents is at a minimum. This kind of reaction suggests active aggression as a release from external conformity and the hostility-guilt complex of parent-child relationships. Dominance, aggression, and exhibitionism, found on previous testing procedures, are amplified and find expression in leisure activities, peer groups, and heterosexual affiliations.

On the question of freedom of argument in the home, fewer

Irish-American disturbed boys feel free to argue than do the boys in the control group (Table 46). However, comparison of the disturbed groups shows there are still more Irish-American boys than Italian-American boys who feel free to argue in their own homes ($p < .10$). A more tightly bound schedule of rules and a reduction of the freedom to argue may relate to increased maternal dominance and maternal identification, with greater dependency upon the mother. It is conceivable that some of the Irish-American mothers, bearing the burdens of raising their children alone and separated from paternal help, are more stringent in enforcing the regulations of the home and are more aggressive in their demands for obedience. The Italian-American disturbed boys feel even less able to argue in their own homes than do the boys in the control group. This is a foreseeable finding in view of the fact that there is less identification with the father and less participative family feeling, with harsher paternal authority and consequent tendencies to seek wider community horizons.

If, according to Erikson (28), the development of a stable autonomous maturity is based on an initial foundation of trust, then the ego-ideal construct is shaped by the way of life of the ethnic family pattern. A meaningful resemblance between what the adolescent has come to see in himself and what others judge him to be produces the self-concept and identity starting within the family culture. In this study, the psycho-social image is patterned in basic subcultural relationships. Where the adolescents do not resolve their strains within the family, the Irish-American boy isolates himself and enters only stereotyped conforming relationships, while the Italian-American boy attempts to seek social relationships outside the family with sometimes improbable and delinquent partners.

Evidence of increased maternal domination in the disturbed groups corroborates and amplifies the Life-Space Drawing. The Irish-American boys show loss of father identification and loss of security in relationship with the father, while the Italian-American disturbed group sees the father as a harsher disciplinarian and as one whom the boy serves with confusion and defiance.

The differences in paternal relationships set up differences in masculine identification. In the Irish-American group, masculine identification is poor, and dependency and subordination are directed toward the mother. In the Italian-American group, masculine identification is confusing and the boys appear to imitate the dominance and aggression of the father in an attempt at masculine identification, while affection is directed to an ingratiating mother.

From this analysis of intrafamilial relationships and familial rituals, we can infer that the adolescent struggles with the symbol of authority within his ethnic subculture. The adolescent searches for a personal identity and autonomy as he sets up an ideal image of himself within the primary pattern of his family. This ideal image is extended into his community of peers.

If, as Coleman (19) states, adolescents look to their own peer groups to help shape their interests, these peer-group relationships grow out of previous adolescent subcultures that began in the home. The Irish-American and the Italian-American boys determine interpersonal relationships within peer groups differently, the Irish-American by passive aggression, the Italian-American by active aggression.

Conceptions of Self in Relation to One's World

Uncertainty Principle

In this section of the questionnaire we tried to see how restrictions in the home affect a boy's needs, his release of hostile impulses, and the necessary prerequisites for change.

We tried to determine adolescent daydreams, fantasies, and attitudinal perceptions that indicate in what way boys will respond to environmental presses. We also tried to determine any preconceived ideas of life itself and the philosophical speculations of the adolescent, particularly with reference to pragmatism or idealism in coping with stress. Pragmatic or idealistic conceptions of reality will reveal themselves in attitudinal responses to questions involving beliefs and principles of conduct.

The Control Groups

The tabulations indicate that the Irish-American and the Italian-American control groups differ significantly in response to the honesty-dishonesty principle. Although the majority of the boys in both groups state that in real life one cannot be completely honest, a larger majority of the Irish-American boys state that there is no necessity for being dishonest in real life.

One should notice that the answer to the category "don't know"

Table 47
"Do you agree with the statement that honesty is the best policy,
but in real life one can't be completely honest?"

Response Set	Social Class		Irish-American Control	Italian-American Control	Social Class	
	I–III	IV–V			I–III	IV–V
	%	%	%	%	%	%
Yes	66.66	68.18	65.00	53.00	71.42	40.00
No	33.34	22.72	27.50	17.64	00.00	30.00
Don't know	00.00	00.00	00.00	2.94	00.00	00.00
Uncertain	00.00	9.00	7.50	26.47	28.58	30.00
Total	100.00	99.90	100.00	100.05	100.00	100.00
			N = 40	N = 34		

Last two categories combined for chi-square analysis.

$x^2 = 1.45$, 1 d.f.; $x^2 = 6.22$, 2 d.f.; $x^2 = 3.25$, 1 d.f.;

$p = $ N.S. $p < .05$ $p < .10$

is practically non-existent. This probably indicates that the maturing boy has given the question of honesty in real life some thought. We can infer that there is a significantly higher idealistic rejection of dishonesty among the Irish-American boys, while the Italian-American shows a more concrete willingness to consider the question of honesty-dishonesty in life. This consideration stands out in exaggeration in the disturbed groups. Perhaps the somewhat greater religious conformity of the Irish-American boys may account for their rejecting the need for dishonesty. There has been a consistent tendency in this study for the Irish-American boys to exhibit greater internal conformity and a more rigid acceptance of moral principles of conduct, which may well be a factor in differentiating this group from the Italian-American group where external conformity is matched by autonomy and dominance in interpersonal philosophies of life. The Italian-American boys would sacrifice honesty, if necessary, to gain ascendence in social intercourse.

The Italian-American group again has suggestive social class differences with regard to the conflict between honesty and dishonesty. The differences are in line with previous data indicating greater parental discipline to conformity and greater physical punishment. Apparently more of the upper-class boys approve of dealing with life in a pragmatic manner, a mode they may have learned by experience through avoiding parental discipline by giving shrewd, less-than-honest, replies. In the lower classes, where there is less frequent and less severe physical punishment, there is less need for dishonesty.

The Disturbed Groups

In disturbance, certainty and uncertainty with regard to the principle of honesty shows an exaggeration of the control group pattern. The disturbed Irish-American boys adhere more rigidly to the principles of right and wrong, while the Italian-American boys adhere more to the principle of overt manipulation of the social environment which can include dishonesty to gain one's ends. There is a very crude tendency for both groups to respond more positively to the question of dishonesty in the lower classes $(p > .10)$.

The ethnic differences found with regard to dishonesty confirm the clinical differentiations and symptomology described in a previous section. That section gave evidence of more aggressive and delinquent patterns for the Italian-American disturbed boys and greater socially conforming patterns for the Irish-American disturbed boys. The principle or philosophy upon which these boys answered this question of honesty falls in line with their behavioral pattern in disturbance and reflects ethnic tendencies in everyday life.

Dependent conforming tendencies, as opposed to active-aggressive

Table 48
"Do you agree with the statement that honesty is the best policy,
but in real life one can't be completely honest?"

Response	Irish-American Disturbed	Italian-American Disturbed
	%	%
Yes	48.00	66.66
No	44.00	8.33
Uncertain	8.00	24.90
Don't know	00.00	00.00
Total	100.00	99.89
	N = 25	N = 24

Last two categories combined for x^2
$x^2 = 6.65$, 2 d.f.; $p < .05$

Table 49
Difficulty in Making Decisions

Response Set	Irish-American Disturbed	Italian-American Disturbed
	%	%
Yes	64.00	29.16
No	36.00	45.83
Uncertain	00.00	24.99
Total	100.00	99.98
	N = 25	N = 24

Last two categories combined for chi-square analysis.
$x^2 = 5.95$, 1 d.f.; $p < .02$

tendencies, again appear in response to the question on "difficulty in making decisions." Whereas there were no significant differences between the control groups in difficulty in making decisions or in what to make decisions about, the disturbed Irish-American boys showed heightened exaggerations of dependency in this regard while the Italian-Americans showed greater independence.

Two-thirds of the Irish-American boys feel that they have difficulty in making decisions. The disturbed boys lose autonomy and the ability to think independently as they become increasingly more conforming and dependent in their interpersonal relationships. We

Table 50
"What kind of things is it often difficult
for you to make up your mind about?"

Response	Irish-American Disturbed	Italian-American Disturbed
	%	%
Many things	32.00	8.33
Career choice	8.00	24.00
Religion and the goodness of life	00.00	8.33
The reason why other people behave differently	8.00	00.00
Girls and dates	12.00	12.00
Total	60.00	52.66

can infer passivity and dependent compulsive doubting as well, both from the clinical differentiations and from the high degree of desire for order and deference for authority.

When asked to define the content of their difficulties, 32 percent of the Irish-American boys stated that they had difficulty in making up their minds about "many things." This category consisted of such statements as "I imagine so many ways of doing the same thing," "I wonder if my homework is good," "I have to make up my mind to study and how to figure out problems," "Where to go in my spare time," and "If I like a guy." While 32 percent of the Irish-American boys made these kinds of statements, 24 percent of the Italian-American boys expressed consistent tension about career choice and the wish for successful completion of career goals. It is rather interesting to note that while a very small percentage of the Italian-American boys had doubts about religion and the goodness of life, the Irish-American boys, who had no doubts about this, had difficulties in making up their minds about why other people behaved differently. A large percentage of the boys did not answer this question; but when these categories are contrasted to those of the control groups, there is an increased response in various difficulties presented by the Irish-American boys.

Daydreams

Fifty percent of the Italian-American groups and approximately 70 percent of the Irish-American groups acknowledged daydreaming as a frequent phenomenon. It is the content of the daydream that is significant; whether the content is essentially pragmatic or idealistic. The idealistic daydream is concerned with the experiences of the good life that transcend the usual human experiences and that are not usually achievable in the imperfect world of reality. The pragmatic daydream refers to ruminations about one's practical life and its possibilities within the limits of reality.

The Control Groups

The Irish-American boys activate aggressive fantasies and wishful thinking for change, which cannot always be realized in reality. Daydreaming allows them to transcend reality while they externally practice conforming behavior.

Table 51
Content of Daydreams

Response	Irish-American Disturbed	Italian-American Disturbed	Irish-American Control	Italian-American Control
	%	%	%	%
Pragmatic	32.00	45.83	40.00	70.74
Idealistic	40.00	16.60	42.50	14.74
No Response	28.00	37.50	17.50	14.70
Total	100.00	99.93	100.00	100.18
	N = 25	N = 24	N = 40	N = 34

$x^2 = 3.25$, 2 d.f.; % < .20 $\qquad$ $x^2 = 7.82$, 2 d.f.; % < .02

The following categorization of idealistic and pragmatic daydream material contrasts the Irish-American control group with the Italian-American control group.

Idealistic: Irish-American Control Group

1. Being successful and admired by everybody
2. Being good and going to heaven
3. Being good enough to go to heaven
4. Being a president of the United States and having great power
5. Being with God and being saved
6. Being somebody else and being very important
7. Being the smartest and the happiest guy on earth

Pragmatic: Irish-American Control Group

1. Being a big guy who can do a lot for others
2. Thinking about girls I'd like to marry
3. Getting a good education and being loved
4. Being a successful college graduate
5. Dreaming of what to do to be good and how life could be better
6. Traveling and seeing the world
7. Being popular and good
8. Being successful and happy

Idealistic: Italian-American Control Group

1. Being big with no problems
2. Things I could do if my life were different
3. Being close to God and being good
4. Being successful and a great athlete who can conquer all

Pragmatic: Italian-American Control Group

1. How rich I would be if I were smart enough
2. The girl I'd like to marry and to date
3. Owning a home, getting married, and raising a family
4. Being very good at baseball
5. Many things; jobs I'd like, girls I'd like to date, being a success
6. Being someone important and knowing what life is all about
7. Being a professional person
8. All the good times I had in the past
9. Having lots of money and being popular with girls
10. Getting a good education and being smart

The Irish-American control boys have more concern with a good and different life. Their daydreams concern goodness, happiness, the good life, a different life, and popularity. Desires for self-esteem and respect from others transcend material pleasures. Fifteen percent of the Irish-American boys express religiosity and goodness in contrast to only 3 percent of the Italian-American boys. They do not stress material rewards but do equate intelligence and happiness with self-importance and self-esteem. The daydreams of these boys show self-glorification and transcend reality to the higher authority of a good life and to the pinnacle of success, esteem, and happiness where admiration by others is a natural consequence.

Although 60 percent of the boys in both groups acknowledge daydreaming, each group patterns itself differently in achieving its ends. One visualizes worldly success in a dream of wishes; the other visualizes a dream apart from usual reality.

Significantly more Italian-American control boys are concerned with the immediate environment and immediate future goals. The important things for these boys are not only success in the future but also desires for more material pleasures, within which wealth and "smartness" are equated. They relate a sense of personal esteem and respect from others to popularity, intelligence, and wealth. The daydreams are, for the most part, concrete and attached to life, and have some realistic chance of fulfillment.

The Disturbed Groups

In disturbance the boys show the same tendencies toward pragmatic and idealistic thinking as do the control groups. However, a decreased contrast is due to the fact that many more boys were reticent in stating the content of their daydreams, probably because of the decreased ability to communicate of the self-isolating Irish-American boys, and the defiance in communication with authority figures of the more rebellious Italian-American boys.

Idealistic: Irish-American Distrubed Group

1. I am concerned with the future; I'll be so educated nobody can touch me
2. About praying to God to make me good
3. Being the most popular baseball player and being a hero
4. Being famous
5. Being a hero and everyone has to look up to me
6. Being a popular hero who can do a lot for others
7. Being as big as the president of the United States

Pragmatic: Irish-American Disturbed Group

1. Having a happy family and going home
2. Being successful at a profession when I'm older
3. Dating girls
4. Traveling and seeing the world

Idealistic: Italian-American Disturbed Group

1. Being independent and very famous
2. Being in heaven with God, away from wicked people
3. How can I be successful and have everyone look up to me
4. My father returning who is dead

Pragmatic: Italian-American Disturbed Group

1. Getting out of father's clutches and being big to show up my father

2. Self-confidence and know what I want to do in the future
3. Where I would place myself on leaving the institution
4. Dating girls
5. Recreation in the future when I can make my own recreation
6. Success in future career
7. Owning a car and taking a trip

The boys in the Irish-American disturbed group are concerned with change from the present situation of low self-esteem and unhappiness to a world in which self-glorification and kinship ties are more desirable events. They are concerned with being different from what they are, being good, having happy families (in the face of parental separations), and being compensatory popular heroes to replace commonplace selves. They wish to give help to achieve a good life and approval from others.

In his pragmatic responses, the Irish-American boy wants to change from his present predicament in the foster home or institution to a more ideal and better family and social life that he assumes other boys have. He daydreams about that which he does not have and that which he hopes to have in the attainable reality. Like the boys in the control group, he wants to travel. He seeks changes in his social relations, whereby he can gain self-esteem and respect from other people, and regain a sense of being wanted and loved. This is compensated for by fantasies of being admired through education and heroism, fantasies which indicate some feeling of inferiority and a sense of low self-esteem.

In the Italian-American disturbed groups, 45 percent of the responses relate to wishful planning of immediate and future life, and they concern independence, autonomy, and social security. One boy was placed in the idealistic category because he dreamed of the return of his deceased father. In this group's pragmatic daydreams there are elements of self-confidence and self-realization in the world of reality, elements of defiance of authority with desires for independence and autonomy, and elements that reveal feelings of insecurity. As with the control group, there is wishful fantasy for future success, but there is also emphasis upon defiance and desire for independence from authority.

Both disturbed groups are less concerned with religiosity than with better lives than they now have. Both groups desire realistic self-improvement and increased self-esteem.

Most Important Thing

As a corollary to self-awareness and to the analysis of daydreams, the boys differentiated themselves once again through their statements on what is the most important thing in life to them.

The Control Groups

About half of the boys in both control groups wish to achieve success in future career plans. Table 52 shows that over 32 percent of Italian-American boys want material pleasures in addition to pragmatic career orientations. This outnumbers the Irish-American boys, who try to attain personal satisfaction and personal esteem on internal levels. The Italian-American boys more often equate money and material desires with happiness. They also more often display status-seeking and recognition-seeking behavior, because of the pleased response they receive.

The Disturbed Groups

There are no significant differences between the disturbed adolescents in terms of what they consider most important. The Irish-American disturbed group does not differ from the control group in desiring self-esteem. Significantly more Italian-American disturbed boys desire self-esteem and respect from others and want to improve themselves to please others. In this fashion the Italian-American disturbed group differs from its control group and is similar to the Irish-American group. In both disturbed groups there is an absolute minimal desire for material pleasures.

Disturbance makes these boys want esteem and respect from other people, and they want to improve themselves in order to please other people. However, the groups differ in how they accomplish this. Each disturbed group copies the perceptual attitudes of its control group. The model Irish-American disturbed boy thinks in terms of being a great person, of going to heaven (following daydream material), and of being a leader and being respected by other people. He is out to attain personal inner satisfaction in a less concrete way than the Italian-American boy. This is in line with the symptomatology of his disturbance (isolation and withdrawal tendencies toward autistic fantasy) and also with a more rigid moral-ethical balance and the need for an inner equilibrating force in order to gain external acceptance. The modal Italian-American dis-

Table 52
Distribution of the Control Boys with Regard
to What is Considered Most Important in Their Lives

Most Important Desire	Irish-American Control	Italian-American Control
	%	%
Sense of Esteem and Respect from Others:		
Be something to be respected for	5.00	00.00
Do good and be popular	00.00	2.90
To be loved by a swell girl	00.00	5.90
Improvement of the Self in an Effort to Please Others:		
Learn to be with people	2.50	00.00
Attain personal satisfaction	5.00	00.00
Get on the honor roll	00.00	2.90
Know what I want to do and go after it—will please mother	00.00	2.90
Marriage	12.50	5.90
Go to Heaven	15.00	5.90
Material Pleasures:		
To have money and happiness	5.00	20.60
Get rich	00.00	5.90
Own a car	00.00	5.90
Achieve Success in Future Plans:		
Go to college	25.00	17.64
Get a good job	22.50	8.80
Be secure in the job	2.50	00.00
Be promoted on the job	5.00	14.50
Total	100.00	99.74

First four categories combined for chi-square analysis.
$x^2 = 9.49$, 2 d.f.; $p < .01$

turbed boy attempts to increase his self-esteem and respect from other people by dreams of being popular, independent, married and rich. The boys in both disturbed groups are concerned with being at home with happy families. This nostalgia is most evident among Irish-American boys, who more frequently come from broken homes. This is evident in the Life-Space Drawing, where extended family members become figures of choice.

There is somewhat more religious emphasis in the Irish-American home than there is in the Italian-American home. Intergenerational communication of fantasies of pleasure and self-glorification are evident in the Irish-American boy, in spite of the fact that there are dependent conforming patterns and repressed rebellion in his home. Materialistic pressures in solving the problems of life differentiate the Italian-American adolescent's perception of his social situation from the Irish-American adolescent's perception.

Achievement Orientation

The most basic assumption in this study is that a youth must forge for himself some central perspective and unified direction out of the affective remnants of his childhood and family and his hopes of anticipated adulthood. Eventually a meaningful resemblance should appear between how the adolescent views himself and what others judge him to be.

The basic assumption in this section is that there is a systematic variation, in the realm of achievement orientation, that stems from the ethnically oriented adolescent's traditional institutions. These institutions help to determine his perspectives and the motivations for his adult future. Value orientations, for both the present and anticipated future, are complex, patterned principles resulting from the transactional interplay of the cognitive, the affective, and the directive elements of one's life pattern. These give order and direction to the stream of human problems facing the individual youth.

We can assume that the rate and the degree of assimilation of an ethnic group to the dominant American culture will depend in large part upon the compatibility of the group's own rank ordering of achievement orientations in that of the dominant culture. Rosen (96) indicates that upward mobility rates of eight racial and ethnic groups in America have been markedly dissimilar when compared with one another and with some white-Protestant groups. He postulates that social mobility within ethnic groups depends in large part upon the individual's psychological and cultural orientation toward achievement. Rosen attributes differences in individuals to educational-vocational aspirations derived from the individual's ethnic subculture. In his summary analysis, social class is an influential component of the racial and religious factor.

The Control Groups

Our analysis rests on the premise that standards of excellence imposed on the child by the parents as representatives of the culture are interwoven with affective interpersonal relationships with the parents. Patterns of parental behavior determine what the next generation will do in terms of responses and actions in future anticipation. The younger generation of sons will, by their responses and actions, tell the older generation whether life as represented by the older generation has meaning, will renew this parental meaning and regenerate it in terms of self-fulfillment, or will rebel against it. This often spells the difference between a healthy youth and an emotionally disturbed youth with "identity diffusion" (29).

Of the control adolescents enrolled in college preparatory courses, there were more Italian-American boys. More Irish-American boys enrolled in general and business courses. Again, while there is no significant difference between the two groups, 88 percent of the Italian-American boys stated that they would attend college if financially able, compared to 70 percent of the Irish-American boys who would do so. Responses to this question were reinforced by the fact that more Italian-American boys in the lower socioeconomic classes were attending schools to prepare for college and stated that they would attend college if financially able (85 percent of class IV, and 67 percent of class V). Italian-American boys have particularly greater mobility orientations, since, to the last boy, 100 percent of those in the upper classes stated they would attend college if they could. Conversely, more Irish-American boys would not go, or are indecisive as the social classes decrease in rank order. As noted in the description of social class, second generation Italian-American parents on all social levels value and achieve high school graduation. This consistent finding leads to the general proposal that Italian-Americans, on all levels, give achievement values higher pragmatic status than Irish-Americans. Although over 60 percent of the lower-class boys in both groups stated that they would attend college if financially able, it is possible that the motivation arose from encouragement by the school based on the student's scholarship and ability. Yet, this motivation has to be encouraged in the home if the boy is to enter and persist in a college entrance program. It is conceivable that in the Italian-American group, second-generation parents with unskilled labor have encouraged these boys toward professional security as a goal in life.

We must also consider that achievement in any realm depends upon ability and motivation to reach the goal. If people in the lower social classes of both groups believe that they have the opportunity and hold the values that help them to achieve their goal, then they may move to achieve the goal successfully. A subtle factor in the achievement orientation of the boys in these groups may be the reference group of the individual. It is conceivable that the lower-class individuals are identifying with upper-class individuals and absorbing the value systems of the upper-class groups. This is apparent with classes IV and V in the Italian-American control group, and with class IV in the Irish-American control group. Encouragement by school authorities, coupled with encouragement by parents and with positive peer group associations may move boys to motivations in academic and vocational careers that exceed the vocational limitations of their own parents. Religious and spiritual counselling, coupled with vocational inspiration, also may motivate the boys in the control groups toward achievement orientation in line with other classmates.

The findings on achievement orientations for the Italian-American control group differ from the findings of Rosen (96). He indicated, in his analysis of ethnic groups, that the Italian groups place less emphasis on achievement training than do the Protestants, Jews, and Greeks. In this study, as in Strodtbeck (108), there is no evidence that the Italian-American or Irish-American groups differ from the general population in achievement orientation. However, the findings on social class analyses in this study differ from the findings of Strodtbeck (108). This study illustrates higher achievement motivations in both upper and lower classes. Italian-American class V achievement orientations in this study are in line with heightened mean achievement orientations in class V Italian boys studied by Strodtbeck (108).

Glazer and Moynihan (44) point out that Italian-American people, in efforts to achieve middle-class status in American culture, adopt religious affiliations. Children of Italian immigrants found important symbols of new status as middle-class Americans in new ethnically mixed Roman Catholic churches of the suburbs, and consequently adopted the parochial school. Glazer and Moynihan propose that the Italian people saw education as important in preparing for professions, such as engineering or the free professions. American Catholicism, too, encouraged such practical pursuits.

A study of interests in careers reveals that there is no significant difference between the two groups in their choice of a professional career over mechanical and service careers. Two-thirds to three-quarters of the boys in both groups desire professional careers involving at least a college degree or more. The only social class difference lies in the Italian-American group. In this group, all of the boys in the upper classes desire professional careers, while the lower-class boys follow the examples in the literature on lower-class aspiration (73). In this lower social class, only 45 percent of the boys desire professional careers, while 30 percent of them have not resolved vocational decisions.

Boys with lesser professional aspirations in the lower classes of

Table 53
Italian-American Control Social Class Differentiation
in Choice of Career

Class	Professional	Mechanical	Don't Know	Total
	%	%	%	%
I–III	100.00	00.00	00.00	100.00
IV–V	45.00	25.00	30.00	100.00

$x^2 = 11.08$, 1 d.f.; $p < .001$

both control groups chose professional ball playing, teaching, pharmacy, journalism, and clergy. Their mechanical or service choices were small business, office work, and electrician training. Higher professional aspirations included medicine, law, journalism, and accounting.

The Irish-American and the Italian-American groups differ somewhat in their vocational goals. The Italian-American boys chose so-called free professions that provide for interpersonal communication, self-esteem, and monetary return to a greater extent than some other professions. These professions are dentistry, medicine, accounting, and pharmacy. On the whole, vocational aspirations of the Italian-American boys are above the achievement of their parents, who are described as employed in unskilled and semiskilled work. This holds as well for the Irish-American boys, whose aspirations surpassed that of parental achievement. Irish-American boys, although they chose certain interpersonal professions, such as medicine and law, also had aspirations in the fields of history, research, and the military. We interpreted these latter goals as egocentric because the boys stated that they wanted to be professors of law, professors of history, and historians. These scholarly pursuits of isolated creative tasks, and military service (in which the self is altruistically tied to the group as a whole), were not mentioned at all by the Italian-American boys.

There may be discrepancies between aspirations and actual achievements among the Irish-American lower-class boys. Occupational aspirations of boys in the lower classes are influenced not only by upper-class classmates but also by parental approval and encouragement, together with some form of financial aid for achievement of professorial and research aims. One can foresee that aspirations may far exceed actual accomplishments. If dependency and passivity are potential reactions in the group's lower class, and if maternal domination is also a potential, then the aggressive masculinity necessary for educational and occupational success depends in large part upon maternal values. Maternal domination could, in view of this dependent trait, hinder the development of the independence and initiative needed to attain the discipline required in the intensive study of law or history. On the other hand, the educational achievements of mothers in this social class are above those of their husbands, and if they work, they are economic assets to their households and college aspiration models for their children.

In the description of the sample, the mothers of the class IV Irish-American control boys are presented as women gainfully employed in teaching, sales, clerical work, and nursing. While 50 percent of the mothers are high school graduates, 27 percent of them completed college. Krauss (68) proposes that when the working-class mother holds a non-manual job and has some college training, while her husband has only completed high school, the mother's education and interests strongly affect the child's interest in college. When the mother has married "down," as indicated by her having more education than her husband, most of the offspring plan to attend college. Krauss also predicts that college-oriented students will gravitate toward others with similar interests. Such peer-group associations are likely to reinforce college aspirations. He suggests that middle-class schools are likely to identify with the middle class. Such middle-class interests and values shared by lower-class students who plan to attend college reflect anticipatory socialization in reference group behavior. These factors may thus reflect upward striving in the lower-class family.

Although the factors above may be appropriate in an evaluation of lower-class youth, ethnic factors appear to indicate certain variation. In the Italian-American group, the lower classes are significantly less interested in the professions and are more service oriented and more indecisive about desired vocations. The majority of the youth, however, would go to college if they were financially able. This is noticeable in the Italian-American lower-class youth, where there is some indication that although the parents in the lower classes are not college oriented, there is greater parental pressure for professional achievement, in contrast to the Irish-American group pressures. The Irish-American working-class boy appears to be more mobility oriented than his parents are.

There is no significant difference on an ethnic basis in parental interest in school achievement. The only significant difference lies in the Italian-American group's social classes. In this group, 43 percent of upper-class boys feel that their mothers are interested in their achievements, while 35 percent feel both parents are interested. In the lower classes, only 20 percent of the boys perceive combined parental interest, while 80 percent are equally divided between maternal and paternal interest (U.C.-L.C.-$x^2 = 7.18$, 2 d.f.; x^2 $p < .02$). The Italian-American group does not perceive interest on the part of both parents to be as great as it is in the Irish-American group (26 percent as contrasted with 43 percent). As shown by the previous data, there is some perceived difference in parental roles.

The Irish-American boys remain consistent in their perceptions of parental unity in family function and discipline. We should remember that they identify closely with their fathers and bring them into discussions on serious personal problems. The Irish-American control group family provided more democratic intrafamilial relationships than the Italian-American control group, where the father was more authoritarian. It appears that in the Italian-American lower classes, autonomous adolescent decisions conflict with parental orientations.

The Irish-American boys, in the main, do not feel that their parents urge specific job choices upon them while almost 30 percent of the boys in the Italian-American group state that their parents have specific employment plans for them. There is no class difference in this respect. Apparently in the Italian-American group the parents are either emphatic about goals for their child, or they are indifferent altogether.

In response to the question of whether or not the Irish-American parents applied career planning pressure, the youths reported "no parental pressure," "what I do is up to me," "they want me to do my best and to make decisions on my own," and "they want me to be successful in whatever I do." The few indications of parental pressure were represented by "they want me to go to college," "they want me to be a doctor," and "they want me to be an electrician and earn a good living."

In the Italian-American control group, 46 percent of the parents want their sons to go to college, a figure considerably higher than the Irish-American parents (26 percent). In the Italian-American group, the percentage of parents planning and desiring professional careers for their sons decreases through the lower classes until class V which exhibits a deviant response in an attitude of whole hearted support from the parents, with serious attention paid to both counselling and planning with the boys for their future. These boys perceive their parents' attitudes as ones that encourage attending college and make them feel capable and motivated. However, in the lower classes of the Italian-American group as a whole, the boys appear to have the least amount of plans made for them by their parents, and from their statements they seem to be in conflict with these plans. Only 35 percent of the parents in this class want their boys to go to college, while more of the boys themselves plan to go to college. Two boys in this class stated that their parents do not care, but they do want to go to college. Two other boys stated that they do not like their parents' advice because although the boys want to go to college, their parents do not want them to. One boy stated that if he chose college, his parents declared they would provide no financial assistance. This kind of conflict may be the reason for the high "don't know" category, where confusion between aspiration and reality is apparent. High adolescent motivation for college in the Italian-American lower-class structure also conflicts with the fact that only 57 percent of the boys are actually enrolled in college preparatory courses. This is in contrast to 86 percent who would go to college if they were financially able. Most of the fathers in this social class are skilled workers who may be trying to mold their sons in their own image, for they assume a high school degree and skilled labor are totally adequate. Pride in one's manual skill

Table 54
Categorization of Adolescent Perception of Parental Attitudes
Regarding Vocational Aspirations

Perceived Parental Attitudes	Irish-American Control	Italian-American Control
	%	%
Social Classes I to III		
My parents want me to go to college	33.33	65.00
They want me to be successful in whatever I choose to do	38.88	28.57
Father is going to see I get a good education	12.50	00.00
They are satisfied with my professional plans	5.00	00.00
They want me to get a good job and to have security	00.00	7.00
Don't know	10.00	00.00
Total	99.71	100.57
Social Classes IV and V		
My parents want me to go to college	18.10	45.00
I want to go to college—parents don't care	00.00	14.23
They want me to have a good job or a career of some kind	18.00	00.00
They want me to be professional	9.00	00.00
They want me to do what I think I would enjoy and am suited for	27.00	20.00
They are satisfied with my plans	4.50	00.00
My parents care—I don't like their advice I want to go to college	00.00	10.00
Don't know	22.50	11.40
Total	99.10	100.63

and work, together with some semblance of future economic security, could be transferred to the son for achievement identification. At the same time, a father's traditional hierarchical authority in the home could very well be threatened by a son with more education. The Italian-American group also have a greater emphasis upon pragmatic economic and vocational security. More Italian-American boys would rather have jobs that afford economic security and long-range employment, even with lower salaries. In contrast, the

Irish-American boys prefer more idealistic and adventurous vocations in life, which is in keeping with their daydream material and their desire for change. Reliance upon desire, whether reality permits it or not, is of greater force in the Irish-American boy's life.

We should note that the majority of the boys in both groups have loftier aspirations than their parents, in spite of the fact that there are ethnic variations in parental authority toward vocational achievement. In view of greater parental permissiveness on the part of the Irish-American group, and greater authoritarian influence in the Italian-American group, it is pertinent for us to discuss Merton's (78) influential analysis on social structure and normlessness. He discusses the syndrome of lofty goals and limited realistic opportunities patterns inviting deviant behavior (78:148). In his discussion, lower class individuals internalize cultural goals of success, but they realize that the means to success are not available to them. The lower class adolescent who internalizes middle-class norms will be frustrated if he hasn't the means to achieve his goals, but his frustration will recede if he thinks that the means for future success *are* available.

Whether or not the high aspirations of the control group boys in the lower classes prove frustrating is not within the scope of this book. The study does indicate, however, that ethnic considerations in the class system help dictate vocational choices. The two ethnic control groups vary from each other in terms of achievement orientation, adolescent choice of vocation, and parental pressure towards achievement.

The Disturbed Groups

In keeping with the frame of reference of this study, essential ethnic orientations to achievement are both maintained and exaggerated when these boys become emotionally disturbed.

Statistical counts indicate that in contrast to the control groups, considerably fewer boys in the disturbed groups are in high school for college preparation. This is partly because approximately 30 percent of the boys in each ethnic group are not yet enrolled in high school. At the beginning of this study, we noted that the disturbed boys were one to two years younger than the control boys and were behind in their school work because of constant shifting, changing of schools, and failure in achievement due to disturbance. Even so, the Italian-American disturbed group still has more boys enrolled in college preparatory courses (38 percent), as contrasted to the greater percentage of Irish-American boys in business (20 percent business as opposed to 4 percent college preparatory). Although statistical manipulations are nonsignificant in this respect, this characteristic is in keeping with the control groups.

Actually, considerably fewer boys in both ethnic groups are college oriented and motivated as compared with their control groups. Conversely, there are more boys in the disturbed groups who are preparing for jobs. Approximately 20 percent of the boys in the disturbed groups are going to school because they have to.

An analysis by social class indicates that 50 percent of both groups upper classes are preparing for college, while 50 percent of them are preparing for jobs. More disturbed upper class boys are preparing for jobs than in the control group boys. In view of the small number of boys in each social class and of the greater variability inherent in small samples, these findings are held in reserve. It is possible, however, that disturbed boys on all social-economic levels more often shy away from college preparation. This is logical considering the poor family relationships, fears of failure, and feelings of inadequacy these boys have, together with all of the frustrations inherent in achievement orientation. Again the Irish-American group shows somewhat greater parental participation, for 24 percent of these boys acknowledge parental guidance, while only 8 percent of the Italian-American boys do so.

The data on school attendance and achievement orientation point out that these boys have sufficient awareness of reality to accommodate themselves to lesser opportunities in view of parental separation and discord. By reducing their aspirations, the boys guard against failure and frustration. A very interesting phenomenon noted here is that almost 60 percent of the boys in both groups would go to college if they could afford it. The boys are equally divided in their mobility orientations between the upper and lower social classes.

Again, like its control group, the class IV boys of the Italian-American group would, in the great majority (86 percent), go to college if they could afford it, yet only about 43 percent of these boys are enrolled in college preparatory courses. Like its control group, the class IV boys appear to be the most mobility oriented of their ethnic group, and they appear to be more mobility oriented than the class IV boys of the Irish-American group, 69 percent of whom would attend college if they could. The largest element of "don't know" answers regarding the question of motivation with financial ability appears to be in the lower class. In the upper class of the Italian-American group, 36 percent of the boys would *not* attend college, even if they could afford it. These boys do not appear to be as mobility oriented as their parents, who are in managerial and professional occupations. In the Irish-American groups the number of boys desiring college decreases with social status, but not significantly so.

In summary, we can generally state that the boys in all socioeconomic classes of both disturbed groups are not as achievement oriented as their parents, nor are they as achievement oriented as the boys in both control groups. In spite of this, the lower-class boys in both disturbed groups tend to show more mobility orientation than their own parents. The lower-class boys maintain the mobility orientations discovered in the lower classes of the control group, with the Italian-American disturbed lower classes maintaining higher mobility orientations than those of the Irish-American groups.

A sizeable percentage of the boys in both disturbed groups are oriented toward mechanical and service careers in the various trades (36 and 33 percent). This is evident in all of the socioeconomic classes. A sizeable percentage of the boys in both disturbed groups have not yet made up their minds as to future vocations (28 and 38 percent). In this respect, both disturbed groups differ significantly from control groups ($p < .02$).

We enumerated and studied specific vocational aspirations expressed by the boys in an effort to determine qualitative differences in vocational choice. A study of the boys in the different social classes indicated the following tendencies. In the lower classes, the majority of the Italian-American boys chose teaching positions; for example, teachers of history and mathematics. In this respect they appear to be far more mobility oriented than their own parents, who are skilled and unskilled laborers. While 57 percent of the boys in class IV chose the professions, 43 percent stated that they had not yet made up their minds as to specific vocational choice. However, in class V, the lowest social class, 83 percent of the boys chose such mechanical and service careers as carpenter, auto mechanic, electrician, fireman, and plumber.

In contrast to the Italian-American disturbed group's lower class, 35 percent of the Irish-American boys in the lower classes desire college and professions in contrast to their own fathers. Forty-one percent of the boys in class IV of the Irish-American group state that they "don't know" what career interests them. The Irish-American boys were apparently restless, for approximately 20 percent of the boys in all classes were making miscellaneous temporary plans for the future (such as travel, military service, and racing car driving). In the lowest class of the Irish-American group, 75 percent want to enter military service, apparently in order to postpone making long-term future plans. The immediate attractions of this choice are perhaps the adventure and the security to be found in the larger paternal order of the army. Military service is desirable among the Irish-American boys in all of the social classes. Tabulations show that the upper-class Irish-American boys not only desire military service, but also want to be physicians or to pursue scholarly careers in mathematics, language, and physics. These professional desires are again in contrast to the more pragmatic professional pursuits of the Italian-American disturbed boys who desire to be physicians, engineers, and clergymen.

In previous sections of this study, we noted that the upper-class Italian-American parents handled their boys in a more authoritarian way in an effort to bring about greater conformity to rules and regulations in the home and social world. Once again, some defiance and resistance on the part of the upper-class boys appear evident in disturbance, which is in keeping also with the symptomatology of active aggression and defiance of authority in the upper-class authoritarian family. However, those who make career choices do so showing practicality and service to the community along with a desire to achieve self-esteem. The professions chosen indicate some promise of interpersonal communication along with economic and social security.

While both disturbed groups have significantly reduced achievement orientations when compared to the control groups, in both groups a larger number of boys do not know their vocational aspirations. This is especially the case in the Irish-American disturbed group. The Italian-American disturbed boys again appear more mobility oriented in class IV. All of the peculiarities of the singular ethnic traits enumerated above are in line with these findings. Differences in vocational choice indicate contrast of pragmatism and practicality as opposed to military service and scholarly pursuits.

When the boys in both ethnic groups, control and disturbed, were asked whether they preferred jobs with high salaries and travel or those with lower salaries but more reliability, only gross tendencies were apparent in their answers. The control boys' answers to this question indicated a contrast between Irish-American preference for jobs with high salaries and travel as opposed to Italian-American preference for more reliable low-salary positions $(p<.10)$. There was more convergence on this question in the disturbed groups $(p<.25)$. Crude tendencies still existed however, in which the Italian-American boys preferred jobs that gave them more security but lower salaries, while the Irish-American boys preferred travel and change.

A survey of the data allows the following generalizations. Consideration of ethnicity in disturbance reveals that vocational choices are influenced in each social class by ethnic variations that contrast and color the values adopted in an ethnic group's class system, in contrast to another ethnic group's class system. Failure and frustra-

Table 55
"If you were offered a job, which would be more important for you?"

Response	Irish-American Control	Italian-American Control
	%	%
Job with high salary and a lot of travel	55	35
Job with lower salary but which is steady and can be depended upon to keep you employed	45	65
Total	100	100
	N=40	N=40

$x^2=2.90$, 1 d.f.; $p<.10$

tion in the classroom is an extension of the feeling of failure and frustration in the home. This occurs in both ethnic groups, regardless of social class. The boys in the upper classes of the disturbed groups do not have the status orientations evident in their control groups. The boys in the lower classes have achievement orientations that perhaps are more congruent with their own economic and psychological reality.

In terms of ethnic symptomatology, the disturbed Irish-American boys become more isolated and withdrawn while they conform superficially to social norms and resort to fantasy. In this way, self-glorification and romanticism in daydreams of social success compensate for feelings of inadequacy. The Irish-American disturbed boy educational frustrations take on an inner imaginative need to formulate a happier world. The Italian-American disturbed boys select reference groups that will afford them an audience for their domineering and exhibitionistic tendencies. Peer group accommodation of mischievious misdemeanors requires the selection of friends who will fulfill personality needs. Defiance of authority also involves defiance of educational counselling and guidance.

Both ethnic groups defy authority in their own characteristic ways, and their inability to concentrate upon vocational objectives and upon present educational attainments take on different personality characteristics. As a consequence of these variations, counselling of disturbed groups must necessarily consider the concept of reality held by each social class and ethnic structure. Family orientations and identifications, in terms of achievement possibilities and perceptual strivings, are within the scope of psychological counselling, so a knowledge of intrafamilial and parental pressures toward achievement is a useful addition to adequate counselling techniques.

The Italian-American upper-class disturbed boy indicates that the father exhibits the greatest parental interest in school achievement (63 percent), in contrast to the Irish-American boy, who prefers the mother and is more dependent upon maternal interest and upon the mother as a household manager. On the other hand, almost half of the Italian-American lower-class boys perceive both parents as interested in their school achievement. This confirms the upper-class boys' perceptions of paternal authoritarianism in the service of conformity. It also indicates the feeling of greater democratic participation the lower-class boy has in contrast to the upper-class boy in the Italian-American group. With relatively less authoritarianism in the home atmosphere, the more affectively oriented Italian-American boy more often tries open manipulation of the environment in his mobility aspirations. Less authoritarianism in the home leads to reciprocal argument and freedom in defense of the self-image. In class IV of the Italian-American disturbed group, there are indications of father-son conflict with regard to mobility aspiration and desire for college. If motivations exist for this lower-class Italian-American boy, achievement may be possible if he takes the liberty to defend his self-image.

The great majority of the boys in both ethnic groups state that their parents do feel it is important to help them think seriously of jobs for which they should prepare. The great majority of the boys in all social classes of the Italian-American disturbed group perceive their parents as highly interested. In contrast to this, all of the boys in the upper class of the Irish-American group perceive their parents to be interested, but 41 percent of the boys in the lower classes do not.

Significantly more Italian-American boys, especially lower-class ones, are pressured on the choice of specific jobs. This parental planning for specific job choice interweaves with the lower-class parent-son conflict. Parental separation in this group is not as great as in the Irish-American disturbed groups, which potentially provides greater parental unity and stable interest. Parental domination, greater in Italian-American upper classes, does not seem to influence the perception of parental pressure in any way. In this group, as in the control group, perception of parental planning for the choice of a specific job does not decrease by class as it does in the Irish-American groups. It is interesting to note again that, as in the control group, class V responses indicated they had by far the greatest amount of parental pressure in choosing a career.

One might question at this point whether increased parental planning in the lower social classes of the Italian-American group is a function of a boy's disturbance and perceived parental need to dominate a boy's future direction, or whether the disturbance is a consequence of increased parental pressure. Authoritarianism produces defiance and confusion, but authoritarianism in the home has appeared as an ethnic trait in the Italian-American groups, both control and disturbed. This trait colors and covers the class variable in its mobility orientation, however the disturbed boys see their parents as exerting pressure for negative reasons, while the control group do not feel it to be negative. This perception of parental pressure as negative is particularly more prominent in the lower classes.

In contrast to the Italian-American disturbed boys, 89 percent of the lower-class Irish-American boys have less parental pressure exerted upon them either for thinking seriously of employment for the first time or for choosing a specific job. This lack of parental pressure in the lower classes is in line with the class pattern of the Irish-American control group where decreasing pressure for college education and increasing permissiveness in the choice of vocation are evident. We can hypothesize that separation of parents and a larger number of working mothers, coupled with nuclear family orientations that provide less extended family help, leave these mothers busy and helpless in the face of disturbance and their own anxieties. Counselling and aid in vocational matters is often left to the schools and institutions. In further support of this inference, the majority of the boys in the Irish-American disturbed group (in exaggeration of its control group) state that their parents fail to help in choosing a specific job, a failure they seem to perceive as indifference on their parents' part. This lower interest on the part of their parents, however, means the boys have much less pressure for the choice of future careers.

The Life-Space Drawing showed that the Italian-American disturbed boys prefer peers to collateral family. In view of the Italian-American disturbed boy's symptomatology, it was reiterated that this boy needs selective associations to appease his traits of active aggression and exhibitionism. His family and peer pressures probably promote pragmatic and aggressive orientations in his conquest of economic and social problems. He seeks autonomy in spite of parental dominance and it becomes defiantly exaggerated. In contrast, in the Irish-American groups, vocational choices are made by both parents and the boy. Professional orientation and educational attainment go down with decreasing social status, and the class system, as a system of values, is more apparent among the Irish-American boys.

Achievement orientations, as witnessed in the mean score values on the Edwards Personal Preference Schedule, were not different from each other, nor were ethnic mean scores different from the representative scores. Although the achievement orientation scores were not different, actual vocational aspirations and self-projected perceptions showed variation and difference by ethnicity.

Discussion

Achievement orientation is a complex phenomenon involving ethnic groups, social classes, and religious affiliations. A study by Srole and Opler (105) indicates that the most mobility-oriented individuals are the healthiest, while whose with less social mobility have more impaired mental health. Kleiner and Parker (64) discuss the relationship of psychopathology to social status, social mobility, and mobility orientation. In an extensive review of the literature they indicate that there is no clear relationship between social class and neuroses or psychoses. In their review of the relationships among social class, social mobility, and illness, they cite evidence that points to a tendency for emotionally disturbed subjects to either over- or under-aspire, compared to those who have made better adjustments.

One can argue that maladjusted persons have high anxiety and high fears of failure, that they attempt to minimize by selecting a task so easy they cannot fail, or so difficult that failure would be no cause for self-blame. Another plausible argument is that the high level of anxiety experienced by maladjusted persons prevents them from realistically evaluating their own abilities in reaching certain goals.

The evidence cited in this study shows both ethnic disturbed groups to under-aspire in contrast to their healthy counterparts. Under-aspirations, however, must be seen in the context of high anxiety with isolation and fantasies in the Irish-American disturbed boys, and high anxiety and active aggression in the Italian-American disturbed boys.

In keeping with F. Kluckhohn (66), the Italian-American and the Irish-American boys in this study are moving away from the collateral and the linear relationships of families. They are also moving away from subjection-to-nature with its orientation upon the present. In both groups the adolescents appear to be future-oriented and individualistic.

In agreement with Kluckhohn, there are differences in both the rate and the kind of movement between the sick and the healthy families—especially in the Italian-American groups. In the sick Italian-American family, there is a breakdown of collateral relational ties, whereas in the healthy family these ties are still quite strong. It is one thing to try to change from a non-planning, present-time, and present-being oriented position when one has the cushion of a solid family tie to support and sustain one in the case of failure, but it is quite another thing when this cushion is lacking. In the Italian-American disturbed group, collateral ties have been partially or wholly destroyed. Harsher intrafamilial relationships force the boy to project on the outside world and authority his own confusion and his own difficulty in integrating the social and authoritarian demands. The denial and escape defense mechanisms of the Irish-American boys enable them to emphasize the perfectibility of good and evil by the pattern of withdrawal and daydreaming.

Elder (24) indicates that social class and ethnic variations account in part for differences in achievement orientations among men. In the present study it appears that family structure and educational attainment, along with stylistic family patterns on subcultural bases, influence the way in which adolescents go about forming aspirations in the different social classes. In Elder's discussion of familial authority and familial democracy, he states that high educational attainment is most prevalent among persons who report democratic relationships with the parents and equalitarian relationships between the mother and father. Strodtbeck (108) found that those who experienced democratic relationships with their parents and reported equality between parents were most likely to value independent mastery and achievement. This study does not corroborate those findings.

In this study, there is more paternal authoritarian discipline in the Italian-American groups, particularly in the upper classes, yet the boys in these classes show greatest professional motivation. Somewhat higher achievement orientations and desire for educational attainment are apparent in the Italian-American groups than in the Irish-American subculture which has more democratic intrafamilial discussion patterns. Strodtbeck (108) states that high achievement orientation is associated with masculine identification, in which the boys perceive their fathers as friendly and as persons with whom they would discuss their personal problems. This statement may explain the high achievement orientations of the control groups but these conditions do not obtain for the disturbed groups where maternal dominations are most prevalent and where paternal identifications lack both opportunity and impetus. Aggressive father-son conflicts are especially prevalent among the Italian-American boys. Hostility to the collateral family and moving out into the larger community are also more prevalent among the Italian-American disturbed boys.

It appears that although masculine identification and father-son relationships are important, especially in view of the central conflicts of these boys, there are yet other factors stemming from the familial and ethnic style of a subculture that provide impetus for achievement motivation. The basic assumption in this study is that achievement orientation stems from the subtle interplay of parents and children within the family. This interplay involves value transmission through successive generations in the process of socialization. We originally hypothesized that intergenerational communication began in the Old World and continued its subtle transmission in the new world. An important contribution to ethnic variability is the communication from parent to son in a certain subcultural base. The fitting of an ethnic group within the larger American culture and a loss of its manifest traits does not entail the loss of its latent influence in dealing with the experiences of life. Personal stress arises from an initial mode of life in a subcultural setting. Inbreeding a mode of life provides inbreeding of a characteristic reaction to environmental press.

Movement and Endurance Toward Achievement

In the previous section, the analysis of achievement motivations indicated qualitative contrasts between the two ethnic groups. At the same time, disturbance points out a discrepancy between the potential for achievement and achievement motivation. In considering the adolescent's interpersonal and extended social environments, there are differences in cultural conditioning within the families in movements toward achievement goals.

Self-fulfilling prophecies may produce discrepancies between a boy's potential for achievement and his actual achievement. In prophesizing that "I feel I am not, therefore I am not," this incongruous prediction in disturbance lessens achievement motivation and reduces endurance to the task at hand. The traits (as measured on the EPPS) of endurance and orderliness are more intense in the Irish-American boys, especially in disturbance. These traits are confirmed with regard to the performance of homework in the service of achievement. However, it was shown the Irish-American boys put more endurance into withdrawal, inner-imaginative fantasy and self-glorification. Less endurance in the Italian-American disturbed group was due to active aggression with impulsivity in the service of compensatory omnipotence for feelings of inadequacy.

The Control Groups

In American society, the ability to stick to a task and to organize one's homework for successful achievement are considered good study habits. This creates a secure optimism that the achievement goal will reach successful completion. It tends to enhance the private world since the private feelings of self-esteem are in keeping with the demands of society. In answer to the question "Do your parents usually have to supervise you in order for you to do your homework?" a very high percentage of the boys in both control groups stated that their parents did not have to supervise them in their homework. In the Italian-American group there are suggestively more boys in the lower classes who have to be supervised by their parents. These adolescents have more dominant heterosexual and social inclinations.

While 50 percent of the Irish-American boys would not neglect their homework for social relationships, only 29 percent of Italian-American boys would not do so and another 30 percent are uncertain about this. When the question is asked, "If you have homework to do, do you very often spend more time watching television by yourself or doing other things by yourself than you spend in doing your homework?" there is again some statistical suggestion ($p<.20$) that more Italian-American boys are distracted by television (68 percent), and that more lower-class Italian-American boys are offenders ($p<.20$). Italian-American boys show not only less endurance and consistency for the demands of the task, but also less parental supervision in the accomplishment of homework assignments. This and previous data suggest a contrast between ethnic home environments. The one environment presents a more compulsive atmosphere as opposed to the other where self-responsibility is organized relatively less around routine schedules. Conscious awareness of easy diversion from responsibilities and of ambiguities in conflict situations is more prominent in the Italian-American boys, especially in the lower classes.

The Disturbed Groups

These groups are uniform in their feelings that they need their homework supervised, thereby differing significantly from the control groups. This is understandable considering the difficulties of concentration these boys have due to restlessness and anxiety. This leads to underachievement problems and difficulties in maintaining themselves in one school for any length of time which further reduces their capacity to concentrate. There is a certain hopelessness attached to their reaction patterns.

The boys of the disturbed groups do not neglect their homework to be with friends or to watch television. In this respect the Italian-American disturbed boys differ from their control group ($p<.05$). In the questionnaire section on "Most important thing in life," these boys were concerned with self-improvement in the eyes of others. And the Irish-American disturbed boys show increased compliance along with orderliness and endurance, which should provide the character traits necessary to attend to homework without diversion. However, autistic withdrawal and potential for fantasy foster poor achievement orientations and superficial compliance, without inner psychological compliance.

Social and Recreational Activities

Approximately 65 to 70 percent of the boys in both groups spend one to two evenings a week out with friends. The limited number of evenings out with friends was explained by the majority of boys in both groups as a rule set down by parents. A somewhat larger percentage of boys in the Italian-American lower classes are out of the home three to five evenings a week. This is not mathematically significant, but falls in line with findings of other subcultural data.

The Control Groups

There are no differences between the control groups with regard to the total number and kinds of extracurricular activities engaged in at school. Approximately 75 percent of the boys in both groups engage in sports, academic and fine arts clubs, and social clubs. Fifty percent of the boys in both groups engage in sports, while approximately 30 percent belong to school clubs. Approximately 25 percent have no extracurricular activities in school.

In amplification of previous data, table 56 indicates that both Irish-American and Italian-American boys tend to maintain their own characteristic styles of school and community participation. The Italian-American control boys persist in their affiliative tendencies to belong somewhere. Over 50 percent of them belong to school activities and community clubs, with leanings toward outside community organization activity. Only about 12 percent engage in extracurricular school activities as a sole source of recreation. In contrast, 55 percent of the Irish-American boys belong either to community clubs or to school clubs, while only 32 percent engage in both school activities and school organizations.

Italian-American sociocentricity and predilection for diversified competitive enterprises are part and parcel of this group's very nature, with its affiliative, domineering, and exhibitionistic tendencies. Amplification of these tendencies is shown when a typical Italian-American boy is capable of being distracted from his homework assignment in favor of socializing with friends, and in favor of pleasurable identifications with personages on television programs.

Table 56
Extracurricular Activities in School and Community

Activity	Irish-American Control	Italian-American Control	Irish-American Disturbed	Italian-American Disturbed
	%	%	%	%
No school activity— but community clubs	20.00	14.70	4.00	29.16
In-school activity— no community clubs	35.50	11.76	44.00	12.50
In-school activity and community clubs	32.50	55.88	28.00	41.66
No extracurricular activity	12.00	17.64	24.00	16.66
Total	100.00	99.98	100.00	99.98
	N=40	N=34	N=25	N=24

$x^2 = 6.00$, 3 d.f.;
$p. < .10$

$x^2 = 5.94$, 2 d.f.;
$p. < .05$

The Disturbed Groups

In contrast to the control groups, 50 percent of the boys in both disturbed groups spend three to five nights of the school week out with friends. This is an especially significant change on the part of the Irish-American disturbed boys ($p < .05$), where affiliation rises in disturbance, and confirms the increased mean affiliation score found on the Edwards Personal Preference Schedule. Again, we infer that the disturbed Irish-American boy complies with authority in the home, but he finds his acceptance and understanding with his own peer groups in the community. Although the boys in both disturbed groups have domestic conflicts in the home involving separation and divorce, in their own characteristic ways they appease their anxieties and apprehensions in affiliative discourses. The boys in both disturbed groups test their roles, earning rewards or punishments from those of their peers whose opinions count the most for self-esteem and whose respect is important for evolving self-improvement. In turning from their disturbed homes to outer community relationships, the Irish-American disturbed boys enhance their self-esteem through compliance and group participation among peers.

Peer-group orientations, thus, maintain the contrasting behavioral modalities for the Irish-American and the Italian-American boys. Passive-aggressive compliance for the Irish-American boy differentiates his role in the peer group from the active-aggressive participation of the Italian-American boy.

The Use of Leisure Time

The questionnaire affirmed that the Irish-American and Italian-American boys handled the release of aggressions caused by restrictions and frustrations differently. We also postulated that release of aggression and increased succorance needs may be manipulated through leisure activities and peer-group relationships.

A review of previous instruments yields a picture of the Italian-American boys as more dominant, exhibitionistic, and affiliative than those in the Irish-American group. We postulated decreased succorance partially as a consequence of the therapeutic situation which provides the support of the physician and other additional attention in the long-term therapeutic regime. We also proposed that decreased succorance requirements resulted from adjustment mechanisms that produced in turn increased detachment in the Irish-American boys and defiance of authority in the Italian-American boys. Irish-American aggression was associated with the need for change and resulted in idealistic daydreaming. The Italian-American boys have given up succorance and nurturance for defiance and rebellion. By so doing, they increase their dominance and exhibitionism in peer-group relationships in the maintenance of active aggression and in order to win approval and admiration.

As a result of the foregoing deductions, we could assume that the egocentric desires of the Irish-American boys would lead them to have more intense attachments in smaller groups, while the Italian-American boys would have more sociocentrically oriented references to the wider field of social relationships.

The Control Groups

In response to the question "do you usually like to spend your leisure time with other people in clubs, fraternities, or groups of fellows?" there is a significant difference between the boys in the ethnic groups ($x^2 = 7.85$, 1 d.f., $p < .01$). Over 50 percent of the Irish-American boys state that they like to affiliate with others in formal or informal groups, while over 85 percent of the Italian-American boys do so. The Italian-American boys have no negative responses to this question, nor do they show social class differences. In the Irish-American group there is a suggestive social class difference ($x^2 = 3.42$, 1 d.f., <.10), with greater socializing in the lower class.

More Italian-American boys belong to fraternities, 38 percent of them affiliating as compared to only 15 percent of the Irish-American boys. On the other hand, in all social classes, the Irish-American boys mention more athletic clubs and Catholic organizations. While only 28 percent of Italian-American adolescents state that they do not belong to organizations, over 42 percent of the Irish-American boys give negative replies to affiliation with larger formal groups.

Amplification of this answer, revealing more overt socializing by the Italian-American boys, comes in response to the question relating to the size of the group they affiliate with. Although statistical tests were not significant ($p < .20$), three-quarters of the Irish-American group state that they belong to groups with only one to six people, while 50 percent of Italian-American adolescents belong to social groups of seven to twelve people. Again, there are no differences between social classes for Italian-American boys, while more lower-class Irish-American boys affiliate with larger groups (37 percent to 16 percent, N.S.).

The Italian-American control boys not only appear to affiliate more with other adolescents and to join more social organizations but also appear to find it easier to keep up with the crowd. Very few of the Italian-American boys find it absolutely difficult to keep

Table 57
"Do you feel it is hard to keep up
with your crowd?"

Response	Irish-American Control	Italian-American Control
	%	%
Yes	35.00	17.64
No	57.50	47.05
Sometimes	7.50	35.30
Total	100.00	99.99
	N = 40	N = 34

$x^2 = 9.42$, 2 d.f.; $p < .01$

up with the crowd, while one-third of these boys state that it is sometimes difficult. The "sometimes" answer can be assumed to be a rather normal answer for most individuals who sometimes find it difficult for one reason or another.

Meaningful group participation with one's peers is particularly accentuated when we note that 90 percent of the Italian-American boys are either one of the crowd or a leader; significantly more Italian-American boys are leaders than are Irish-American boys. Significantly more Irish-American boys designate themselves as neither leaders nor participative members. This would lead one to infer that in view of previous data which reveals fewer organizational attachments and smaller groups, these boys are more or less self-felt

Table 58
"In a crowd of boys, are you usually one
of the crowd or are you often a leader?"

Response	Irish-American Control	Italian-American Control
	%	%
One of Crowd	32.50	55.88
Leader	27.50	35.30
Neither	40.00	8.82
Total	100.00	100.00
	N = 40	N = 34

$x^2 = 9.61$, 2 d.f.;
$p < .01$

isolationists. It appears that 40 percent of these boys do not consider themselves group-oriented.

As usual, more leaders in the Italian-American group come from the lower class ($p < .20$), where 45 percent of the boys designate themselves as leaders, while 71 percent of the upper-class boys designate themselves as one of the crowd.

Neighborhood Affiliation

In an effort to determine whether affiliation in the neighborhood and ethnicity of the neighborhood were correlated, the Tetrachoric correlation coefficient was computed by the methods of the computing diagrams of L. L. Thurstone and others (15).

There is only a low positive correlation in the Italian-American group between affiliation in one's own neighborhood and ethnicity. While 32 percent of the Italian-American boys affiliate in their own neighborhood, 35 percent of the boys also affiliate in non-Italian neighborhoods. This finding is exaggerated in the disturbed group, where more leave their neighborhoods. In the Irish-American group there is no association between one's neighborhood affiliation and ethnicity. Ethnic affiliation does not appear to influence neighborhood affiliation in any group to any extent. Italian-American boys tend to affiliate more with neighborhood boys, regardless of ethnic background. The Irish-American boys tend to affiliate more with boys in community organizations outside of the neighborhood, regardless of neighborhood ethnicity.

Table 59
Affiliation or Non-affiliation in Own Ethnic Neighborhood

Control Group Affiliation	Italian-American		Irish-American	
	Italian	Non-Italian	Irish	Non-Irish
	%	%	%	%
Yes	32.00	35.00 = 67.00	7.00	30.00 = 37.00
No	9.00	24.00 = 33.00	13.00	50.00 = 63.00
Total	41.00	59.00 100.00	20.00	80.00 100.00
		N = 34		N = 40

$$rt. = +.352 \qquad\qquad rt. = -.137$$

The Italian-American boys socialize more with peers in informal ways. Gans (42) describes these boys as those who seek exciting opportunities in the social world, who are "action seekers." However, in this study, there is a deeper meaning to "action seeking." These boys seek supplies from the environment for self-esteem and gratification of desires. They seek gratifications through domineering and exhibitionistic behavioral modalities. Aggression as a result of frustration is appeased by some degree of social dominance. The Italian-American boys attempt to exert social control through nurturance and the reception of succorance from people in the environment.

Among the Irish boys there is greater detachment from larger wholes in social intercourse, with greater attachment to small groups. Perhaps more Irish-American boys place themselves upon the periphery of group participation where they can easily step away from the group members if they so desire. Large community organizations do not foster intimate peer group relationships.

Passive social activities are essentially those actions that may be performed with others, but are aimed mainly at self-enhancement or private pleasure as opposed to social interaction and interpersonal enhancement. We defined passive social activities, in the main, as watching television, going to the movies and theatre, and drinking and smoking. These passive activities were indulged in by the Irish-American boys, while passive activities for the Italian-American boys were indicated by work in the chemistry laboratory and by the statement "do nothing much."

Table 60
Tabulation of Leisure Activities with Friends

Activity	Irish-American Control	Italian-American Control	Irish-American Disturbed	Italian-American Disturbed
	%	%	%	%
Passive Social	40.50	17.64	54.16	37.93
Active Social	60.00	76.44	45.84	62.02
No Response	00.00	5.92	00.00	00.00
Total	100.50	100.00	100.00	99.95
	$N=40$	$N=34$	$N=25$	$N=24$

$$x^2 = 4.28, 1 \text{ d.f.,} \qquad x^2 = 3.08, 1 \text{ d.f.,}$$
$$p < .05 \qquad\qquad p < .10$$

Active social activities included talking things over with fellows on moral and religious issues. This was mentioned by 23 percent of the Italian-American boys as opposed to 7.5 percent of the Irish-American boys. In addition, approximately 12 percent of the Italian-American boys dated girls, and over 20 percent of them went to parties and dances. Of the Irish-American boys, 8 percent dated girls and approximately 12 percent attended parties and dances.

More Irish-American boys attended the YMCA, sports stadiums, plays, theatres, and evening classes. More Italian-American boys attended neighborhood houses, concerts, and public lectures. These ethnic traits become highly exaggerated in disturbance.

Hobbies

There is a highly significant difference between the two ethnic groups in the definitive selection of hobbies.

Egocentric creation refers to hobbies that are usually performed alone for self-enhancement and pleasure. These include stamp and coin collecting, reading, hunting, fishing, and skin diving, all of which the Irish-American boys choose in contrast to the Italian-American boys. From the egocentric-creative frame of reference, the Italian-American boys selected model airplane and car building, listening to the phonograph, caring for a fish aquarium, and reading more often as hobbies. Hunting, fishing, and skin diving, enjoyed

Table 61
Frequency of Hobbies that Enhance Self-Isolation

Egocentric Social Potential	Irish-American Control	Italian-American Control
	%	%
Egocentric-Creative Potential	55.00	38.23
Social-Creative Potential	45.00	26.47
Sometimes Egocentric	00.00	35.29
Total	100.00	99.99
	N = 40	N = 34

$x^2 = 16.89$, 2 d.f.; $p < .001$

by the Irish-American boys, may be attuned to solitary aggressive conquests consistent with aggressive feelings of the Irish-American control group. Caring for fish in an aquarium, as an Italian-American hobby, displays nurturance and control. While the Italian-American boys engage in self-enhancement hobbies "sometimes," this is mingled with social group activity and interpersonal associations, so that privately shared hobbies can alternate with interpersonal events. In contrast to the Italian-American group, it is possible that many of the boys in the Irish-American group are engaged in solitary pursuits as compensations for less social joining and fewer organizational affiliations.

Socio-creative potentials are those hobbies that can be shared readily with others or require joint efforts to accomplish. The Italian-American boys, in the main, play musical instruments and belong to school orchestras; one writes music. A utilitarian socio-creative phenomenon exists in an example where the Italian-American boys fix car engines with the help of their fathers. In the Irish-American group, socio-creative hobbies are wood-working with fathers, radio-electronics, and the operation of ham radios.

The greater accent on egocentric hobbies by the Irish-American boy is consistent with the suppression of aggression and private fantasy. The greater selection of hobbies with social-creative potential is in line with the greater accent on interpersonal communication in the Italian-American group. Aggressive release in both ethnic groups takes on potentially different patterns, a manifestation of which is exhibited by the selection and the pursuance of hobbies. The proportional ratio of the kinds of hobbies selected is increased in disturbance.

The Disturbed Groups

Desire for informal and formal group associations by the Irish-American disturbed boys differs only slightly, if at all, from the control group, with about one-half of the group desiring to spend its leisure time in socializing with groups of fellows. (Again, socializing is insignificantly increased in the lower classes.) In contrast to the control group, the Italian-American disturbed boys desire less socializing. Where the great majority of the Italian-American control boys desire formal and informal group participation, 50 percent of the disturbed boys require this. However, these boys do state that they would "sometimes" like to socialize. Again, as with the control group, there are no differences between the social classes.

When formal organization membership is analyzed, the Italian-American disturbed group gives up more informal associations and favors joining community clubs with more formal organization. The Italian-American disturbed boys choose smaller crowds of fellows for informal relationships and they are, in this regard, on a par with the Irish-American boys. The disturbed boys do not belong to fraternities because they are one to two years younger than the control boys. The pattern of community organization membership is still the same as with the control group. The Irish-American boys belong to the YMCA and certain athletic clubs, while the Italian-American boys belong to the neighborhood houses, neighborhood boys clubs, and music clubs.

On the whole, the differences between small and larger group af-

Table 62
Membership in Community Clubs and Organizations

Response	Irish-American Control	Italian-American Control	Irish-American Disturbed	Italian-American Disturbed
	%	%	%	%
Joiners	52.50	73.53	32.00	66.66
Non-Jointers	47.50	26.47	68.00	33.34
Total	100.00	100.00	100.00	100.00
	N=40	N=34	N=25	N=24

$$x^2 = 3.12, \text{1 d.f.;} \qquad x^2 = 5.87, \text{1 d.f.;}$$
$$p < .10 \qquad\qquad p < .02$$

filiations are maintained, although the Italian-American boys, to a somewhat larger but yet non-significant extent, favor smaller informal groups. Tendencies for aggression and dominance make it more difficult for Italian-American youth to belong to participative social clubs where dominance and aggression are often stifled. In contrast, the Irish-American disturbed boys have fewer friends and join less community organizations. This boy becomes more egocentric and unable to give of himself socially without inhibition and fear of exhibition.

Approximately 50 percent of the boys in both disturbed groups feel that it is "difficult to keep up with the crowd." The Irish-American disturbed boys have not changed in this regard from their control group but the Italian-American boys do differ from their control group by finding it definitely difficult to keep up with the crowd. This answer from the Italian-American disturbed youths forms a natural consequence of their behavioral modality; that is, they decline to join community organizations. Defiance of authority, coupled with domineering and exhibitionistic traits in the service of aggression, requires a group that a disturbed youth can fit into where these traits will be accepted. With these personal drives, a youth prefers to choose his own informal group where he can choose and modify membership characteristics in the interest of mutual suitability.

In the Irish-American disturbed group, affiliation is more pronounced, as are the qualities of nurturance and endurance. These qualities, together with a limited choice of only a few participative friends, help the boy to keep his fewer friendships without undue hardship. It is interesting that in the Irish-American group, the upper-class boys have, throughout, chosen fewer friends, have joined fewer organizations, and have found it harder to keep up with the crowd than have the lower-class boys.

The Italian-American disturbed boys have exaggerated the Italian-American pattern of identifying with neither crowd nor leader. Increased isolation and lack of identification with one's group in the community are linked with this group's difficulty in keeping up with the crowd and with its own defiant and aggressive pattern. This behavioral modality involves poor qualitative participation and cooperation with others, and it may involve characteristics of argument and resentment of group authority. Such people may be seen as marginal men, who fit neatly into no group unless they can adapt the group to their will or adapt the group's function to their own ventilative desires. The Italian-American disturbed boys have increased needs for defiant isolation and for independence that allows one to be beholden to no one. At this point, we have a picture of the sullen, resentful Italian-American disturbed boy and the compliant, dependent Irish-American disturbed boy. These are patterns that have been amplified throughout this study.

Tetrachoric correlation coefficients accomplished with each disturbed group indicates that ethnic affinity in the neighborhood, in exaggeration of the control groups, does not appear to influence affiliation in the neighborhood. In both groups there is a negative correlation between neighborhood affiliation and ethnicity (Italian-American, $-.37$; Irish-American, $-.862$). The Irish-American boys affiliate more in non-Irish-American neighborhoods, although they engage in their own neighborhood affiliations to a greater degree than their control group or the Italian-American group.

Passive-dependence in the Irish-American disturbed boys forfeits wider community identifications. While only 32 percent of the boys belong to formal community organizations, they affiliate with both neighborhood and non-neighborhood friends. The more passive and compliant boy conceivably cooperates with those people in the vicinity of home, school, and church as a way of gaining social approval. The boy who is compliant and shy surrounds himself with familiar friends in the neighborhood.

The Italian-American disturbed boys are not so clearly interested in neighborhood participation, and seek identifying friendships in community groups elsewhere as they stalk the city for selective participation best suited to their emotional modalities. They turn from the groups in their own neighborhoods in order to seek more likely and fitting groups outside the neighborhood. The boy who resentfully removes himself from participative and cooperative functions, and who is filled with aggressive needs that require relief, strays from home to find selective crowds. The boy who is aggressive seeks wider horizons in unknown territory, where even his family will not know his actions.

Discussion

While the compliant personality tends to appease and to nourish the goodwill of other people, the active-aggressive personality does everything he can to be a good fighter. He is alert and keen and will go out of his way to launch an argument for the sake of proving he is right. This is consistent with his attitude of having to fight against a malevolent world. The compliant type seeks to avoid fights with others and moves toward humane ideals.

The assertive, aggressive type moves toward a "law of the jungle" philosophy. In assuming this philosophy, the Italian-American boy moves with shrewdness and cunning in order to insure self-sufficiency and, at the same time, privacy. In this way, the Italian-American disturbed boy moves beyond the neighborhood to unknown places, where he can welcome the compliant types as they subordinate themselves to his own dominance and resourcefulness. If the Italian-American disturbed boy inclines toward detachment, he will shun any direct domination of his activities because it brings him into too close contact with others.

Means and ways of spending leisure time concur with the disturbance characteristics of the boys in both groups, and with changes in social relationships. The data suggest that the Irish-American disturbed boys have more passive-social leisure activities than the Italian-American groups ($p<.10$), although the Italian-American disturbed boys engage in more passive social activities than their own control group. These boys describe their activities as watching television, seeing plays at the theatre, and "doing nothing." More of these boys date girls and go to parties than do the Irish-American boys and they frequent neighborhood houses more often.

Even though there is less community participation by the disturbed Italian-American boys, they mention active social leisure activities as frequently as the control group. In particular, serious discussions on politics, religion, girls, and cars are more frequent among these boys. There is greater skepticism in freer interpersonal discussion that often leads to serious ethical and moral discussions. The street corner congregations and the card playing of the Irish-American boys are not rated as activity preferences by the Italian-American boys, while the interest and participation in musical activities of Italian-American boys is not mentioned by the Irish-American boys. Italian-American adolescents do not mention such solitary activities as skin diving, engaged in by Irish-American boys. Heterosexual striving during leisure time is significantly more an active Italian-American role rather than an Irish-American one. Italian-Americans participate more in competitive sports as a pastime, in contrast to "observation or watching" football and baseball games by the Irish-American boys. On the other hand, more Irish-American boys mention public lectures in the community as a means of egocentric fulfillment.

The pursuance of egocentric hobbies exaggerates and clarifies decreased socializing tendencies in both disturbed groups. Seventy-five percent of the Irish-American disturbed boys pursue hobbies of an egocentric nature, while 66 percent of the Italian-American boys do so. There are no social class differences in this respect. The Italian-American disturbed group has significantly more boys pursuing solitary hobbies than the control group. This finding supports the assumption that the disturbed Italian-American boys are not wholly identified with group membership roles, but remain resentful and rebellious while they assume sullen and hostile individuality. Aggressive behavior of the Italian-American boys, in problems associated with dominant affiliation roles, does not lead to the selection of hobbies that can be socially shared. Defiance and hostility often lead to private hobbies.

However, despite these considerations, the Italian-Americans have more sociocentrically creative hobbies and hobbies that retain more of a native ethnic nature. These boys are still utilitarian-minded in helping their fathers and grandfathers with woodbuilding, woodcarving, and household repair, hobbies that can be reserved for future use in their own married lives and possible employment. Occupations developed both in music and in the practical arts are not necessarily outgrown.

The Italian-American disturbed boys might be said to exhibit Dionysian tendencies in which one annihilates the ordinary bounds and limits of existence in order to break through into another order of experience. The Irish-American disturbed boys, if they can be pictured as Apollonian individuals, try to stay within the powerful influences of tradition. The Italian-American disturbed boys move against people in attempting to rise above ordinary experience. The Irish-American disturbed boys strive for social acceptance by the preservation of tradition and of values that bring social approval. The Irish-American boys are interested not so much in diverse social participation as in the approval of fellow group members and steady, reliable friendships.

Dating Patterns and Attitudes

The Control Groups

Approximately 83 percent of the Irish-American and the Italian-American control boys date girls, while over 90 percent of the boys in both groups enjoy associating with girls. These boys have strong father identifications and have heterosexual striving scores on the Edwards Personal Preference Schedule approximating the normative high school and college scores.

There are, however, significantly more Irish-American boys in the older age category who do not date than in the Italian-American group.

The Italian-American control group, like the disturbed group, has boys of thirteen and fourteen who have not yet begun active dating. These boys apparently are sexually immature, so that attraction to the opposite sex is not yet a reality. The Irish-American

Table 63
Control Boys Who Do Not Date, by Age Level

	Age in Years and Months		
	13–15.11	16–19.11	Total
	%	%	
CONTROL:			
Irish-American	14.29	85.71	100.00
Italian-American	83.33	16.67	100.00

Fisher — Yates $= p = <.05$

boys who do not date would rather socialize with a crowd of fellows than with a mixed crowd, and they prefer to associate with plain and serious girls rather than pretty and popular girls. They feel that "girls are hard to get to know well." The younger Italian-American boys generally look forward to dating, and usually feel "blind dates may be fun."

The Disturbed Groups

Fifty percent of the Italian-American disturbed boys actively date girls, as opposed to only 24 percent of the Irish-American disturbed boys ($p < .10$). While adolescents in both disturbed groups date girls less than do the boys in the control groups, this phenomenon may be partially due to sexual immaturity. However, where masculine identifications are confused or lacking, the Italian-American boys still actively date significantly more than do the Irish-American boys. When we make analyses of the age dating began, there are significant differences between the ethnic groups. Over 83 percent of the Italian-American boys began dating at the age of thirteen, while 75 percent of the Irish-American boys began dating at ages fifteen to sixteen. Age level of the boys who never dated is shown in table 64.

In contrast to the Italian-American boys, 88 percent of the Irish-American boys from ages thirteen to sixteen do not date (only four are thirteen years of age). There are not only more boys in this group who do not date, but 50 percent of the sixteen year olds and 20 percent of the seventeen to nineteen year olds do not date. In general, dating starts one to two years later than in the Italian-American group.

In the Irish-American disturbed group there is a significant difference between the social classes in dating patterns. Dating is more

Table 64
Disturbed Boys Who Do Not Date, by Age Level

	Age in Years and Months		
	13–13.11	14	Total
	%	%	
DISTURBED:			
Irish-American	25.00	75.00	100.00
Italian-American	83.33	16.66	99.99

Fisher—Yates $p = <.01$

frequent among upper-class boys and non-dating among the lower-class boys ($p<.05$). This finding appears somewhat contradictory, in that the lower classes socialize somewhat more than the upper classes, but socializing may occur with other boys rather than with girls.

The Italian-American boys do not exhibit class differences in dating patterns. There is, however, a non-significant tendency in both control and disturbed groups for more dating in the lower classes, which coincides with lower stress placed upon conformity and authoritarian control.

Even in disturbance, the non-dating Italian-American boys feel that girls are friendly and fun; they enjoy associating with girls, and they enjoy mixed crowds. They look forward, with a sense of competitive spirit, to dating pretty and popular girls. The Irish-American disturbed boys who do not date prefer girls who are plain but serious. They are not given to blind date adventure, and they feel that girls are difficult to get to know, while 75 percent of the Italian-American disturbed boys feel that girls are not hard to know. Seventy percent of the Italian-American boys date at least once a week while 70 percent of the Irish-American boys date once every two weeks. The Italian-American disturbed boys, who socialize less than their control boys, still appear to show greater tendencies toward heterosexual socializing than the Irish-American disturbed boys.

Even though the boys in both disturbed groups have difficulties with masculine identification, it becomes evident throughout this study that the mechanisms of adjustment are different. The Irish-American boys, with fewer friends, greater inhibitions, and more small group affiliations, find it harder to play the aggressive masculine role in dating. We can even infer that the Irish-American boy substitutes those of the same sex for those of the opposite sex in efforts at masculine identification. Exchanging sexual stories with other boys provides an initiation into sexuality without fear of inadequacy in heterosexual experience. The active aggressive defiance of the Italian-American disturbed boys allows them to date girls for reassurance of masculinity.

The Irish-American boys prefer the more plain and serious girls, as do the Italian-American disturbed boys, who in the last analysis relate better to the serious girl for discussion of their life problems. In disturbance, both groups—one aggressive and defiant, the other withdrawn and introverted—choose serious girls whom they feel they can relate to and trust in their attachments. Competitive heterosexual spirit in each disturbed group has decreased, so perhaps they try to achieve masculine identification with understanding girls who are less competitive. The dire need for proof of masculine adequacy comes at the same time these boys need a friend who can compensate for the troubled home atmosphere and for an undesirable self-image.

The Irish-American disturbed boys exhibited in the questionnaire the traits of order and deference for authority first identified on the Edwards Personal Preference Schedule. The great need for order and conformity in Irish-American boys explains why they do not welcome blind dates or events that are not planned in advance. The Irish-American disturbed boys frequently date more serious girls in more passive dependent ways to ensure security and dependency, thereby transferring his maternal dependency to a girl his own age.

Summary

The questionnaire amplified the previous research instruments by its particularization of the differently ordered family lives and attitudinal frames of reference in which these boys developed. It described mechanisms of familial interaction, achievement orientations, peer-group associations, recreational and social intercourse, and heterosexual activities.

Analyses of the data indicated that the social frames of reference pointed to in-group direction for the Italian-American boys and less in-group direction for the Irish-American boys. The questionnaire amplified problems of masculinity in the various areas of social life as well as differential ethnic mechanisms of appeasing anxiety and hostility. Social class differentiations appeared in the more conforming social behavior of the upper classes Italian-Americans as contrasted to their lower classes. Irish-American boys socialized more in lower social classes while exhibiting more tenacity in task achievement.

In general, the questionnaire amplified the research instruments by further confirming the idealistic and egocentric frames of reference for the Irish-American groups as opposed to the more pragmatic and sociocentric frames of reference for the Italian-American groups.

10

Summary and Conclusions

Summation

The concern of this study was to determine whether there were significant differences in adolescent adjustment processes between ethnic groupings. This study maintained that, even though diluted through generations of living in a dominant American culture, value orientations vary between ethnic groups, and as a consequence we postulated that adolescent patterns of adjustment would vary ethnically and that adolescent disturbances would intensify the ethnic behavioral modalities. We held that social class factors are necessary considerations but subject to the variant values of the ethnic groups. Considering these factors, we inferred that there would be differences in disturbance modalities between Irish-American and Italian-American adolescents.

We developed frames of reference as areas for hypothetical proposals and for research purposes which included relationship to family authority, sexual identification, relationship to peers, hostility and anxiety, emotional expression, role and behavior, and patterns of values.

Four research instruments delineated the variant predispositions of the adolescent's perceptual fields. This polydimensional approach was an attempt to depict personality, family interaction, and role perception as Gestaltic rather than as an aggregate of isolated needs. At the same time we performed tests of significance between the social class structures as these were held constant within the context of each ethnic group.

The ultimate conclusion of this study was that intergenerational communication of attitudes and values in the home leaves the contemporary Irish-American and Italian-American adolescent with a heritage of stylistic cognitions and behavioral patterns that are stimulated differently in the two different kinds of homes.

The Irish-American Groups

Irish-American youths obtain higher mean scores in deference for authority, in desire for change, and in aggression. In contrast to Italian-American boys, aggressive heterosexuality and exhibitionism are low. Aggressive drives in an Irish-American youth repress heterosexuality and release compensatory reactions of conforming behavior. Higher needs for change and lower needs for order complement each other in pointing towards desires for new loyalties and preferences. Increased aggression, coupled with deference for authority, relegates dependent-independent conflicts to passive resistance where desires for a change are relegated to fantasy.

In the Life-Space Drawing, Irish-American youths draw significantly smaller "Me" circles than do Italian-American youths, which we interpreted to mean that they see themselves as less significant in the social field and perceive themselves in a mirror as other people react to them. This is corroborated in the self-concept scale, where difficulties in identity and moral-ethical areas are illustrated. Irish-American youths compartmentalize themselves in the various areas of social field in efforts to obtain social approval for conforming modalities.

Irish-American youths have somewhat greater father identifications than do Italian-American youths, but they select mothers as the closest relationship regardless of separation or employment. Not only are nuclear family orientations prevalent, but extrafamilial orientations precede extended family relationships. Irish-American family life is more democratic than Italian-American family life. Mother domination is evident, not only as the first proximal choice and as the one whose disapproval is the most feared, but also as the one who sets the more compulsive and more important rules and regulations in the home. In spite of the home regime, Irish-American youths feel that their fathers are active in praise and encouragement and that both parents are interested in them.

The questionnaire revealed that mobility aspirations in Irish-American youths are higher in all social classes than are the vocational interests of the parents. In contrast to Italian-American youths, who are inclined to the free professions, Irish-American youths show interest in scholarly activities and professional military experience. Parental pressure toward achievement orientation did not appear to be as great as that in Italian-American groups;

however, positive non-directed parental pressure was evident to a greater extent.

The Irish-American boys tend to congregate in smaller social groups than the Italian-Americans, and several of them prefer isolation. More Irish-American boys place themselves upon the periphery of group organizations. Hobby activity is on more egocentric levels, and socially shared activities, such as music, were not indicated in the Irish-American groups. There is greater need for solitary activity, such as skin diving, hunting, and fishing. Irish-American youths are not as prone to heterosexual and mixed crowd activity as are the Italian-American boys, and Irish-American youths who did not date girls included older boys, unlike Italian-Americans.

Irish-American youths do not openly oppose authority, but rather they conform socially and engage for compensation in egocentric imaginative reflections. They compartmentalize their ego identities in accordance with the demanded conformity to differentiated social groups. Ego unity is used to gain social approval; they pay compulsive attention to detail and give primary reference to an idealistic form of ethics in the interest of social approval. Aggression and heterosexuality are suppressed in favor of the fantasy of self-glorification and in compliance to authority.

In disturbance, Irish-American youths significantly exaggerate deference for authority in subordination to counsel and direction. Significantly increased orderliness and conformity to details place Irish-American youths in dependent positions and act as reaction formations against suppressed hostilities and feelings of guilt. Aggressive impulses are significantly diminished, with further reductions in heterosexuality, as compared to control boys. Aggression and desires for change are suppressed through the process of autistic withdrawal and self-glorifying fantasy. Dependency is further exaggerated by decreases in dominance. The passive aggression of this youth is in direct contrast to the active aggression of Italian-American youth.

In spite of maternal employment or separation, there is marked maternal identification among disturbed Irish-American youths. Although the Irish-American parents are more often separated or divorced, there is a nostalgic clinging to the maternal image and to extended family figures. This is in contrast to the Irish-American control group and indicates need for family unity and security. Lack of an adequate masculine role model is correlated with high identification with the mother and with female proximity choices.

In disturbance, Irish-American youths describe the same strict home rules but democratic intrafamilial processes contrast to the responses of the Italian-American boys. We attribute their greater endurance in task achievement to autistic thinking and fantasies of self-glorification where withdrawal and autism are symptoms of emotional disturbance. These fantasies allow the boy to feel omnipotent and admired. This form of rebellion contrasts to the defiant rebellion of the Italian-American youths. Stress upon conformity and stress upon an idealistic self-image in fantasy are exaggerations of the patterns of the control Irish-American youths.

In disturbance, Irish-American youths continue to socialize in small groups, and belong to fewer clubs and informal groups. Also, these boys prefer a sense of belonging to leadership, and depend upon group membership for social approval. Leadership, as lower-class behavior, is not confirmed in this study of Irish-American youth. Irish-American youths date girls far less than do Italian-American youths, and they begin dating at an older age. In actuality, the Irish-Americans prefer crowds of fellows and they do not look forward to heterosexual adventure. Leisure and hobby activities remain egocentrically oriented and are pursued alone. Identity diffusion exists with reference to "what he is" in the general state of things. Irish-American youths focus upon external criteria for evaluation, especially in the areas of the social and the family self. They base self-criticism of the moral-ethical ideal primarily upon what they are in contrast to what they should be.

In general, Irish-American youths move toward a benevolent world, with great detachment in defense against social disappointment. Leisure time activities and hobbies are private. Maternal images are internalized, and demands for expiation on maternally dominated guilts provide poor masculine identification. Suppressing aggression in order to comply with authority works only if they get social approval. If not, and if the sense of order as a reactive defense against aggression is weakened, their ego control breaks down and suppressed aggression may cause masochistic phenomena. Autistic withdrawal into the world of fantasy, in which adolescence assumes heroic proportions, compensates for ego inadequacy and deflation.

The Italian-American Groups

The Italian-American youths, in their modality, require less change in habits and routine, less of the new and experimental;

they desire prearranged designs of behavior and organizational work patterns. They have greater drive for succorance, while there is also substantial drive to give nurturance to those in distress. Aggressiveness in heterosexuality and exhibitionism is greater with Italian-American boys than with Irish-American boys. The Italian-American modal pattern of behavior is less consistent, indicating an impulsive quality with greater responsiveness and impulsiveness in social interaction. This combination of personal attributes signifies initiative in social action and a tendency to convert aggression into affectionate and domineering relationships.

In the Life-Space Drawing, Italian-American youth include more collateral kin in perceptual proximity choices. They also draw significantly larger circles of "Me" than the Irish-American boys, which was amplified on the Fitts self-concept scale, where ego unity and internal balance were found to synthesize from the outer social environment.

The questionnaire reveals that Italian-American boys choose their fathers for identification, although the mother is seen as a loving and ingratiating figure. The modality of Italian-American home life reveals fewer clock-bound schedules of activities, with evidence of greater paternal authoritarianism. In contrast to the Irish-American groups, significantly more boys in this group are physically punished, and situations of conflict at home make the adolescents avoid the parents in favor of outer community relationships. They also seek release of active aggression outside the family.

Their achievement orientations involve pragmatic goals, and their mobility aspirations are higher than those achieved by the parents. Evidence of parental pressure toward achievement exists in all social classes.

In contrast to the Irish-American groups, there is greater predilection for social attachments with more participation in both formal and informal community groups. Leisure time activities are socially shared, and hobbies take on active social overtones. The enjoyment of heterosexual activities is more apparent, and they seek heterosexual striving, succorance, and nurturance in social intercourse. With the diminution of these traits, exhibitionistic, domineering, and aggressive drives increase in efforts to raise self-esteem. Without the ingratiating accompaniment of succorance and nurturance, assertive drives are used to serve personal power and to defy authority. Increased desire for change initiates desire for new affiliative and object conquests. These assertive drives deny feelings of inadequacy. Exhibitionism replaces succorance by forcing attention upon the subject and his talent. Successful exhibitionism compensates for feelings of masculine and social inadequacy. Increased action orientation in the social field with peers who appreciate exhibitionistic and domineering strivings lead to sociopathic escapades and conflicts with the law. Since abasement mean scores remain on normative levels, conscience keeps dependent-independent adolescent conflict on levels of impressive misdemeanors.

In disturbance, Italian-American youths draw somewhat smaller circles of "Me" than the control group, but the configurations are still larger than those of the Irish-American groups. Social punishment for aggressive misdemeanors tends to make these disturbed youths somewhat less ego-inflative than control youths, but more selective in social affiliation. In disturbance, Italian-American youths tend to leave collateral family relationships in favor of peer-group associations, and positive maternal choice is associated conversely with parental separation.

Analysis of the questionnaire illustrates that in disturbance, Italian-American youths lack adequate masculine identification. While female identification is not as strong as it is in the Irish-American disturbed youths, prominent and authoritative figures initiate confusing masculine identifications. Authoritarian discipline of the father and subservience of the mother initiate strong lack of trust in paternal relationships. Conflicts in masculine identification promote active peer group identifications as substitutes for paternal images, and peer groups act as testing grounds for exchange of feelings.

In disturbance, authoritarianism in the home increases and the father is a harsher disciplinarian. Italian-American youths tend to feel that their parents do not understand them, and there are more overt disagreements with parents. These appear as inabilities to live up to the expiation demands of authoritarian parents.

Defiance of authority diverts aggressive impulses to peer groups, where Italian-American youths attempt to gain social control through peer-group admiration. Leisure time activities and hobbies are more passively social and more egocentric than those of control boys. However, disturbed youths fit neatly into no group unless the group is adapted to their own emotional drives. Behavioral modalities of the disturbed boys show increased affiliation beyond the neighborhood boundaries because they seek peer groups in line with their own behavioral modalities. Italian-American youths deny need for expiation and fight a world perceived as malevolent with shrewdness and cunning in the interest of self-sufficiency. They shun direct domination of activities and seek respect from selective friendships. Heterosexual affiliations are greater than in Irish-American groups; Italian-American youths date girls at an earlier age and prefer heterosexual adventure. In disturbance, Italian-American youths still have more sociocentric activities and socially shared hobbies than do the Irish-American groups. The socially shared hobbies maintain the utilitarian and pragmatic base.

Failing to get a sense of basic trust from parents in the home, Italian-American youths distrust others. In rebellion, they strive for autonomy and for a narcissistic sense of importance in the social world. They fight coercion and move against people in the seemingly malevolent world. Where Italian-American youths do not resolve their identity problems, they seek identity through omnipotent relationships with sometimes improbable and delinquent partners. Self-identity is placed in the service of extraceptive manipulation.

Social Classes

The study has pointed out the importance of social class factors, subject to the influence of ethnicity. The social class system as a system of values is more apparent among the Irish-American boys. In this ethnic group, achievement orientation went down, and overt manipulation of the environment increased with lower social class status.

The Italian-American upper-class group had greater authoritarianism in the home, coupled with physical punishment and stern demand for conforming behavior. Italian-American achievement orientations remain high in all social classes, as does parental pressure for achievement.

Clinical differentiation of the boys does not discriminate between the social classes in terms of frequency or the depth of delinquent acts. The boys in the lower classes of both ethnic groups have greater mobility orientation than their parents, with consequent conflict in this regard. The Italian-American boys were exhibitionistic and aggressive in all social classes, without significant differences. The supposition that in the upper classes withdrawn behavior with tendencies to daydream causes a decline in leadership so that leadership may be class-linked behavior, has not been confirmed. Dominant patterns of withdrawal by the Irish Groups, occur in all social classes, and dominant patterns of delinquency by the Italian group occur in all social classes. While leadership patterns are not confirmed on a class basis in the Italian group the ethnic variable points to leadership tendencies.

Summary:

In keeping with the hypotheses of this study, subtle intergenerational communication directs the Irish-American boy to show dependent conforming behavior toward an idealistically benevolent world. When the way of life becomes disappointing, the boy's behavior becomes less conforming and more detached. In accordance with the hypothetical frames of reference, the Italian-American boy builds his self-image through overt manipulation of his environment and in accordance with a sociocentric ideology derived from his home. In exaggeration of control boys, disturbed adolescents maintain their particular ethnic patterns, but rigidify them in efforts to achieve personal identity.

Although the rank ordering of a subculture within the larger dominant society may be affected by its ability to harmonize with and blend with the larger American society, an important addition to ethnic theory is the communication from parent to son in a maintained subcultural base. The fitting of an ethnic group to the larger American culture and a loss of the group's manifest traits do not necessitate the loss of its latent influence in dealing with life. Personal stress begins in a family which has a particular subcultural setting, and the modes of living learned there will provide a characteristic reaction to environmental stress.

Although masculine identification and father-son relationships are important, especially in view of the central conflicts of these boys, there are yet other factors stemming from the familial and ethnic styles of a subculture that provide impetus for all of the achievement and conforming factors of life. Values are organizing ends, organizing precisely because many other satisfactions and actions are subordinate to them. The Irish-American boys, who seek imaginative and spiritual values, aim to stand in membership with as many things among people in the field of experience as possible. If the Irish-American boy is unsure of the possibility of attaining real satisfaction for instance, he will try to act respectably, regardless of conflict.

The one who seeks interpersonal social values may be faced with inconsistencies in the prevailing cultural climate. Relations with a larger society can present the modal Italian-American boy with great problems of adaptation and interpersonal consistency which are necessary to achieve concrete social harmony in keeping with his needs. Since an Italian-American boy's moral-ethical code is built on the ambiguities of society, his inner emotional equilibrium is preserved at the cost of a labile social shrewdness.

In our diverse and varied society, we need both kinds of personalities. We need both the materialistic thinker and pragmatic utilitarian who is concerned with the present and everyday problems, and we need the imaginative person who dreams of the future and of a better present, who asks "why" about the general state of things, and who queries imaginatively how to make a better world.

Implications for Social Psychiatry

The Family and Social Roles

As a bridge between the processes of intrapsychic life and those of social participation, sociologists, social psychologists, and anthropologists often employ the concept of role. They apply this term to prescribed and ascribed functions in different social status positions. In addition, they often draw distinctions between inner and outer selves. Thus, the individual is characterized as tending to see himself as others see him, and in this way he defines the situation in which he is a vital part. These conceptual assumptions mean that personality and society cannot be considered separately if the fullness of a total being is to be accurately assessed. Human adaptation is shaped both by the organization of personal internal forces and by the external forces of society. Success or failure of adaptation depends partly upon the support the individual derives from his reference group relationships.

There is an essential continuity between identity and stability in the family group. The family is the oldest and most important reference group in an adolescent's personal and social environment. An adolescent will always have internalized the norms and values of his parents which he will modify or replace by values growing out of his own experiences. Identifications with and affection for his parents are related on a continuum from harmonious dualities to opposing factions. The child's world is different from his parents', and realization of this forces upon him change and ideologies commensurate with his abilities, but intergenerational communication still defines adaptational values, which are the subtle ways that he defines a situation, and his essential adaptational maneuvers to environmental stress.

Given these commonly accepted concepts, clinical observation brings to life dramatic examples of interlocking psychopathology and family relationships. Such observations underscore mutually dependent psychoses in parents or in parents and children. Perhaps the concept of role is not sufficient from an interpersonal frame of reference. Masculine identifications do not become so simply because boys are masculine. Masculine identifications and constructive parent-child relationships also do not necessarily involve both parents. The remaining parent, after divorce or widowhood, can develop relationships so that the adolescent can prepare his own unique personal identity concomitant with a sense of significance and self-esteem. The development of personal identity and the relationship of this to parental and family identity are critically important phenomena in adolescence.

Perhaps the critical factor in adolescent maturation is the consideration of the parents themselves. The parents, as key members of ethnic nuclear groups, transmit to the child his world outlook, his expectations, and his obligations. Adolescents do have an identity with some values and with some system of morality. Where the subcultural orientation induces confusing values, there is a diffusion of identity and the perception of a malevolent world.

In this study on ethnicity, the boys with delinquent behavior have both internalized parental values and incorporated a welter of aggressive and hostile feelings toward themselves. In his efforts at masculine identification, the modal Italian-American boy struggles for survival in a world, perceived as malevolent, where he feels misunderstood by his own father. In doing so, he develops an emotional and cognitive pattern resembling that of his dominant and punishing parent. Perhaps we can say that when a father refuses to allow his son to grow up and to rework the old standards through mutual reciprocity, the attempt at maturity will proceed with defiance and rebellion. This defiance and rebellion is adapted from the affective overtone of the boy's family. In contrast, the Irish-American boy displays unilateral respect but cannot, without reciprocity, develop an autonomous mature value system. Where a strong ethical code is intrajected and dependency encouraged, hostile aggression and anxiety move against the self; the conscience remains juvenile.

In keeping with the principal premise of this study, experiences within the family denote styles of attending, perceiving, communicating, and thinking in family transactions that promote cognitive and emotional development of the offspring in certain directions, either by serving as models for identification or by eliciting certain complementary behaviors. Experiences within the family are to a certain extent derived by internalization, in which ways of thinking, derived meanings, anxieties, irrationalities, and confusions are expressed in the shared mechanism of the family. Since people cannot avoid dealing with the problems of relationship control, a child's ability to gain trust through verbal communications, as a means of mutual understanding and reciprocity, is determined largely by a parent's respect for the child's need of gradually increasing independence. If his needs for increasing autonomy are not met, he is forced into a more complete dependence on the family and the parental patterns of behavior. In the final analysis, the parents themselves determine the child's role patterns.

Further Research

The findings in this study demonstrate that the disturbed adolescents were reared under conditions adverse to good mental health. However, they had brothers and sisters, reared under similar conditions, who did not become ill, so the question arises whether sex status and ordinal position in the family are influential components in the development of mental illness.

In the description of the samples, the Italian-American boys were, in many instances, the oldest children. The Irish-American boys were in many instances the middle siblings. It was proposed that in the Irish family there was long standing and brewing undertones of discontent due to the inhibition of affective display. In this way family crisis rumbled before the explosion of parental discord. In the Italian home there were overt affective overtones which served to create explosive eruptions, quickly subsiding. This occurred in extended families with close kinship bonds. This does not answer the question of why one family member was exposed to those conditions more than other family members. It does not answer the question of why the patient and not his siblings became ill. It raises the question of how much constitutional factors contribute to a person's reaction patterns.

Secondly, we indicated that even where social class differences were considered within the context of the two ethnic groups, ethnic styles overlaid the social-class structure. We indicated that the Irish-American upper classes were somewhat more egocentric than the lower classes, and we emphasized that the Italian-American upper classes were more authoritarian than the lower classes. In disturbance, the social classes tended to fuse in favor of ethnic phenomena. The relatively small number of adolescents within each social class, and the consequent increased variability around the mean, suggests that further research should be done with larger ethnic and social class groupings. This would reduce the variability and sharpen the tests of significance.

This study further suggests that a comprehensive understanding of psychiatric illness in American society needs to include not only social class variables, but also ethnic orientations to which familial functions are linked. Organic, interpersonal, and intrapsychic factors alone are not sufficient to explain the development or formulate the treatment of mental illness. A closer study of the kind of mental illness that we can expect in adolescence may stem from the study of stylistic patterns of behavior in ethnicity. Through consistent expectations from subcultural orientations, therapy can proceed with knowledge of the basic complementary role relationships within the family. By simply describing role relationships as falling along a continuum from rigidity to looseness or from mutuality to hostility, or from the mathematical view of increasing social distance, we are missing the deeper interpretations of reality, the true *Verstehan* or perspicacity which penetrates to the intangible, almost wordless, perspective of human relations. Beyond the measurement of parental rigidity or flexibility lies the entire wordless communication that exists between child and parent. The "meaning" behind this nonverbal communication does not always lie in words. A child's denial of any meaning is just as important as the distorted interpretation of meaning. A fencing match between parent and child is not always outspoken.

A Consideration of Disorganization and Delinquency

Since this study was completed, new questions and hypotheses have come to mind regarding delinquency and disorganization. Perhaps sociology should shift emphasis from the external cultural approach to the subcultural approach combined with the psychological orientation of the adolescent.

Where social disorganization exists, one might ask if there actually are no norms, for so long as there is life, there is a psychological motivation to reintegrate a value system. Reintegration might take the form of overt manipulation of the environment or such other forms as self-imposed inner aggression. Whatever the form of coping with environmental stress, the individual does not remain in a position of status quo.

According to the Durkheimian viewpoint, anomie (losss of value-orientation) is made external to the individual and radically sociological. While social influences are important in bringing about anomie feelings, one can question whether the standard sociological explanations (social dysfunction, malintegration between cultural goals and institutionalized means) are necessary or sufficient conditions for anomie, or whether they are totally appropriate concepts for explaining this lack of norms.

To Durkheim, anomie suggested a weakening of restraints, giving men the feeling of wandering with no landmarks from which to take their bearings or by which to set a course of action. As a result a person becomes confused and tired; the struggle appears futile, life loses its value, and many anomic people finally commit suicide.

Social dysfunction and anomie are popular themes in the discussion of juvenile delinquency, family disruption, and unemployment. The norms of a society are, of course, learned as are the feelings of the individual that there are no norms. Feelings of anomie are said to be most intense among older people, widows, and divorced and separated persons of low education and low income.

Anomic conditions may be perceived in a distorted way by people who are depressed. These people may suffer from impaired cognitive functioning and an inability to structure the world and to react in a realistic manner. Psychological states of this kind may be especially important in the growth of anomie. Far from denying the existence of sociological factors that contribute to anomic problems, it is suggested that we need to assess the contribution of personality to anomie as a necessary step toward clarifying the social influences in bringing about anomic feelings.

If consideration is given to the psychological orientation in anomie, we can visualize not only a normless sociological process external to the individual but also as a process that includes internal socialization and subcultural backgrounds of socialization. In this way we see personality factors may make some people highly resistant to anomic conditions, while others may be highly vulnerable. Some people may see anomie as a form of social stress, in that certain sociological conditions are frustrating for the successful achievement of aspirations. Others may see anomie as either a product or an instigator of certain personality disturbances.

From the psychological viewpoint, the Irish-American egocentric way and the Italian-American sociocentric way involve two different ways of dealing with perceived family and social dysfunction. If the child is a product of a sequence of experiences, present adjustment, and future anticipations, then these reaction patterns stem from one's whole life experiences beginning in one's first relationships to authoritarian adults. Thus, egocentrism involves a subjective attitude that is engendered by strong personal feelings and self-reference. The individual with this frame of reference may be individualistic in his personal speculations. Severe social stress of any form that involves feelings of inadequacy and frustration may cause withdrawal and isolation to a perceived better world of one's own imaginative construction. On the other hand, a utilitarian attitude emphasizes a pragmatic overt mechanism in coming to grips with social stress.

We are led, in consequence, to a consideration of delinquency from both pragmatic and theoretical viewpoints. Cloward's (18) and Short's (102) concepts of opportunity structures in the individual's milieu emphasize the opportunities that exist in a deviant environment to learn and perform deviant action, and the moral support given the deviant when he breaks with conventional norms. Merton (78) stresses institutional means as appropriate adaptive mechanisms to goals of action.

This study indicates that a study of deviance in society requires more specifically described personal constructs especially as they relate to the subcultural base of the family. As Reckless and Murray (89) have said, some boys may not as readily become delinquent as others, in spite of similar opportunities. Personal constructs involve differentiated self-concepts that help to determine how individuals will use their social fields. In the same neighborhood or census tract of a city in which there is a high incidence of delinquency, there are many boys who do not become delinquent. Robins (92) states that the antisocial behavior determines class status rather than the reverse; he analyses age, sex, and ethnic values to determine the kinds of deviance expressed.

The question of delinquency requires more research on socialization processes, which might explain both delinquency and non-delinquency with a single set of variables. For instance, in the Irish-American group, a poor self-concept does not necessarily lead the boy to use environmental opportunities for delinquency. On the contrary, this boy clings to certain people and an idealistic framework while generally detaching himself from the larger culture. The Italian-American boy has a more positive self-concept, but this boy is more prone to aggressive acts that may be delinquent.

A plausible explanation of delinquency or non-delinquency may concern the relationship between the self-concept and the perception of the mother as a very significant person during the adolescent years. Where a boy does not become (as with the Irish-American boy) delinquent, failure to give up the mother as the most dominant individual may conceivably reduce the possibility that delinquent boys, who might control his behavior or change his moral-ethical code, become important in his environment. We propose that the cognitive structure that intervenes between opportunity and delinquency is a function of unique subcultural socialization experiences relevant to a family's orientation. Proneness to delinquency may be a function of a confused self-image coupled with social spontaneity, impulsivity, overwhelming aggression, and the desire for omnipotence.

Freedom for Creative Intelligence

The interpretive emphasis in this study has been on how sociocultural backgrounds may produce different definitions and responses to essentially the same emotional experiences. The strongest evidence in support of this argument is the variation in ethnic perceptions for essentially the same diagnostic category. While it is well known that not all people react in a similar fashion to the same disease process, and even though the diagnostic category was nebulous, it is rather striking that the pattern of response varied with the ethnic background in this study as consistently as it did.

This study suggests that a comprehensive understanding of psychiatric illness in our society needs to include subcultural orientations to which familial functions are linked. Awareness of the influence of social factors can be of considerable aid in effecting understanding and constructive physician-patient relationships, for it may enable the physician to respond in certain ways and to catch important diagnostic cues.

We hope that this study will shed some light on the fact that an individual's variability (derived from social, family, ethnic, and other factors) in response to human relationships makes the practice of medicine and psychiatry more difficult unless we are aware of these embedded systems of values. Perhaps our greatest danger lies in becoming attached to any exclusive interpretation of reality; but the second greatest danger remains in abandoning the search for reality. This holds for all professional workers: physicians, nurses, public health workers, social workers, and community recreational organizations. Without more inclusive knowledge, professional workers cannot gain entrance into the home with effectual treatment measures. In addition, in order for people to accept treatment and to relate their symptomatology, they must be accepted in their own right and understood through their own frame of reference.

Adolescence is a period of breaking away from what is parental and what is old. Extreme emotional immaturity, registered as dependency, prevents an individual from accepting what is new. Emotional immaturity, represented as adolescent narcissism and rebellion, prevents him from accepting what is old. There should be a thrill in trying the new (within the limits of no danger to self or society), and adolescents can be helped to see the value of the old and traditional, while they adjust to necessary change.

Our cultural and social institutions need to be appraised in the light of what each institution means to those growing boys. If the personality is as much the result of the elements of its cultural pattern as it is of its own past life, then psychiatry must know that cultural pattern as it knows the patient's life. If those in psychiatry set out to improve the lives of adolescents so that they will constructively meet every new problem and innovation, then they must also focus on alterations of cultural patterns in terms of relevancy to the prevention of adolescent disturbances. For social workers and nurses this means that they can explain environmental presses and help adolescents to cope with social stresses in a better way. In turn, they can explain the subcultural and family mental health problems to society. The adolescent sees the world in terms of what kind of parents it has given him and in terms of how these parents set the stage for reciprocal associations.

This study found mental stress to arise from inconsistent Italian-

American parental roles and authoritarian paternal roles that exceeded the expectations of the Italian-American boys and made them vulnerable to conflict. In contrast, maternal domination in the Irish-American family allowed little room for paternal identification and the assumption of gradual autonomy in the process of maturation. We can say that these combinations of circumstances produce these combinations of problems and styles of disturbances. But the particular variations in personality and situation, even on subcultural levels, leave room for conjecture as to how these combinations of family interactions are contrived on either quantitative or qualitative bases.

At what point does stress become imminent and disturbing in each life style? If stress on ethnic levels proceeds from incompatibility with American culture in general, how much of this stress can be tolerated before disturbance ensues? What variables soften or harden this stress? What parts of the Old World heritage can be made conscious, so adaptation to the new world can constructively include what is valued by the child's parents? Conceptually, this study points to certain practical considerations in the care of those who are emotionally disturbed.

We could say that the Italian-American boy needs help in redeveloping nurturance toward others and the ability to receive succorance from interested and significant others. He needs help in redirecting his "maladaptive" aggression into more constructive channels of achievement orientations, changing his attitude of outer world malevolence to a more trusting one of benevolence. He needs to be given the opportunity and the encouragement to develop reciprocal social respect in group interaction. The Irish-American boy's egocentric activity needs to be shared concretely with others on a realistic basis. His aggressive impulses and need for change can be directed into channels other than fantasizing. He needs to be encouraged to use his imaginative and intraceptive powers for creative and artistic tasks.

The educational forces of our society have a tremendous responsibility for the young people of today. It does not seem quite enough to nurture rationality. This is too sterile a separation of thought from the richness of a child's experiences. The kind of rationality that teachers in our educational system should strive for should come from the healthy craving for contact with reality. The child leaves the home seeking order and system in his world. It is the educator's responsibility to engender a willingness to face and judge all of reality, no matter how threatening, irrational, or trival. It is only in this way that the child frees himself from that which is frightening. It is in this way that the teacher gives focus to a child's present experiences and to the past out of which he came. By widening the attitudes of the home, the educator enables the child to focus upon his questions with creativity. All of this demands from the teacher new perspectives that come from the study of children.

The study of juveniles should be aimed at collecting original statements from them in the various subcultures that describe the circumstances under which they grew up. There is nothing that juveniles know that they cannot somehow say in word and action.

Appendixes

Appendix I

Supplementary Tables

Table 1

Distribution of Ethnic Groups in Monsignor Carr
Institute by White Male Adolescent Population in
November 1963, and Comparison with Same Ethnic
Groups of First and Second Generation White
Males in Census 1960 (90:Table 99).

Ethnic Group	% Institute Patients	% Census Population
German	14	14
Irish *	45	4
Italian	24	20
Polish	15	22

* Represents 4th–5th generation
$x^2 = 40.50$, 3 d.f.; $p < .001$

Table 2

Distribution of Adolescents' Fathers' Occupations
in Institute Sampling of November 1963 by U.S.
Census 1960 Occupational Categories; and
Comparison with Census Proportions of 1960 Detailed
Characteristics of New York State.

	Institute Adoles. Fathers	Census W.M. Labor Force
Professional, Technical, and kindred	12	10
Mangers, offices, and proprietors	12	10
Clerical and kindred workers	09	07.5
Sales workers	09	06.7
Craftsmen, foremen and kindred	22	24
Operatives and kindred workers	12	23
Private household workers	00	00.6
Service (exclusive of private homes)	14	05.6
Laborers—except mine workers	06.6	09
No occupation reported	03.6	03.6
Total	100.00	100.00

$x^2 = 7.50$, 8 d.f.; $p > .05$

Table 3

Distribution of Education Completed by Adolescents'
Fathers in Institute Sample and Comparison with
Education Completed by Persons 25 years and
over in SMA Buffalo, Census 1960 (90:15)

Education Completed	Institute Father	Census Population
College	13	069
Partial College	05	07
High School	55	24
Partial High School	12	24
Elementary School	146	17
Total Subjects	78	603,000

$x^2 = 64.5$, 4 d.f.; $p < .001$

Significant Self Concept Tables

Table 4
Mean Value Scores by Ethnicity on Self-Criticism [1]

Ethnic Group	X	N
CONTROL:		
Irish-American	39.00	37
Italian-American	37.29	34
DISTURBED:		
Irish-American	33.16	25
Italian-American	33.00	23

Normative Group: -35.54
Patient Group: -36.00

Overall Effect: $F_{3,115} = 5.95 \ p < .001$
Main Effect, Nationality: $F_{1,116} = .07 \ p = \text{N.S.}$
Main Effect, Disturbed-Control: $F_{1,116} = 16.97 \ p < .001$
Interaction Effect: $F_{1,115} = .16 \ p = \text{N.S.}$

[1] Due to the disproportionate numbers in social groupings between the Irish-Italian and the Control-Disturbed groups, these data were analyzed by *t* tests rather than incorporated in the analyses of variance. This applies to all tabular analyses.

Table 5
Mean Value Scores for the Social Self by Ethnicity and Social Class

Ethnic Group	Social Class I–III	Social Class IV–V	Ethnic X–S.D.	N	Class "t"
CONTROL:					
Irish-American	10.50	15.85	13.32– 9.16	37	1.83 *
Italian-American	13.42	15.00	14.05– 6.12	34	N.S.
DISTURBED:					
Irish-American	9.30	11.25	10.84–10.40	25	N.S.
Italian-American	15.46	13.75	14.86– 7.52	23	N.S.

$* \ p < .10$

Normative Group: -14.07
Patient Group: -11.00

Overall Effect: $F_{3,115} = 2.038 \ p > .10$
Main Effect, Nationality: $F_{1,116} = 4.547 \ p < .05$
Main Effect, Disturbed-Control: $F_{1,116} = 1.251 \ p = \text{N.S.}$
Interaction Effect: $F_{1,115} = .302 \ p = \text{N.S.}$

Table 6
Mean Value Scores for Identity by Ethnicity

Ethnic Group	X–S.D.	N
CONTROL:		
Irish-American	33.81–11.4	37
Italian-American	35.47– 7.92	34
DISTURBED:		
Irish-American	26.84–17.20	25
Italian-American	31.48– 8.44	23

No Social Class Difference   Normative Group: -37.10
Patient Group: -26.20

Overall Effect: $F_{3,115} = 3.680 \ p < .025$
Main Effect, Nationality: $F_{1,115} = 1.787 \ p = \text{N.S.}$
Main Effect, Disturbed-Control: $F_{1,115} = 6.475 \ p < .001$
Interaction Effect: $F_{1,115} = 2.777 \ p < .10$

Table 7
Mean Value Scores for Total Consistency by Ethnicity

Ethnic Group	X–S.D.	N
CONTROL:		
Irish-American	43.62–11.64	37
Italian-American	49.26–12.20	34
DISTURBED:		
Irish-American	40.64– 8.76	25
Italian-American	43.17–11.64	23

No Social Class Differences   Normative Group: -49.03
Patient Group: -51.60

Overall Effect: $F_{3,115} = 7.79 \ p < .001$
Main Effect, Nationality: $F_{1,116} = 10.99 \ p < .01$
Main Effect, Disturbed Control: $F_{1,116} = 11.00 \ p < .01$
Interaction Effect: $F_{1,115} = 1.34 \ p > .10$

Table 8
Mean Value Scores for Internal Consistency
by Ethnicity and Social Class

Ethnic Group	Social Class I–III	Social Class IV–V	Ethnic X–S.D.	N	Class "t"
CONTROL:					
Irish-American	27.22	21.05	24.32–6.44	37	1.92 *
Italian-American	32.14	26.50	30.73–7.30	34	2.19 **
DISTURBED:					
Irish-American	22.66	19.00	20.76–7.08	25	N.S.
Italian-American	29.54	24.16	26.82–9.48	23	1.40 *

* $p < .10$, ** $p < .05$

Normative Group: -29.50
Patient Group: -28.60

Overall Effect: $F_{3,115} = 4.61\ p < .01$
Main Effect, Nationality: $F_{1,116} = 10.39\ p < .01$
Main Effect, Disturbed-Control: $F_{1,116} = 2.72\ p < .10$
Interaction Effect: $F_{1,115} = .75\ p = N.S.$

Table 9
Mean Value Scores of External Consistency
by Ethnicity and Social Class

Ethnic Group	Social Class I–III	Social Class IV–V	Ethnic X–S.D.	N	Class "t"
CONTROL:					
Irish-American	22.22	19.52	20.29–7.84	37	N.S.
Italian-American	20.71	16.00	18.47–6.05	34	N.S.
DISTURBED:					
Irish-American	20.00	21.25	20.72–7.08	25	N.S.
Italian-American	20.45	22.50	21.95–5.68	23	N.S.

Normative Group: -19.60
Patient Group: -23.00

Overall Effect: $F_{3,115} = 1.50\ p > .10$
Main Effect, Nationality: $F_{1,116} = .97\ p = N.S.$
Main Effect, Disturbed-Control: $F_{1,116} = 2.56\ p > .10$
Interaction Effect: $F_{1,115} = 1.00\ p = N.S.$

Appendix II

Edwards Personal Preference Variables Defined (20:5).

1. *Achievement:* To do one's best, to be successful, to accomplish tasks requiring skill and effort, to be a recognized authority, to accomplish something of great significance, to do a difficult job well, to solve difficult problems and puzzles, to be able to do things better than others, to write a great novel or play.

2. *Deference:* To get suggestions from others, to find out what others think, to follow instructions and do what is expected, to praise others, to tell others that they have done a good job, to accept the leadership of others, to read about great men, to conform to custom and avoid the unconventional, to let others make decisions.

3. *Order:* To have written work neat and organized, to make plans before starting on a difficult task, to have things organized, to keep things neat and orderly, to make advance plans when taking a trip, to organize details of work, to keep letters and files according to some system, to have meals organized and a definite time for eating, to have things arranged so that they run smoothly without change.

4. *Exhibition:* To say witty and clever things, to tell amusing jokes and stories, to talk about personal adventures and experiences, to have others notice and comment upon one's appearance, to say things just to see what effect it will have on others, to talk about personal achievements, to be the center of attention, to use words that others do not know the meaning of, to ask questions others cannot answer.

5. *Autonomy:* To be able to come and go as desired, to say what one thinks about things, to be independent of others in making decisions, to feel free to do what one wants, to do things that are unconventional, to avoid situations where one is expected to conform, to do things without regard to what others may think, to criticize those in positions of authority, to avoid responsibilities and obligations.

6. *Affiliation:* To be loyal to friends, to participate in friendly groups, to do things for friends, to form new friendships, to make as many friends as possible, to share things with friends, to do things with friends rather than alone, to form strong attachments, to write letters to friends.

7. *Intraception:* To analyze one's motives and feelings, to observe others, to understand how others feel about problems, to put one's self in another's place, to judge people by why they do things rather than by what they do, to analyze the behavior of others, to analyze the motives of others, to predict how others will act.

8. *Succorance:* To have others provide help when in trouble, to seek encouragement from others, to have others be kindly, to have others be sympathetic and understanding about personal problems, to receive a great deal of affection from others, to have others do favors cheerfully, to be helped by others when depressed, to have others feel sorry when one is sick, to have a fuss made over one when hurt.

9. *Dominance:* To argue for one's point of view, to be a leader in groups to which one belongs, to be regarded by others as a leader, to be elected or appointed chairman of committees, to make group decisions, to settle arguments and disputes between others, to persuade and influence others to do what one wants, to supervise and direct the actions of others, to tell others how to do their job.

10. *Abasement:* To feel guilty when one does something wrong, to accept blame when things do not go right, to feel that personal pain and misery suffered does more good than harm, to feel the need for punishment for wrong doing, to feel better when giving in and avoiding a fight than when having one's own way, to feel the need for confession of errors, to feel depressed by inability to handle situations, to feel timid in the presence of superiors, to feel inferior to others in most respects.

11. *Nurturance:* To help friends when they are in trouble, to assist others less fortunate, to treat others with kindness and sympathy, to forgive others, to do small favors for others, to be generous with others, to sympathize with others who are hurt or sick, to show a great deal of affection toward others, to have others confide in one about personal problems.

12. *Change:* To do new and different things, to travel, to meet new people, to experience novelty and change in daily routine, to experiment and try new things, to eat in new and different places, to try new and different jobs, to move about the country and live in different places, to participate in new fads and fashions.

13. *Endurance:* To keep at a job until it is finished, to complete any job undertaken, to work hard at a task, to keep at a puzzle or problem until it is solved, to work at a single job before taking on others, to stay up late working in order to get a job done, to put in long hours of work without distraction, to stick at a problem even though it may seem as if no progress is being made, to avoid being interrupted while at work.

14. *Heterosexuality:* To go out with members of the opposite sex, to engage in social activities with the opposite sex, to be in love with someone of the opposite sex, to kiss those of the opposite sex, to be regarded as physically attractive by those of the opposite sex, to participate in discussions about sex, to read books and plays involving sex, to listen to or to tell jokes involving sex, to become sexually excited.

15. *Aggression:* To attack contrary points of view, to tell others what one thinks about them, to criticize others publicly, to make fun of others, to tell others off when disagreeing with them, to get revenge for insults, to become angry, to blame others when things go wrong, to read newspaper accounts of violence.

Appendix III

Clinical Abstract—Presenting Problem

Identification Number: _____

Address: _____

Date of Referral: _____

Referred by Whom: _____

Reason for Referral: _____

Physical Illness: _____

Diagnosis: _____

Living with Parents? _____

    Explain:

Member of Family Seen by a Psychiatrist? _____

  I. Summary of Psychological Tests:

 II. Clinical Observations:

     A. Emotional Expression

        1. Kind

        2. Direction of: to self or other

        3. Control: impulsivity, conscious suppression

     B. Behavior: Aggressive, compliant, other

     C. Anxieties and Hostilities:

     D. Attitude to Authority and to Mental Health Clinic

Summary: Central conflicts: relation of conflicts and symptoms with modes of interpersonal adaptation.

Appendix IV

The Questionnaire

Number of Subject: Group:
                                                               Group C _____
                                                               Group D _____

   Different people have different ways of looking at things. We'd like
some information on some of the questions we have down here. This is a
takeoff from the tests you took. There are no right or wrong answers and
this is not a test. We just want to know how you feel about some of the
situations that are brought up. You will be able to explain what you
mean and how you feel about the situations which are brought up. No
names will be given; simply note your identification number at the top of
this sheet.

Family and Authority:

1. Please indicate below if you are living at home with:
     1. parents _____
     2. foster parents _____
     3. step-parent (indicate which one)_____
     4. adopted parents

2. Indicate below the number of brothers and sisters you have and if
   they are older or younger than you.

3. State below which relatives you are in close contact with and see
   often. Indicate if these relatives are on your mother's or your father's
   side.

4. Which of the above relatives lives at home with you?

5. All children have rules to go by in their homes (such as those for a
   time to eat, sleep, doing homework, going to church, etc.). Is there a
   strict set of rules set down by your parents or guardians in your
   home?

1. Yes _____
2. No _____

What are the strict rules in your home which are set down for you?

Which parent or guardian makes sure you obey these rules?

Which parent punishes you *more* for not obeying?

Which parent punishes you more severely for not obeying?

6. Do your Parents (or guardians) *often* punish you for not obeying the rules?
   1. Yes _____
   2. No _____

What kind of rules do they punish you for not obeying?

7. When you are punished, are you:
   1. Scolded only
   2. Scolded with privileges removed
   3. Physically hit only
   4. Physically hit with other punishment

Does this punishment occur:
   1. More than once a week
   2. More than once in two weeks
   3. More than once a month
   4. More than once in six months
   5. Less than the above

8. *Underline:*

Which person do you think and act like the most?
   1. Mother
   2. Father
   3. Uncle, aunt, grandmother, grandfather
   4. Other (name)_____

9. Which person do you feel closest to?
   1. Mother
   2. Father
   3. Uncle, Aunt, Grandmother, Grandfather, Cousin, Sister, Brother
   4. Friend
   5. Other

10. Would you say that your parents or guardians usually praise you when you do a good job?
    1. Usually yes_____
    2. Usually No_____
    3. Other (specify)_____

Which parent or guardian praises you more?

11. Do you feel that usually your parent or guardian is very interested in your problems and helps you to work them out?
    1. Usually yes_____
    2. Usually no_____
    3. Don't know_____
    Which parent or guardian is more interested in helping you?

    Indicate which person you prefer to talk things over with when you have a personal problem. Indicate anyone in or out of the family.

12. Would you say that your parents or guardians are interested in having you do well in school?
    1. Yes_____
    2. No_____
    3. Don't know_____
    4. Indifferent_____

    State which parent or guardian takes more interest in your schooling.

13. Do your parents or guardians feel that it is important to help you think seriously of jobs you should think about and prepare for as a means of earning a living?
    1. Yes_____
    2. No_____
    3. Don't know_____
    4. Indifferent_____

    Do your parents or guardians have plans for you in the choice of a *specific* job or kind of career?
    1. Yes_____
    2. No_____
    3. They are indifferent_____

    State how they feel about your plans for the future.

14. Do you worry about what your parents think of you?
    1. Yes_____
    2. No_____
    3. Don't know_____
    4. Indifferent_____

15. Do you usually try to please your parents if you can?
    1. Yes_____
    2. No_____
    3. Indifferent_____

    State below in what ways you try to please them.

    Do you feel that your parents understand you?
    1. Yes_____
    2. No_____
    3. Indifferent_____

16. If you had a problem of a serious nature and wanted to discuss it with someone, which of the following would you prefer to talk things over with?
    1. Father or guardian_____
    2. Mother or guardian_____
    3. Friend_____
    4. Relative (specify which)_____

17. If your parents or your friends disapproved of something you did, which one would it be harder to take the disapproval of?
    1. Mother or guardian_____
    2. Father or guardian_____
    3. Friend_____

18. Do you feel free to argue with members of your family when you think you are right?
    1. Yes_____
    2. No_____

School and Achievement:

1. What program are you taking in school?
   1. Manual Training_____
   2. College Preparatory_____
   3. Other (specify)_____

   Was the program selected by:
   1. You_____
   2. Parents or Guardian_____
   3. Counsellor or other (specify)_____

2. Are you attending school to?
   1. Prepare for job_____
   2. Prepare for College_____
   3. Because you have to go to school_____

3. If you had a choice, which would you rather be?
   1. Skilled person in working with hands_____
   2. A scholar_____
   3. A Professional Person_____

4. If you could swing it financially, would you think about going to college?
   1. Yes_____
   2. No_____
   3. Indifferent_____
   4. Don't know_____

   State in a few sentences what your plans are for the future and what you want to do for a living.

5. Do your parents usually have to supervise you in order for you to do your homework?
   1. Yes_____
   2. No_____

6. If you don't have time to keep up with your homework and be with your friends, would you neglect your homework in order to be with your friends?_____
   1. Usually yes_____
   2. Usually no _____
   3. Don't know

7. If you have homework to do, do you *very often* spend more time watching television by yourself and doing other things by yourself than you spend in doing your homework?
   1. Yes_____
   2. No_____

8. How many evenings a week during school days do you spend out with your friends?
   1. One-two evenings_____
   2. Three-four evenings_____
   3. Five evenings_____

9. Would you say that it is very important to take part in school activities, such as athletics and school clubs?
   1. Yes_____
   2. No_____
   3. Indifferent_____

   What extracurricular activities are you engaged in at school?

10. If you were offered a job, which would be more important for you?
    1. A job with a high salary and a lot of travel_____
    2. A job with a lower salary, but which is steady and can be depended upon to keep you employed_____

Leisure and Peers:

1. Do you usually like to spend your leisure time with other people in clubs, fraternities, or groups of fellows?
   1. Yes_____
   2. No_____
   3. Sometimes_____
   4. Never_____

   What clubs or organizations do you belong to?

2. How many fellows are there in your crowd?
   1. Less than few fellows (1–3)_____
   2. Few fellows (4–6)_____
   3. Several fellows (7–12)_____

3. Do you have hobbies of your own that keep you busy and by yourself a great deal?
    1. Yes _____
    2. No _____
    3. Sometimes _____

Do you belong to hobby clubs?
Name them:

What hobbies do you have?

4. Does your neighborhood have mostly:
    1. Irish People _____
    2. Italian people _____
    3. German people _____
    4. English or French people _____
    5. Puerto Rican _____
    6. Other _____
    7. All kinds of nationalities _____

5. Are you closer to boys in your neighborhood rather than to those in the rest of the city that you meet through such organizations as scouts, church, YMCA, etc.?
    1. Yes _____
    2. No _____
    3. Some of both _____

6. Some people feel that it is hard to keep up with the crowd. Do you agree with this in relation to the crowds you go with?
    1. Yes _____
    2. No _____
    3. Sometimes _____

7. In a crowd of boys are you usually one of the gang, or are you often a leader?
    1. One of the gang _____
    2. Leader _____
    3. Neither _____

8. State in a few sentences what you and your friends do for pastime.

9. Do you go to any of the following places in the city?
    YMCA _____
    Neighborhood house _____
    Concerts, musicals, art displays _____
    Museums _____
    Public lectures _____
    Evening classes _____
    Sports Events _____
    Other (specify) _____

Heterosexuality:

1. Do you date?

   Yes_____

   No_____

2. Could you say that you enjoy associating with girls?
   1. Yes_____
   2. No_____
   3. Don't know_____
   4. Indifferent_____

   How often do you date girls?

   Do you go steady with any girl?

   Yes_____

   No_____

3. If you were set up on a blind date by your friends, would you consider it to be fun?
   1. Yes_____
   2. No_____
   3. Indifferent_____

4. If you had a choice between going out with a crowd of fellows or a mixed crowd of fellows and girls, which would you rather choose?
   1. Crowd of fellows alone_____
   2. Mixed crowd_____

5. If you had a choice between a plain looking but serious minded girl and a very pretty and popular girl, which one would you rather take out?
   1. The plain but serious girl_____
   2. The pretty and popular girl_____
   3. Both_____

6. Some fellows state that girls are hard to get to know. Do you agree with this?
   1. Yes_____
   2. No_____
   3. Don't know_____
   4. Indifferent_____

7. If someone made the statement that girls are silly and gossipy, and someone else said that girls are friendly and fun to take out which statement would you agree with?
   1. Silly and gossipy_____
   2. Friendly and fun_____
   3. Both_____

Self Percept:

1. Some people daydream a lot. Would you say you do this very often?
   1. Yes_____
   2. No_____

   What do you daydream about?

2. Do you agree with the statement that "Honesty is the best policy but in real life one can't be completely honest?
   1. Yes_____
   2. No_____
   3. Don't know_____
   4. Uncertain_____

3. Some people think that it is always difficult to make up their minds about things. Would you agree with this statement about yourself?
   1. Yes_____
   2. No_____
   3. Uncertain_____

4. What kind of things is it often difficult for you to make up your mind about?

5. What is the best and most important thing that could happen to you?

Bibliography

1. Ackerman, Nathan. *The Psychodynamics of Family Life*. New York: Basic Books, 1958.
2. American Psychiatric Association. *Mental Disorders, Diagnostic and Statistical Manual*. Washington D.C., 1952.
3. Arensberg, Conrad, and Solon T. Kimball. *Family and Community in Ireland*. Cambridge: Harvard University Press, 1948.
4. Barrabee, Paul, and Otto Von Mering. "Ethnic Variations in Mental Stress in Families with Psychotic Children," *Social Problems*. Vol. 1, 1953–1954, pp. 48–53.
5. Beaglehole, Ernest. "Cultural Complexity and Psychological Problems," in *A Study of Interpersonal Relations*, edited by Patrick Mullahy. New York: Hermitage Press, 1949.
6. Bell, Norman and Ezra F. Vogel, eds. *A Modern Introduction to the Family*. Illinois: The Free Press of Glencoe, 1960.
7. Benedict, Ruth. "Continuities and Discontinuities in Cultural Conditioning," in *Personality in Nature, Society and Culture*, edited by Clyde Kluckhohn and H. E. Murray. New York: Alfred K. Knopf, 1949, pp. 414–423.
8. ———. *Patterns of Culture*. New York: New Amsterdam Library, 1959.
9. Brittain, Clay. "Adolescent Choices and Parent-Peer Cross Pressures," *American Journal of Sociology*, Vol. 28, No. 3, June 1963, pp. 385–391.
10. Cameron, Norman. *The Psychology of the Behavior Disorders: a Biosocial Interpretation*. Boston: Houghton-Mifflin, 1947.
11. Campisi, Paul F. "The Italian Family in the United States," in *Social Perspectives on Behavior*, edited by Herman Stein and Richard Cloward. Illinois: The Free Press of Glencoe, 1958. pp. 76–81.
12. Carleton, William. *Traits and Stories of the Irish Peasantry*. Vol. 1. London: William Tegg, 1864.
13. Carothers, J. C. "A Study of Mental Derangement in Africans and an Attempt to Explain Its Peculiarities to Life," *Journal of Mental Science*, Vol. 93, 1947, pp. 548–560.

14. Centers, Richard. "Children of the New Deal: Social Stratification and Adolescent Attitudes," in *Class, Status and Power,* edited by Reinhard Bendix and Seymour Lipset. Illinois: The Free Press of Glencoe, 1953, pp. 359–370.
15. Chesire, Leone, Milton Saffir and L. L. Thurstone. *Computing Diagrams for the Tetrachoric Correlation Coefficient.* Chicago: University of Chicago Press, 1933.
16. Child, Irvin L. *Italian or American? The Second Generation in Conflict.* New Haven: Yale University Press, 1943.
17. Clark, Robert E. "Psychoses, Income and Occupational Prestige," in *Class, Status and Power,* edited by Reinhard Bendix and Seymour M. Lipset. Illinois: The Free Press of Glencoe, 1953.
18. Cloward, Richard A. "Illegitimate Means, Anomic and Deviant Behavior," *Americal Sociological Review,* Vol. 24, No. 4, 1959, p. 164–176.
19. Coleman, James. *The Adolescent Society.* Illinois: The Free Press of Glencoe, 1961.
20. Crowne, Douglas P., and Mark W. Stephens. "Self Acceptance and Self Evaluation Behavior: A Critique of Methodology," *Psychological Bulletin,* 1961, pp. 104–121.
21. Davis, Allison. "Socialization and Adolescent Personality," in *Readings in Social Psychology,* edited by T. M. Newcomb and E. L. Hartley. New York: Henry Holt, 1947, pp. 139–150.
22. Davis, Allison, and Robert J. Havighurst. "Social Class and Color Differences in Child Rearing," in *Personality in Nature, Society and Culture,* edited by H. A. Murray and C. Kluckhohn. New York: Alfred K. Knopf, 1949. pp. 252–266.
23. Edwards, Allen L. *Edwards Personal Preference Schedule. A Manual.* New York: The Psychological Corporation, 1954.
24. Elder, Glen H. "Family Structure and Educational Attainment," *American Sociological Review,* Vol. 30, No. 1, February 1965, pp. 81–96.
25. Engel, Mary. "The Stability of the Self Concept in Adolescence," *Journal of Abnormal Psychology,* Vol. 58, 1959, pp. 211–215.
26. Erikson, E. H. *Childhood and Society.* New York: W. W. Norton & Co., 1950.
27. ———. "Ego Development and Historical Change," *The Psychoanalytic Study of the Child,* Vol. II, New York, International University Press, 1946.
28. ———. "The Problem of Ego Identity," *Journal of American Psychoanalytic Association.* Vol. IV, No. 1, 1956, pp. 58–121.
29. ———. *Young Man Luther.* New York: W. W. Norton & Co., 1958.
30. ———. *Youth: Change and Challenge.* New York: Basic Books, 1963.
31. Fenichel, Otto. *The Psychoanalytic Theory of Neurosis.* New York: W. W. Norton & Co., 1945.

32. Finney, D. J. "The Fisher-Yates Test of Significance in 2 X 2 Contingency Tables," *Biometrika,* 35, 1948, pp. 145–156.

33. Fisher, Seymour, and David Mendell. "The Communication of Neurotic Patterns Over Two and Three Generations," in *The Family,* edited by N. Bell and E. F. Vogel. Illinois: The Free Press of Glencoe, 1960, pp. 616–622.

34. Fishman, Joshua A. "Childhood Indoctrination for Minority Group Membership," *Daedalus,* Vol. 90, 1961, pp. 329–349.

35. Fitts, William H. *Tennessee Self-Concept Scale. A Manual.* Nashville: Counsellor and Recording Tests, 1965.

36. Fleming, C. M. *Adolescence, Its Social Psychology.* New York: Grove Press, 1962.

37. Freud, Anna. *The Ego and the Mechanisms of Defense.* New York: International University Press, 1956.

38. Freud, Sigmund. *The Basic Writings of Sigmund Freud.* edited by A. A. Brill. New York: Modern Library, 1938.

39. Fried, Jacob. "Acculturation and Mental Health Among Indian Migrants in Peru," in *Culture and Mental Health,* edited by M. K. Opler. New York: Macmillan, 1959, pp. 119–140.

40. Friedenberg, E. Z. *The Vanishing Adolescent.* Boston: Beacon Press, 1959.

41. Fromm, Erich. "Individual and Social Origin of Neurosis," in *Personality in Nature, Society and Culture,* edited by C. Kluchkohn and H. A. Murray. New York: Alfred Knopf, 1949.

42. Gans, Herbert J. *The Urban Villagers.* Illinois: The Free Press of Glencoe, 1962.

43. Gellhorn, Ernest. *Physiological Foundations of Neurology and Psychiatry.* Minneapolis: University of Minnesota Press, 1953.

44. Glazer, Nathan, and Daniel Patrick Moynihan. *Beyond the Melting Pot.* Cambridge: M.I.T. Press, 1963.

45. Gordon, Milton. "Assimilation in America: Theory and Reality," *Daedulus,* Vol. 90, Spring 1961, pp. 263–285.

46. Gouldner, Alvin. *Enter Plato.* New York Basic Books, 1965.

47. Grinder, Robert, ed. *Studies in Adolescence.* New York: Macmillan Co., 1963.

48. Handlin, Oscar. *Boston's Immigrants.* Cambridge: Harvard University Press, 1941.

49. ———. *The Uprooted.* Boston: Little Brown, 1951.

50. Hansen, Marcus L. "The Search for Continuity," in *Social Perspectives on Behavior,* edited by H. Stein and R. Cloward. Illinois: The Free Press of Glencoe, 1958.

51. Hartmann, Heinz. *Ego Psychology and the Problem of Adaptation.* New York: International University Press, 1958.

52. Havighurst, R. J., and Hilda Taba. *Adolescent Character and Personality.* New York: John Wiley and Sons, 1963.

53. Hollingshead, August B. "Cultural Factors in the Selection of Marriage Mates," *American Sociological Review*, October 1950, pp. 627–642.
54. Hollingshead, August B. *Elmtown's Youth*. New York: John Wiley & Sons, 1949.
55. Hollingshead, August B., and Frederick C. Redlich. *Social Class and Mental Illness*. New York: John Wiley & Sons, 1958.
56. Hollingshead, August B. *Two Factor Index of Social Position. A Manual*. New Haven: 1965 Yale Station, 1957.
57. Horney, Karen. *The Neurotic Personality of Our Time*. New York: W. W. Norton & Co., 1945.
58. ———. *Our Inner Conflicts*. New York: W. W. Norton & Co., 1945.
59. Howorth, H. *The Irish Writers 1880–1940*. New York: Hill and Wang, 1958.
60. Hsu, Francis L. K., Blanche G. Watrous, and Edith M. Lord. "Culture Pattern and Adolescent Behavior," in *Studies in Adolescence*, edited by Robert E. Grinder. New York: The Macmillan Co., 1963, pp. 59–74.
61. Hyman, Herbert H. "The Value Systems of Different Classes: A Social Psychological Contribution to the Analysis of Stratification," in *Class, Status and Power*, edited by R. Bendix and S. M. Lipset. Illinois: The Free Press, 1953, pp. 426–441.
62. Joyce, James. "A Little Cloud," in *Masters of the Modern Short Story*. edited by Walter Havighurst. New York: Harcourt Brace, 1955, pp. 119–131.
63. Kennedy, Ruby J. Reeves. "Single or Triple Melting Pot, Intermarriage Trends in New Haven 1870–1940," *American Sociological Review*, Vol. I, 1944, pp. 339.
64. Kleiner, Robert J., and Seymour Parker. "Goal-Striving, Social Status and Mental Disorder: A Research Review," *American Sociological Review*, Vol. 28, No. 2, April 1963, pp. 189–202.
65. Klett, James. "Performance of High School Students in Edwards Personal Preference Schedule," *Journal of Consulting Psychology*. Vol. 21, No. 1, 1957, pp. 68–72.
66. Kluckhohn, Florence Rockwood. "Family Diagnosis: Variations in the Basic Values of Family Systems," *Social Casework*, XXXIX, February to March 1958, pp. 63–72.
67. Kluckhohn, Florence, and Fred L. Strodtbeck. *Variations in Value Orientations*. New York: Row Peterson, 1961.
68. Krauss, Irving. "Educational Aspirations Among Working Class Youth," *American Sociological Review*, Vol. 29, No. 6, December 1964, pp. 867–879.
69. Lewin, Kurt. *A Dynamic Theory of Personality*. New York: McGraw Hill, 1935.
70. ———. *Resolving Social Conflicts*. New York: Harper Bros., 1948.

71. Lief, A. *The Commonsense Psychiatry of Adolf Meyer.* New York: McGraw Hill, 1948.
72. Linton, Ralph. "Concepts of Role and Status," in *Readings in Social Psychology,* edited by T. Newcomb and E. L. Hartley. New York: Henry Holt, 1947.
73. Lipset, Seymour, and Reinhard Bendix, eds. *Class, Status and Power,* Illinois: The Free Press, 1953.
74. Lord, Eliot, John J. Trenor, and Samuel J. Barrows. *The Italians in America.* New York: B. F. Buck and Co., 1906.
75. Lynd, Helen M. *On Shame and Search for Identity.* New York: Harcourt Brace, 1958.
76. Mead, Margaret. "Adolescence in Primitive and Modern Society," in *Readings In Social Psychology,* edited by T. Newcomb and E. L. Hartley. New York: Henry Holt, 1947, pp. 6–13.
77. McClelland, David, John W. Atkinson, Russell Clark and Edgar Lowell. *The Achievement Motive.* New York: Appleton Century-Crofts, 1953.
78. Merton, Robert K. *Social Theory and Social Structure.* Illinois: The Free Press, 1957.
79. Mintz, N., and D. Schwartz. "Urban Ecology and Psychosis: Community Factors in the Incidence of Schizophrenia and Manic Depression Among Italians in Greater Boston," *International Journal of Social Psychiatry.* Vol. X, No. 2, Spring 1964, pp. 101–117.
80. Murray, H. A. *Explorations in Personality.* New York: Oxford University Press, 1938.
81. Murray, Henry, and Clyde Kluckhohn. *Personality in Nature, Society and Culture.* New York: Alfred A. Knopf, 1949.
82. Mussen, Paul Henry, and Mary Cover Jones. "Self Conceptions, Motivations and Interpersonal Attitudes of Late and Early Maturing Boys," *Child Development,* Vol. 28, 1957, pp. 243–256.
83. Naegele, Kasper. "Youth and Society," in *Youth: Change and Challenge,* edited by E. H. Erikson. New York: Basic Books, 1963.
84. O'Connor, Frank. "The Uprooted," in *Masters of the Modern Short Story,* edited by Walter Havinghurst. New York: Harcourt Brace, 1955, pp. 99–118.
85. Opler, Marvin K. "Cultural Differences in Mental Disorders: An Italian and Irish Contrast in the Schizophrenics," in *Culture and Mental Health,* edited by M. K. Opler. New York: Macmillan Co., 1959.
86. Patterson, Tom. Abstract of Research Findings on Tennessee Department of Mental Health Project (unpublished mimeographed report).
87. Piedmont, Eugene. "An Investigation of the Influence of Ethnic Grouping Differences in the Development of Schizophrenia," unpublished Ph.D. dissertation, Department of Sociology, University of New York at Buffalo, June 1962.

88. Rank, Otto. *Will Therapy and Truth and Reality*. New York: A. Knopf, 1945.

89. Reckless, Walter C., Simon Dinitz and Ellen Murray. "Self Concept as an Insulator Against Delinquency," *American Sociological Review* 21, 1956, 744–746.

90. Roberts, Bertram, and Jerome K. Myers. *Family and Class Dynamics in Mental Illness*. New York: John Wiley, 1959.

91. Roberts, Bertram, and Jerome K. Myers. "Religion, National Origin, Immigration and Mental Illness," *American Journal of Psychiatry*, Vol. 110, 1954, pp. 759–764.

92. Robins, Lee. *Deviant Children Grow Up*. Baltimore: Wilkins and Wilkins, 1966.

93. Rogers, C. R. *Client Centered Therapy*. Boston: Houghton Mifflin, 1951, pp. 136–150.

94. Rogers, C. R. and Rosalind F. Dymonds. *Psychotherapy and Personality Changes*. Boston: Houghton Mifflin, 1954.

95. Rose, Arnold. "The Prevalence of Mental Disorders in Italy," *International Journal of Social Psychiatry*. Vol. X, No. 2, Spring 1964, pp. 87–100.

96. Rosen, Bernard. "Race, Ethnicity and Achievement Motivation," *American Sociological Review*, Vol. 24, 1959, pp. 47–60.

97. Russell, Dearmund. *The Irish Reader*. New York: Viking Press, 1946.

98. Sanua, Victor D. "Differences in Personality Adjustment Among Different Generations of American Jews and Non-Jews," in *Culture and Mental Health*, edited by M. K. Opler. New York, Macmillan Co., 1959, pp. 443–466.

99. Schemerhorn, R. A. *These Our People*. Boston: D. A. Heathland Co., 1949.

100. Schrier, Arnold. *Ireland and American Emmigration 1850–1900*. Minneapolis: University of Minnesota Press, 1958.

101. Sherif, Muzafur. *Psychology of Ego Involvements*. New York: J. Wiley and Sons, 1947.

102. Short, James E., Ramon Riviera, and Ray A. Tennyson. "Perceived Opportunities, Gang Membership and Delinquency," *American Sociological Review*, Vol. 30, No. 1, 2, 1965, pp. 56–67.

103. Sirjamaki, John. "Culture Configurations in the American Family," in *The Family*, edited by Norman Bell and E. F. Vogel. Illinois: The Free Press, 1960, pp. 295–314.

104. Smith, Walter D., and Dell Lebo. "Some Changing Aspects of the Self Concept of Pubescent Males," *The Journal of Genetic Psychology*, Vol. 88, 1956, pp. 61–75.

105. Srole, Leo, Thomas Langner, Michael Stanley, Marvin Opler, and Thomas Rennie. *Mental Health in the Metropolis*. Vol I. New York: McGraw-Hill Co., 1962.

106. Stein, Herman D., and Richard A. Cloward, eds. *Social Perspectives on Behavior.* Illinois: The Free Press, 1958.
107. Strauss, Anselm. *The Social Psychology of George Herbert Mead.* Chicago: University of Chicago Press, 1956.
108. Strodtbeck, Fred L. "Family Interaction, Values and Achievement." in *Talent and Society,* edited by David McClelland, Alfred Baldwin, Urie Bronfenbrenner and Fred Strodtbeck. Princeton: D. Van Nostrand Co., 1958, pp. 135–191.
109. Sullivan, Harry Stack. *The Contributions of Harry Stack Sullivan,* edited by P. Mullahy. New York: Hermitage House, 1952.
110. Swinehart, James W. "Socio-economic Level, Status Aspiration and Maternal Role," *American Sociological Review,* Vol. 28, No. 3, June 1963, pp. 391–399.
111. United States Bureau of the Census. *United States Census of the Population of New York 1960–Detailed Characteristics.* Washington: Government Printing Office.
112. United States Bureau of the Census. *United States Census of Population and Housing: 1960, Census Tracts Buffalo, N.Y. Standard Metropolitan Statistical Area PHC (1)–21.* Washington: Government Printing Office.
113. Ware, Caroline F. "The Breakdown of Ethnic Solidarity: The Case of the Italian in Greenwich Village," in *Social Perspectives on Behavior,* edited by H. Stein and R. Cloward. Illinois: The Free Press, 1958.
114. Weber, Max. "Religion and Modern Capitalism," In *The Structure of Social Action,* edited by Talcott Parsons. Illinois: The Free Press, 1958.
115. Wittke, Carl. *The Irish in America.* Baton Rouge: Louisiana State University Press, 1956.
116. Wylie, Ruth. *The Self Concept: A Critical Survey of Pertinent Research Literature.* Lincoln: University of Nebraska Press, 1961.
117. Zborowski, Mark. "Cultural Components in Response to Pain," in *Patients, Physicians and Illness,* edited by E. Gartly Jaco. Illinois: The Free Press, 1958, pp. 256–269.
118. Zuckerman, Marvin. "The Validity of Edwards Personal Preference Schedule in the Measurement of Dependency-Rebelliousness." *Journal of Clinical Psychology,* Vol. 14, 1958, pp. 379–382.